Promoting Multilingualism in Schools:

A Framework for Implementing

the Seal of Biliteracy

Kristin J. Davin
University of North Carolina at Charlotte

Amy J. Heineke
Loyola University Chicago

ISBN: 9798985710809
© 2022, ACTFL
1001 North Fairfax Street, Suite 200
Alexandria, VA 22314

Table of Contents

Acknowledgments

This book has been a labor of love during the COVID pandemic, one of the most challenging times in our collective lives. We want to begin by thanking our families and friends for their ongoing support as we conducted research and wrote this book.

We also want to thank the students, teachers, administrators, and policymakers who have participated in our research over the years. This book highlights and draws from the incredible work being done in schools, and these pages would not be possible without the time and efforts of our partners and participants in sharing their expertise and experiences with us. We cannot name them all due to confidentiality promised as a part of the various research studies, but greatly value their continued commitment and work toward supporting students' biliteracy.

Many colleagues supported our writing of this book in various ways, including lending their expert perspectives and providing feedback on chapter drafts. Candace Black, Justin Fisk, and Pamela Wesely graciously read this text in its entirety and offered insightful suggestions that greatly strengthened our work. Others offered important feedback on individual chapters, including Andrew Bowen, Margaret Malone, Jason Martel, Cornelia Okraski, Kim Sallee, Victor Santos, and Annie Wendel. Michele Anciaux Aoki provided in-depth information and feedback on Chapter 3 on multiple occasions. Mary Jo Adams's expertise also strengthened Chapter 3, as did her insights and recommendations related to performance-based rubrics. Other individuals informed vignettes and examples, including Melody Becker, Resha Cardone, Mara Cobe, Justin Fisk, Grant Moss, Roxana Norouzi, Amy Schumann, and Meredith White. This work was also shaped by the support of amazing doctoral students who have supported our research over the years, including Charlotte Hancock, Cornelia Okraski, Joseph Elliott, and Kristen Moore.

Many have informed our work on the Seal of Biliteracy. We hope that this book honors the work of Arthur Chou at SealofBiliteracy.org, who has been a huge source of support over the years as we developed and carried out our research agenda. Other colleagues and scholars have challenged and shaped our thinking over the years, including Guadalupe Valdés, Linda Egnatz, Todd Bowen, Helen Solórzano, Laurie Olsen, Nicole Sherf, Nic Subtirelu, Ursula Lentz, and Phyllis Hardy.

Finally, we are deeply appreciative of Howie Berman and Paul Sandrock at ACTFL for their support of this book.

Preface

This book is based on our experiences as students, educators, and researchers, as well as our shared belief that all students deserve the opportunity to learn and develop multiple languages. We both grew up in small towns, Amy in Wisconsin and Kristin in North Carolina, where we took Spanish classes in school. However, both of our lives changed dramatically as a result of study abroad. Through those experiences, we learned firsthand how it feels to struggle with communicating one's needs, how it feels to make an embarrassing cultural faux pas, and how proficiency in another language fundamentally changes the way one interacts in the world. Those experiences shaped our desires to become teachers—Amy a bilingual kindergarten teacher and Kristin an elementary Spanish teacher.

Becoming teachers opened our eyes to the divergent expectations and opportunities in language education. While teaching in Arizona and North Carolina, we came to realize our privilege as elite bilinguals, the term referring to those from English-speaking homes in the United States who had the opportunity to learn an additional language in school (Valdés & Figueroa, 1994). While colleagues and administrators lauded our bilingualism as White, English-dominant women, their attitudes sometimes changed when framing the competencies of children from immigrant families. These deficit-based perspectives accompanied staunchly different opportunities to develop bilingualism. For example, at Amy's school in Arizona, Spanish-bilingual kindergarteners were placed in English-only classrooms where state policy mandates and related threats from administrators deterred consistent or meaningful home language supports. While immigrant children in South Phoenix had their home language taken away from them in service of assimilation, White students in Scottsdale and Paradise Valley had the opportunity to become bilingual through dual-language immersion programs. These blatant inequities based on race, class, and language background—

which we continued to see in various contexts across our careers—ignited our passions to prepare teachers and engage in research that promotes multilingualism for all students on a broader scale outside of our classrooms.

Whereas this book tackles the implementation of a contemporary language policy, it is the product of our combined decades of work in language education in classrooms, schools, and universities. Despite the rampant monolingualism and elite bilingualism that we too commonly see in policy and practice across the United States, the Seal of Biliteracy (SoBL) offers a mechanism to promote all students' multilingualism and multiliteracies. Building from our prior experiences and passions in the field, we wrote this book to support the language development of all students while paying particular attention to students who arrive at school with rich linguistic resources in languages other than English. We believe that all individuals should have access to high-quality, articulated, research-based language instruction in at least two languages, including one's home language. To that end, we believe that the SoBL movement has the potential to improve the landscape of language education in the United States.

Our collaboration began around 2015, shortly after colleagues in Illinois established the state's SoBL, making it the fourth state to adopt a SoBL policy. At that time, little research existed on the SoBL and many districts in the area were reaching out to us for implementation support. In planning our research agenda, we met with Dr. Anne Nerenz, editor of *Foreign Language Annals* at that time, at the annual ACTFL convention. Over coffee, she conveyed that the field desperately needed an exploratory study of how the SoBL policy differed across states, which we published in 2017 (Davin & Heineke, 2017). That work led to subsequent research on states' policy journeys to implementation (Heineke & Davin,

2020a), administrators' successes and challenges with implementation (Davin et al., 2018), students' perceptions of the policy (Davin & Heineke, 2018), issues of equity and access for students labeled as English learners (Heineke et al., 2018), and characteristics of high-awarding districts (Heineke & Davin, 2021).

Throughout our research and work in partner schools, we saw widely divergent implementation, creating inequitable conditions for students' attainment of the SoBL depending on the state or local context. For example, policy provisions in some states allowed participation in world language study to serve as proof of proficiency, privileging elite bilinguals' access to world language coursework rather than actual language competencies. In other states, however, stakeholders endeavored to provide proficiency assessments in every heritage language used by students and families. At the local level, some overextended world language department chairs charged with SoBL implementation deferred to shortcuts in implementation, such as offering proficiency tests only to students in Advanced Placement courses. At the same time, other leaders leveraged the SoBL to reshape language education across districts, including adding dual- and heritage-language programs in response to home and community languages.

This implementation guide comes from our recognition that administrators, teachers, counselors, and school staff want what is best for students. We understand that SoBL implementation is often shaped by deep-rooted inequities in the U.S. education system, including divergent access to the development of biliteracy, particularly for students of color. We see access to world, heritage, and bilingual education as an issue of social justice and envision the SoBL as a key lever to changing policy and practice across the United States. This book aims to confront these inequities through what we call the 5Ps

Framework: (a) creating a meaningful and equitable **Purpose** for SoBL implementation, (b) offering students equitable access to **Proficiency Assessments**, (c) developing language **Programs** that support SoBL attainment, (d) tapping into **Partners** to broaden access to the SoBL, and (e) using **Promotion** to extend the work across schools and communities.

Throughout this book, we open each chapter with a vignette describing a student we have met in our SoBL research. To underscore the importance of supporting multilingualism and promoting equitable pathways to SoBL attainment for all learners, we close this preface with the words of Uba (a pseudonym). A Somali immigrant who received the SoBL in a Minnesota high school, Uba explained that, to her, the SoBL meant "that my language, that the language that I speak at home isn't so much useless. I'm glad that I have the opportunity to also use my first language to get some credit for my future."

Chapter 1
The Seal of Biliteracy

Fluent in both Somali and Arabic, Kaaha (a pseudonym) came to the United States and enrolled in eighth grade at a middle school with English-only instruction. She explained, "There was so much pressure to learn this new language and then to almost perfect it to get around." She felt like her "other languages didn't really matter as much as English and the only thing that [she was] going to get recognized for is English because you take the ACT [college entrance exam], all these tests." The Seal of Biliteracy provided her first opportunity to use her home languages in school. Her identity that once felt "buried...came back to life" after taking the Seal of Biliteracy assessments in high school. As a freshman in college, Kaaha reflected on her biliteracy development over the past five years. She saw the Seal of Biliteracy as integral to her achievements, including securing a job as a translator at a call center. She recalled the initial interview going poorly until she mentioned her Seal of Biliteracy. She sent a picture of the award to the interviewer, who quickly changed his tone and offered her the job. Kaaha felt that the Seal of Biliteracy provided important proof of her multiliteracy—for herself and for her employer.

Guiding Questions

Why is multiliteracy important?
What is the Seal of Biliteracy?
How does the Seal of Biliteracy vary across states?
How can this text guide implementation efforts?

In today's interconnected world, active engagement requires communication with others across communities, countries, continents—and consequently languages. Consider any professional context in society: business, higher education, hospitality, security, technology, or medicine. Multilingualism—the ability to speak and understand more than one language—emerges as central to engaging with others and supporting productivity to move the world in a positive direction. Approximately 75 percent of the world's population speak languages other than English, necessitating multilingual individuals who foster intercultural interaction and collaboration in daily work and communication (Commission on Language Learning, 2017).

For centuries, multilingualism has been the norm across much of the world, with schools playing integral roles in fostering proficiency in national, regional, and global languages (Bhatia & Ritchie, 2013; Commission of European Communities, 2003; Zsiga et al., 2014). For example, European citizens are entitled to learn multiple languages due to the European Union's emphasis on the individual's mother tongue plus two world languages in school-based programming (Commission of European Communities, 2003). In South Asia, which boasts 650 languages in addition to numerous language varieties and dialects, multilingualism facilitates daily life in the region, as well as international business and the global economy (Bhatia & Ritchie, 2013).

Yet in the United States, monolingual doctrines have driven policy and practice for centuries (Crawford, 2000). Standing in contrast to their global counterparts, U.S. schools have limited availability of early-start, long-sequence world language and immersion programs for *world language learners*, defined as students who opt to learn a language other than English in school. As a result, only one in five students enrolls in world language classes and only about 20 percent of states have world language graduation requirements (American Councils for International Education, 2017). In states with world language requirements, the maximum obligation is two years of high-school coursework (O'Rourke et al., 2016), which results in limited language proficiency (Davin et al., 2014). Because no federal policy exists for kindergarten-through-twelfth-grade (K-12) world language education, state or local administrators make program decisions. Often, schools in wealthier areas with more resources offer more languages over longer sequences than those in less-resourced neighborhoods. As a result, only about 10 percent of English-dominant individuals in the United States are multilingual (Smith et al., 2011).

The current context of language education is also troubling when considering **heritage language learners,** individuals raised in homes among languages other than English who themselves speak or understand the heritage language to some extent (Valdés, 2000). Linguistic diversity abounds across the United States, with Indigenous and immigrant languages enriching the landscape of many communities. Twenty percent of U.S. public school students speak a language other than English (National Center for Educational Statistics [NCES], 2019). But monolingual ideologies pervade, with educators and other stakeholders espousing unexamined ideas about language that then shape their perspectives and "evaluative views about speakers and their language use" (Valdés, 2018, p. 396). Students like Kaaha, introduced in the opening vignette, typically have few opportunities to use or develop home languages in school and may experience exclusion and discrimination as they develop English proficiency.

Many **bilingual programs**, programs in which instruction occurs in two languages, follow **subtractive** models that phase out home languages and prioritize English proficiency, reinforcing the systemic racism and structural barriers that devalue and marginalize students of color (Flores, 2020; Flores & García, 2017). While increasing in number, **additive bilingual programs** that develop students' literacy and content knowledge in home languages in addition to English exist in approximately two percent of schools across the United States (Gross, 2016). However, some of these programs have been criticized for prioritizing English-dominant students' achievement of **elite bilingualism**, the bilingualism of individuals who choose to learn another language

while living in communities that use their home language (Valdés & Figueroa, 1994), rather than students seeking to develop and maintain home and heritage languages (Flores, 2020; Flores & García, 2017; Valdés, 2018; Valdez et al., 2016).

This must change. The benefits of multilingualism, both to the broader global ecosystem and to individuals, families, and communities, are known. Reflective across one's lifetime, these benefits extend beyond the ability to communicate in multiple languages to include social, cognitive, linguistic, and academic dimensions (Kroll & Dussias, 2017). From a cognitive standpoint, proficiency in two languages improves academic achievement (Collier & Thomas, 2017; Lindholm-Leary & Block, 2010) and has been linked to enhanced executive functioning that may result in the delayed onset of dementia (Bialystok, 2007; Bialystok et al., 2007) as well as enhanced working memory (Morales et al., 2013). Additional benefits include increased use and awareness of multiple languages (McLeay, 2003), effective communication skills fostered by the enhancement of perspective taking (Fan et al., 2015), greater intercultural awareness and open-mindedness (Byram, 1997), and increased access to postsecondary education (Kroll & Dussias, 2017).

Bilingualism, typically defined as the ability to speak and understand two languages, is certainly laudable. But **biliteracy**, defined as the ability to read and write in two languages, is equally essential and critical in business and policy circles, with stakeholders asserting a dire need for individuals who are literate in multiple languages. In a recent report by the Commission on Language Learning (2017) entitled *America's Languages: Investing in Language Education for the 21st Century*, the authors pinpointed biliteracy as critical to success in business, research, international relations, and law. In a survey of 289 businesses across California, Callahan and Gándara (2014) found that 66 percent preferred bilingual employees over monolinguals. On a larger scale, survey data from 2,101 businesses across the United States revealed that 41 percent of respondents gave preference to multilingual candidates during recruitment (Damari et al., 2017). Beyond business, the United States needs more multiliterate individuals working in foreign policy. Recent reports have referred to the severe shortage of multiliterate individuals as a national security crisis (A National Security Crisis, 2012).

Understanding the Seal of Biliteracy

It is within this context that the Seal of Biliteracy (SoBL) has emerged as a promising endeavor to promote U.S. students' competencies in multiple languages. The SoBL recognizes high-school graduates who read, write, speak, and listen in English and at least one other language. As of July 2021, high-school graduates in 43 states and the District of Columbia (DC) can receive an emblem placed on the high-school diploma or transcript. Typically awarded by a state department of education, the SoBL provides a clear symbol of bilingualism and biliteracy for future employers and universities (ACTFL et al., 2015; Californians Together et al., 2020).

Unlike many policies mandating practices in U.S. schools, the SoBL movement has been characterized by grass-roots, bottom-up efforts to promote multilingualism (Heineke & Davin, 2020a). Californians initiated the SoBL in response to monolingual policies that historically guided practice with students labeled as *English learners* (ELs; Olsen, 2020). In 1998, the English for the Children campaign resulted in the passage of Proposition 227, which decimated bilingual education. Prioritizing English in place of home languages, the policy yielded challenges for using students' home languages as resources in the classroom, let alone maintaining those languages to promote biliteracy (Olsen, 2020). Seeking to push back against the monolingual ideologies and deficit views of multilingualism, a coalition of advocates, teachers, and civil rights leaders introduced the SoBL, which state legislators enacted in 2011. Organized by the educational advocacy group Californians Together, coalition members embraced a multilingual ideology, seeking to elevate the rich linguistic resources of the state's ELs in the absence of widespread bilingual programs (Olsen, 2020). The concept was that once *multiliteracy*—the ability to read and write in multiple languages—became formally recognized and valued through the SoBL, stakeholders like parents, students, teachers, and administrators would embrace the opportunity to deepen language competencies, ignite demand for bilingual programs, and subsequently elevate a multilingual ideology within schools and communities.

Upon passage of the SoBL in California, word of these pioneering efforts quickly spread to language educators and advocates across the United States who began drawing up plans for their own SoBL efforts, initially with little guidance. By March 2015, when the major national language organizations published the first SoBL guidelines (ACTFL et al., 2015), 11 states had already passed SoBL policies with more on the way. The 2015 Guidelines for Implementing the Seal of Biliteracy described the purpose of the SoBL initiative and included much-needed recommendations for minimum required levels of proficiency and acceptable forms of evidence. Joined by even more organizations, these guidelines were expanded and revised in 2020 (Californians Together et al., 2020). Perhaps in response to critiques that White students from higher socioeconomic backgrounds had greater access to the SoBL than their peers (Subtirelu et al., 2019), the revised version included recommendations related to the promotion of equity and access as well as guidelines for state education agencies, public school districts, and non-public entities.

Since its inception, the SoBL movement has spread across the United States, with states, districts, and schools working to recognize graduating seniors for proficiency in two or more languages. But the SoBL initiative has also expanded to include pathways in early childhood, elementary, and middle schools. *Pathway recognitions* recognize students who are on the path to developing biliteracy across PreK-12 schools, seeking to call attention and motivate children and families around the value of bilingualism from a young age (Seal of Biliteracy, 2021). The preschool pathway aims to nurture pride and excitement in becoming bilingual, as well as to provoke families to consider dual-language options when starting kindergarten. The elementary and middle school recognitions seek to promote ongoing language development with scaffolded proficiency expectations over time. Recognitions may include tiers for participation and attainment to recognize the wide range of students participating in language programming and demonstrating biliteracy in home languages. Implementation of pathway recognitions varies by state, along with other key variances that we explore in the next section.

Exploring the Movement and State-Level Policy Variations

These grassroots efforts across the nation resulted in the current context of the initiative, with different states adopting and enacting their own version of the SoBL with various policy nuances to match their unique context (see Davin & Heineke, 2017). Although policies became more uniform once the guidelines were published, they continued to vary in small yet significant ways. Seemingly minor differences in policy requirements often resulted in major differences in policy implementation.

In this section, we describe these key variations. We include what we are terming **Equity Alerts**, which will appear throughout this text with a scale icon and include critical considerations that relate to how practices can impact equity in implementation. At the end of the chapter, we include questions to guide readers in exploring their state's SoBL policy (see Tool 1.1).

Required Levels of World Language Proficiency

States' SoBL policies vary regarding the minimum level of world language proficiency required to earn a SoBL. **Language proficiency**, discussed more in Chapters 3, 4, and 6, refers to "what individuals can do with language in terms of speaking, writing, listening, and reading in real-world situations in a spontaneous and non-rehearsed context" (ACTFL 2012b, p. 3). The ACTFL Proficiency Guidelines (2012b) consist of five major levels: **Novice, Intermediate, Advanced, Superior,** and **Distinguished** (see Figure 1.1). The first three (Novice, Intermediate, and Advanced) break down into three sublevels: Low, Mid, and High.

Figure 1.1. ACTFL's Proficiency Levels

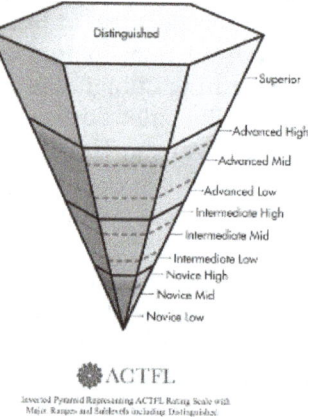

 ACTFL

Inverted Pyramid Representing ACTFL Rating Scale with Major Ranges and Sublevels including Distinguished.

The SoBL guidelines recommend that state policies require a minimum proficiency level of Intermediate Mid in the world language (ACTFL et al., 2015; Californians Together et al., 2020). A speaker at the Intermediate Mid level, for example, "can handle successfully a variety of uncomplicated communicative tasks in straightforward social situations" (ACTFL, 2012b, p. 7). In alignment with these guidelines, policies in most states (24 of 43 as of July 2021) set the minimum at Intermediate Mid. Policies in 13 states set the minimum at Intermediate High, and two (New Mexico and North Carolina) set the minimum at Intermediate Low. Four of the 43 have just recently adopted the SoBL and have not yet set their requirements.

Table 1.1 displays (a) the minimum required world language proficiency level to earn the SoBL in each participating state, (b) descriptions of oral abilities at that level, and (c) corresponding professions for which that level might be suitable. In most states, students must score at or above the minimum required proficiency level in all four language domains (listening, reading, speaking, writing) to receive the SoBL. For example, a student in Washington who scored Intermediate Mid in reading, writing, and listening, but Intermediate Low in speaking, would not receive the SoBL.

As shown in Table 1.1, 14 states have policies with multiple tiers of the SoBL to recognize and distinguish students with varying levels of language proficiency. For example, students in Illinois receive the SoBL for demonstrating the target proficiency level (Intermediate Mid) or they receive a Commendation for demonstrating a slightly lower proficiency level (Intermediate Low). In South Carolina, students earn the SoBL at three different tiers based on language proficiency level: Bronze for Intermediate Mid, Silver for Intermediate High, or Gold for Advanced Low.

In some cases, tiers correspond to differences not related to minimum proficiency level. For example, students in Minnesota earn a Gold or Platinum Bilingual Seal signaling their proficiency in two languages, or a Gold or Platinum Multilingual Seal signaling their proficiency in more than two languages. The District of Columbia also offers two tiers of the SoBL, but the minimum required proficiency level for both is the same. Instead, students who complete a cultural competence activity, such as study abroad or 25 hours of community service in the target language, receive a Seal of Biliteracy with Distinction.

> Lack of consistency in proficiency requirements has the potential to weaken the impact of the SoBL. For students, a SoBL in one state does not mean the same as a SoBL from another state. Consider a student from Michigan and another from New Mexico applying to the same college. Both scored Intermediate Mid on a proficiency assessment, so the New Mexico student earned the SoBL while the Michigan student did not. With all else being equal, this technical difference could influence who is admitted, who earns college credit, and who ultimately graduates with a college degree.

Table 1.1. Minimum Required Level of Proficiency to Earn SoBL in Each State with Descriptions of that Level

REQUIRED PROFICIENCY LEVEL	DESCRIPTION (ACTFL, 2012B)	CORRESPONDING PROFESSIONS (ACTFL, 2015)	STATE
Intermediate Low	Able to handle successfully a limited number of uncomplicated communicative tasks by creating with the language in straightforward social situations, such as topics necessary for survival in the target-language culture (e.g., immediate needs, personal preferences)	None listed	Arizona (in writing and reading for Category IV languages only)*, Illinois (Commendation), Minnesota (World Language Proficiency Certificate), New Mexico, North Carolina, North Dakota (Silver)
Intermediate Mid	Able to handle successfully a variety of uncomplicated communicative tasks in straightforward social situations, such as topics necessary for survival in the target-language culture (e.g., home, social needs)	Cashier Receptionist Sales Clerk	Arizona, Arkansas, California, Colorado, Connecticut, Delaware (Gold), District of Columbia, Florida (Silver), Hawai'i, Illinois (Seal), Iowa, Kansas (Silver), Maine, Mississippi (Silver), Missouri, Nebraska (Silver), Nevada, New Jersey, Oklahoma, Rhode Island, South Carolina (Bronze), Tennessee, Utah, Virginia, Washington
Intermediate High	Able to converse with ease and confidence when dealing with the routine tasks and social situations of the Intermediate level, on topics such as work, school, recreation, particular interests, and areas of competence	Fire Fighter Auto Inspector Missionary Tour Guide	Georgia, Idaho, Indiana, Louisiana, Maryland, Massachusetts (Seal), Michigan, Minnesota (Gold), Nebraska (Gold), New York, North Dakota (Gold), Ohio, Oregon, South Carolina (Silver), Texas, Wisconsin
Advanced Low	Able to handle a variety of communicative tasks on topics such as school, home, and leisure activities, as well as topics related to employment and current events	Language Teacher (K-12), Nurse, Social Worker, Police Officer, Retail Services Personnel	Delaware (Diamond), Florida (Gold), Kansas (Gold), Massachusetts (Seal with distinction), Minnesota (Platinum), Mississippi (Gold), Missouri (Distinguished Seal), South Carolina (Gold), Tennessee (Seal of Biliteracy with Honors)

*Note: Arizona's policy is the only one to distinguish based on the difficulty of the language, setting the minimum at Intermediate Low for Category IV languages in reading and writing. Category IV languages are languages such as Arabic or Chinese that have significant linguistic differences from English thus taking longer to acquire proficiency in reading and writing.

Evidence of World Language Proficiency States also vary regarding what counts as acceptable evidence of language proficiency. In most states, acceptable evidence centers on assessment, where students demonstrate proficiency on an external language assessment (see Appendix 1). These assessments, discussed in more detail in Chapter 3, have an associated cost, occasionally covered by the district but often passed along to students. Alternatively, six states—California, Colorado, Florida, Louisiana, North Carolina, and Texas—allow students to instead demonstrate proficiency with a minimum grade point average (GPA) in a standard course of world language study, often referred to as seat time (Davin & Heineke, 2017).

Each approach has drawbacks. Language assessments can be expensive and may not be available for all language varieties and dialects (Valdés, 2020), as we discuss in Chapter 3. On the other hand, seat time does not ensure a student's ability to read, write, speak, and listen at a minimum proficiency level because countless variables influence language development. With more colleges and universities awarding credit for earning the SoBL and using it to aid language course placement decisions (Davin, 2021b), scores from commercial language assessments enhance the SoBL as a reliable indicator of language abilities.

> Not only does seat time not equate to proficiency, but this variation of the policy favors elite bilinguals who enroll in world language courses, which are typically limited to languages such as Spanish and French. Districts in states that have a seat time policy may offer fewer external assessments in less commonly taught languages, decreasing access for those students who use languages not taught in school.

Moving beyond scores on approved language assessments and seat time, other states have creatively crafted and used SoBL policies to expand recognition of biliteracy. Currently, SoBL policies in 28 states offer **alternative assessment protocols**, such as a language portfolio, through which students demonstrate proficiency by constructing various products in the target language. Most states allow this option for **less commonly tested languages**; that is, for languages that do not have affordable assessments, such as many Indigenous languages. A challenge with the alternative assessment protocol lies in finding individuals capable of scoring the portfolio on a proficiency-based rubric (see Chapter 3). Therefore, alternative assessment protocols often require community partnerships, which we discuss in depth in Chapter 5. In New Mexico and Utah, for example, partnerships with Indigenous groups allow for the certification of proficiency in tribal languages. We explore these flexible approaches to promote equity in SoBL implementation in later chapters, including a template for non-traditional proficiency assessments to support development of options outside of formal tests (see Appendices 3–8).

Evidence of English Language Proficiency
Acceptable evidence of English proficiency also varies across states (see Table 1.2). Currently, SoBL policies in 18 of the 43 participating states require students to pass standardized assessments in English Language Arts (ELA), such as the state's end-of-year tests or American College Testing's (ACT) college readiness assessment. As discussed in Chapter 3, policies in five of these 18 states (Arkansas, Illinois,

Kansas, Nebraska, and Utah) also allow scores from an English proficiency assessment rather than a subject-specific ELA assessment.

> Standardized exams in English, such as the ACT or SAT, were designed to measure ELA content knowledge rather than English proficiency (i.e., one's ability to use a language in real-world contexts). Such tests measure much more than English proficiency, including ELA content knowledge, critical thinking, problem solving, and academic language. Use of ELA content assessments rather than English proficiency assessments creates unfair barriers to SoBL attainment for students.

Seat time is another common form of evidence for the demonstration of English proficiency, adopted by 14 states. Policies in four states require students to score a minimum GPA in high-school ELA courses and five require students to both pass an ELA assessment and achieve a minimum GPA. Policies in three states (Indiana, Nebraska, and New Hampshire) require students to earn a minimum number of ELA credits, without a specified GPA, and pass an English assessment. Still other states have more straightforward requirements, such as accepting a student's graduation from high school as proof of English proficiency. Adopted by 10 of 43 participating states, this SoBL policy provision rests on the assumption that acceptable proficiency in English is a prerequisite to high-school graduation in the United States. However, this policy variation may prohibit students from indicating on college applications that they earned the SoBL, since the recognition is not conferred until graduation.

Various Pathways The SoBL movement has expanded to recognize the developing biliteracy of younger students. Seeking to encourage biliteracy development over time, pathway recognitions can be implemented in preschool, elementary schools, and middle schools with world and dual-language programming. In some states, such as Missouri, the state's SoBL guidelines describe the pathway recognitions, but in others, language organizations such as the Language Opportunity Coalition (LOC) in Massachusetts or the Volunteer State Seal of Biliteracy in Tennessee determine the pathways.

Massachusetts offers a strong example of pathway recognitions established through the collaborative efforts of state professional organizations in world language, bilingual, and EL education (Ritz & Sherf,

Table 1.2. Required Evidence of English Proficiency in Each State

MEET GRADUATION REQUIREMENTS	EARN MINIMUM GPA IN ELA COURSES	PASS ELA ASSESSMENT	OPTION OF ENGLISH PROFICIENCY TEST	MINIMUM GPA AND ELA ASSESSMENT	EARN ELA CREDITS AND PASS ASSESSMENT
Connecticut	Georgia	Delaware	Arkansas	Arizona	Indiana
Florida	Nevada	District of	Illinois	California	Nebraska
Maryland	North Carolina	Columbia	Kansas	Colorado	New Hampshire
Massachusetts	South Carolina	Idaho	Nebraska	Tennessee	
Michigan		Iowa	Utah	Texas	
Minnesota		Louisiana			
New Jersey		Maine			
New Mexico		Mississippi			
Virginia		Montana			
Washington		North Dakota			
		Ohio			
		Oregon			
		Rhode Island			
		Wisconsin			

Table 1.3. Language Opportunity Coalition SoBL Pathway Recognitions in Massachusetts

RECOGNITION	SCHOOL LEVEL	MINIMUM REQUIRED WORLD LANGUAGE PROFICIENCY LEVELT
LOC Bilingual Participation	Preschool, Elementary, and students with disabilities (all grades)	Novice-High proficiency in listening and speaking
LOC Biliteracy Attainment	Elementary and Middle School	Intermediate-Low proficiency in all domains
LOC Biliteracy Achievement	Middle and High School	Intermediate-Mid proficiency in all domains
Massachusetts State Seal of Biliteracy	High School Graduates	Intermediate-High proficiency in all domains
Massachusetts State Seal of Biliteracy with Distinction	High School Graduates	Advanced-Low (and above) proficiency in all domains

Source: LOC, 2021

2021). As students work toward the Massachusetts State SoBL, which requires a rating of Intermediate High, or a Massachusetts State SoBL with Distinction, which requires a rating of Advanced Low, they receive recognition along the way. Table 1.3 displays the various levels of the pathway along with the minimum required world language proficiency level for each.

Participating Schools While the SoBL program originally focused on public and charter schools in many states, policies in 13 states now allow independent (e.g., non-public) schools to participate (see Table 1.4). For example, in Michigan, any student can log into the state's SoBL system and apply for the recognition. This policy variation increases accessibility and allows for community language organizations and weekend language schools to promote the SoBL. Independent schools in states where SoBL policy does not allow for such participation may create and award their own SoBL certificate indicating achievement of the state required level of proficiency or may choose to participate in the *Global Seal of Biliteracy* program, which is associated with a private assessment company.

Program Implementation The SoBL as a policy initiative is still in its infancy. While its novel bot-

Table 1.4. States Allowing Independent Schools to Recognize Biliteracy

Arkansas	Iowa	Nebraska
Connecticut	Michigan	New Hampshire
Delaware	Minnesota	Ohio
Illinois	Montana	Oregon
Indiana		

tom-up approach seems to liberate educators from the typical rigid prescriptions and mandates that come with other educational policies, it also sometimes results in a lack of supports and resources for implementation. By and large, the SoBL movement is unfunded, meaning that districts often receive no state funds to support implementation. As a result, participation is uneven across districts and even across schools within a district. For example, in the 2018-2019 school year, based on the percentage of schools awarding the SoBL from 16 states that provided data, an average of approximately 23 percent of schools participated (Black et al., 2020).

Because funding for the SoBL typically relies upon the local district, emerging evidence suggests that students in well-resourced school districts are more likely to have access to world language education and SoBL attainment (Burnet, 2020; Subtirelu et al., 2019). Stakeholders should work toward wide implementation across districts and high schools.

However, initial data suggests that the number of students earning the SoBL is gradually increasing. Although no centralized database exists with numbers of recognized students, Arthur Chou, the managing director of Velázquez Press and Sealof Biliteracy.org and a pioneer in the SoBL movement, requests this data from participating states annually. In the 2017-2018 school year, 16 participating states contributed data to Chou's report, showing that at least 93,087 students received the SoBL in 56 languages (Chou, 2019). In the 2018-2019 school year, 31 participating states contributed data, showing that at least 108,199 students received the SoBL in 119 languages (Black et al., 2020). This represents approximately 3 percent of high-school graduates in the United States, illustrating the potential for growth in the future. California awarded the most seals (48,311 students) with North Carolina (9,584 students) and Virginia (7,046 students) recognizing

the second and third highest numbers of students. Washington awarded the SoBL in the most languages, with 69 in total.

When considering participation statistics, it is important to consider the demographics of the recognized students to ensure equity by race, class, and language background. To do this, states and districts should not only track numbers of SoBL recipients but disaggregate the data to understand who is receiving the recognition. For the 2017-2018 school year, few states were able to provide the number of current and former ELs earning the SoBL (Chou, 2019). However, by the 2020 report, 20 states provided that data, illustrating that 33,128 current and former ELs, approximately 30 percent of recipients, earned the SoBL (Black et al., 2020). This number was still quite low, suggesting that some state SoBL policies might promote elite bilingualism, representing a critical area for attention.

It is critical that all students have pathways to earning the SoBL, not just students who enroll in world language classes at school. To ensure equity in implementation, stakeholders should track the number of current and former ELs receiving the SoBL.

As evidenced throughout this section, multiple variations in SoBL policies exist across states, and local educators must finesse these nuances to implement the SoBL in their communities. This volume identifies high-leverage practices for SoBL implementation that have emerged from our work with districts across the country. In our initial work with the SoBL, educators described difficulties implementing a policy that came with little guidance beyond the formal state legislation. Although strides have been made in information dissemination in recent years (see SoBL implementation resources from states like Massachusetts, Michigan, Mississippi, and New York), many questions remain around best practices. Districts with the most success connect with national and state language organizations, such as ACTFL, as well as local colleagues to share ideas and learn from one another. In this way, the success of SoBL efforts often relies upon one person with the connections and time to dig around for information and resources (see Marichal et al., 2021 for an inspiring example of how a teacher spearheaded the SoBL in a rural school). Not every school has that person or that time, considering the lack of state and federal funding tied to the SoBL. We hope this book fills that void for school and district stakeholders by sharing research-based practices from SoBL implementation around the country.

Introducing the 5Ps Framework for Implementation

This text presents a five-part framework to guide SoBL implementation and promote multilingualism and multiliteracy for all students (see Figure 1.2). The framework includes five action steps: (a) defining the *Purpose* for the SoBL, (b) determining which *Proficiency Assessments* to use for evaluation of biliteracy, (c) designing *Programs* to support language development, (d) working with *Partners* to facilitate implementation, and (e) using strategies for *Promotion* of the initiative across schools and communities. Throughout the framework, we emphasize an equity lens that seeks to foster the language competencies of ELs as well as world and heritage language learners.

Figure 1.2. Framework for SoBL Implementation

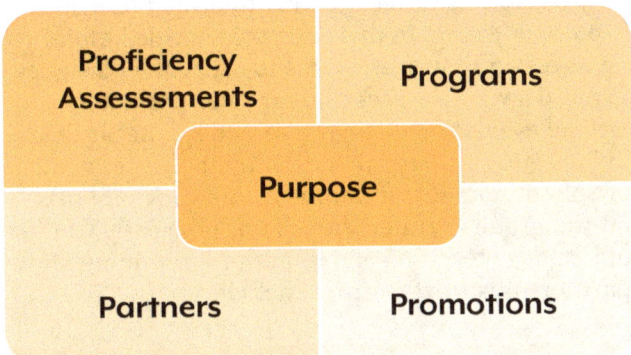

The first facet of the framework centers on *Purpose*. Particularly due to the voluntary nature of the SoBL, districts must adopt this initiative with a clear and shared purpose to promote multiliteracy among their students. In our research, we have discovered that the most successful districts make collaborative decisions about how the SoBL fits within their larger strategic plans and visions (Heineke & Davin, 2021). Whether embracing the SoBL as a lever to bolster enrollment in world language programming, recognize the linguistic assets of ELs, or support the heritage language development of less commonly taught languages, districts need a purpose for embarking upon this work—a purpose that makes sense in their unique context.

The second facet turns to *Proficiency Assessments*. For many, questions emerge related to how to identify students to assess, as well as which assessments to administer, when, and in what location. Our research suggests that implementing proficiency assessments enhances language instruction in schools by providing teachers with valuable data on stu-

dents' language abilities (Davin et al., 2018). Moreover, students value the feedback from these assessments and appreciate the external validation of language proficiency that such tests provide (Davin & Heineke, 2018). However, this facet of the framework presents dangerous equity pitfalls, caused by matters such as cost and the challenges of assessing students who use languages without affordable or convenient assessments. We offer suggestions and tools for readers to avoid these pitfalls.

The third facet of the framework focuses on *Programs*. While some students come to school multiliterate, others benefit from school-based language programming. Language programs, including world language, bilingual, and English language programs, support students in developing language competencies that span listening, speaking, reading, and writing. When used with language programs, the SoBL enhances school and district efforts to reach the overarching goals for students' multiliteracies. Our research has demonstrated that SoBL implementation enhances programs in multiple ways, including extending bilingual education into secondary schools, increasing world language offerings, and promoting instruction for all learners that involves authentic language use, performance assessments, cultural awareness, and community-based service learning (Davin et al., 2018; Heineke & Davin, 2021).

The fourth facet embraces the pertinent role of *Partners*. One readily clear truth about SoBL implementation has emerged across our research: this initiative cannot be the sole responsibility of one person within a school or district (Heineke & Davin, 2021; Okraski et al., 2020). To implement the SoBL in meaningful and effective ways to reach goals and promote equitable access to the recognition, multiple stakeholders must be involved inside and outside of schools. In addition to the primary point person leading the efforts, administrators, teachers, and counselors can encourage SoBL attainment and the requisite language proficiency to achieve it. Families and community partners serve as integral players to offer the recognition in less commonly taught languages. Universities and businesses support pathways to college and career, as well as professional development and the development of assessments. In sum, success comes from an all-hands-on-deck approach to implementing the SoBL.

The fifth and final facet of the framework looks at *Promotion*, referring to ways to expand awareness and access to the SoBL. Our research has demonstrated several ways that schools and districts approach the SoBL to build awareness, convey information, and enhance interest in the recognition (Heineke & Davin, 2021). In addition to more logistical considerations and related ideas like informational flyers, parent communications, and award celebrations, we discuss how to leverage social media to promote the SoBL. This facet provides tangible ideas to immediately enhance SoBL implementation in any context.

Using This Book to Promote Change in Your Unique Context

In the chapters that follow, we explore practices for implementing the SoBL in unique contexts across the United States, organized by the 5Ps framework: Purpose in Chapter 2, Proficiency Assessments in Chapter 3, Programs in Chapter 4, Partners in Chapter 5, and Promotion in Chapter 6. Chapter 7 concludes the text by bringing these facets together to support you in enacting the framework in practice as you plan, implement, and evaluate efforts to promote students' multiliteracy.

It is our hope that this book will be used collaboratively across settings and practitioners, including places just beginning to think about the SoBL, those with more established programs and involving people with advanced expertise in language education, and those with other backgrounds and licensure areas. While diving into the actionable ideas presented in each facet of the 5Ps framework, readers will discover that many of these practices merge overall strong approaches to schooling (e.g., communicating across schools, valuing students' assets, reducing paperwork and barriers) with integral understandings about language and language development (e.g., program models, performance assessments). We hope that teams build on the various areas of expertise brought to the table to use this volume in meaningful and collaborative ways to enhance students' multiliteracy in schools.

To that end, our primary audiences are those working in districts and schools, including world language, bilingual, and EL educators, as well as general-education teachers, coordinators, counselors, and administrators who play integral roles in policy implementation. We include in this audience leaders at community language organizations and faculty in language departments at institutions of higher education. For community language organizations, we discuss how partnerships with local schools to administer the SoBL combat the attrition that often occurs as students progress through high school

(see Chapter 5). For institutions of higher education, we explain how the SoBL informs placement decisions and how, in some contexts, awarding college credit to SoBL recipients increases enrollment (see Chapter 5). Finally, policymakers seeking to adopt or revise state-wide SoBL policy and researchers wishing to investigate SoBL implementation can use this text as a lens on equity in their administration and investigations across school settings.

Exploring Text Features That Promote Learning and Application We have crafted and organized this book for use in leadership teams and professional learning communities. Practitioners can read a chapter, reflect and plan using the provided tools, and come together with colleagues to share ideas as situated in the unique school, district, and community. However, we recognize that this model may be too lofty for some settings, and the SoBL coordinator may be reading independently to bring ideas back to a larger group. In this case, we provide helpful passages, graphics, and tools to use with colleagues to build awareness, seek buy-in, and promote critical evaluation of current practices. Regardless of how you approach this text and the larger work of SoBL implementation, the framework supports on-the-ground refinements of both the daily work of language teaching and larger programming and partnerships. Text features include:

Research-based Vignettes: In each chapter, we provide vignettes to exemplify key concepts and practices. The first vignette in each chapter presents the perspective of a student who earned the SoBL. Subsequent vignettes focus on educators implementing the policy. In most cases, these vignettes come from our research and provide snapshots into each facet of the 5Ps framework. We use pseudonyms for all students, as well as most districts, schools, and educators, except those who provided formal permission to do otherwise.

Guiding Questions: Following the opening vignette, each chapter includes questions, to preview the topics addressed in the chapter. These questions allow you to reflect upon what you already know about the topic, as well as check your understanding following the reading of the chapter.

Consideration of Current Practice: We recognize that readers approach this text at different points of SoBL implementation, with some working to get efforts off the ground and others seeking to refine implementation. We want to start where you are by having you reflect on your current practice in relation to each framework facet to define your own goals and potential applications from the chapter.

Equity Alerts: Throughout each chapter, we include critical considerations that relate to how practices impact equity in implementation. We aim to support you in thinking through how to implement the SoBL in ways that recognize learners' rich and diverse language competencies to promote all students' multiliteracies. Each equity alert is highlighted and marked with a scales of justice icon.

Questions for Discussion and Reflection: At the end of each chapter, we provide a list of questions to help you reflect on the key points of the chapter and apply them to your own context. These questions can also guide discussions in leadership teams and professional learning communities.

Further Reading Lists: Following the discussion questions, we offer suggestions of resources for further reading that delve more deeply into the important concepts presented in the chapter.

Tools: Each chapter is accompanied by a set of tools for stakeholders to adapt and apply to their unique contexts. We designed these tools to help you analyze your existing systems and structures and plan for equitable SoBL implementation.

Appendices: In addition to the tools included with each chapter, we also offer a series of appendices at the end of the text. These include resources to guide assessment prompt creation and action plan examples for SoBL implementation.

Defining Key Terms Used in This Book Throughout this book, when we refer to the *SoBL*, we are referring to states' Seal of Biliteracy policies. The SoBL is typically administered by public departments of education and governed by state-level legislation to recognize students who graduate high school bilingual and biliterate. One business entity gives the Global Seal of Biliteracy to recognize individuals living anywhere in the world who are bilingual and biliterate. Our research to date has focused on state-level SoBL recognitions.

Biliteracy is defined as the ability to read and write in any two languages; however, SoBL policies require students to read, write, speak, and listen in two languages, and in all states except Hawaii, one of those languages must be English. Valdés contends that the SoBL should instead be called the *Seal of Biliteracy and Linguistic Multicompetence*, and that stakeholders should consider phasing out the term "biliteracy" (2020, p. 195). In this book we occasionally use the terms *multiliteracy* and *biliteracy* interchangeably, and likewise the terms *multilingualism* and *bilingualism*, although technically the prefix *bi-* refers to only two whereas *multi-* could be two or more.

Within the SoBL initiative, biliteracy is measured by *language proficiency*, defined by ACTFL as "what individuals can do with language in terms of speaking, writing, listening, and reading in real-world situations in a spontaneous and non-rehearsed context" (2012b, p. 3). While proficiency applies equally well to a single language, two different languages, or even to the integrated use of multiple languages, assessment of language proficiency may not always capture the broader language competencies of multilingual students who may often use *translanguaging* (García & Wei, 2014; Valdés, 2020). Translanguaging occurs when an individual accesses "different linguistic features or various modes of what are described as autonomous languages, in order to maximize communicative potential" (García, 2009, p. 140). However, it can be difficult for language educators to discern the proficiency level of learners who use more than one language within the same language sample. Moreover, the assessments used to award the SoBL are not necessarily designed to account for the broader language competencies of multilingual students who may often use translanguaging, one area of criticism (Rothman & Iverson, 2010). Although we use the term language proficiency in line with state SoBL policies in this book, we also encourage teachers to acknowledge and leverage students' rich and complex language competencies to support their proficiency development during instruction in bilingual education programs in preparation for SoBL assessments.

Throughout this text, we adopt the term *SoBL assessments* to refer to the various language tests that students take to demonstrate world language proficiency. This term encompasses a wide variety of external assessments.

This book consistently considers SoBL implementation for three target groups of students. The term *world language learners* refers to English-dominant students who choose to enroll in language programming to develop proficiency in another language. *Heritage language learners* denotes students whose families use languages other than English and who subsequently develop and use languages connected to their homes and heritage. Within the larger group of heritage learners, students labeled as *English learners* (ELs) are still deemed to be developing proficiency in English as measured by standardized tests (Linquanti & Cook, 2013). While we prefer and consistently use asset-based terms for students in our daily discourse, including *multilingual learners* and *emergent bilinguals* (García, 2009), we use ELs throughout this volume due to readers' familiarity with the institutional label in national and state educational policies.

We also discuss a variety of program types that promote biliteracy. *World language programs* focus on teaching the target language (e.g., Spanish, German). While these programs may reinforce academic content (e.g., math, science, history), they are not responsible for teaching that academic content. Thus, in world language programs, the target language is often both the content and the means of instruction. Whereas world language programs typically prioritize the needs of world language learners, *heritage language programs* are designed specifically for students with exposure to other languages in homes and communities. These programs support students in further developing these languages.

Bilingual programs also play an integral role in SoBL implementation. *Dual-language immersion programs* aim to develop students' proficiency in both home and target languages, with bilingual teachers strategically using both languages to teach academic content. Whereas *two-way immersion programs* involve students from both language groups (e.g., 50% English speakers, 50% Spanish speakers), *one-way immersion programs* involve one language group (Sugarman, 2018). These programs are considered additive in nature, as they seek to develop students' biliteracy over multiple years. *Transitional bilingual programs* emerge from the minimum threshold of bilingual programming required by state policy, which initiates instruction in students' home languages but then transitions them into instruction in English, with predetermined language allocations and home language use decreasing each school year.

English as a Second Language (ESL) programs also factor into SoBL implementation for students labeled as ELs. These programs typically center on English, with pull-out, push-in, and co-teaching models to support ELs in developing English while learning academic content. In *pull-out* program models, ESL teachers pull students out of general education classes for a portion of the school day to provide English instruction. In *push-in* program models, the ESL teacher enters the general education classroom to support ELs while they are engaging in classroom learning, typically for one period of the school day. In *co-teaching* models, the ESL teacher collaborates with the classroom teacher to provide instruction to all learners in the classroom. Although these programs prioritize English by design, we embrace their potential for promoting biliteracy and subsequent access to the SoBL for students labeled as ELs.

Chapter Summary

In this chapter, we have described origins and policy details surrounding the SoBL, which seeks to nurture the multilingualism and multiliteracy of children and adolescents in U.S. schools and communities. We have discussed how SoBL policies vary across the 43 participating states and the District of Columbia, including by minimum required proficiency level, available tiers, accepted evidence of proficiency, and types of schools that participate. These variations shape the number of districts participating in the SoBL program as well as the number of students earning the recognition. Despite these differences, the 5Ps Framework—*Purpose, Proficiency Assessments, Programs, Partners,* and *Promotion*—offers research-based suggestions to implement the SoBL equitably across contexts. That framework is the focus of this book, which has been crafted for you to use independently or collaboratively in your local setting to guide SoBL implementation at the appropriate stage. We look forward to exploring these ideas, tools, and examples with you in the chapters that follow.

Questions for Discussion and Reflection

1. If your state has adopted a SoBL policy, complete Tool 1.1. Discuss the strengths and weaknesses of your state's policy. How might you implement the SoBL to maximize the strengths while accounting for weaknesses? What equity issues might arise based on your state's policy? What revisions would you suggest to policymakers? If your state has not yet adopted a SoBL, examine the policy of a neighboring state, discuss these questions, and consider the best way forward for your own state.

2. Search for additional resources related to SoBL implementation in your state. Determine whether your state-level language organizations have any upcoming conferences with sessions focused on the SoBL. Use Tool 1.2 to connect with another district or school in your state that has experience with SoBL implementation.

3. Think about the 5Ps in the framework for SoBL implementation: *Purpose, Proficiency Assessments, Programs, Partners,* and *Promotion.* Consider each framework facet, informally assessing and reflecting upon your current work in this focal area. Which of these framework facets seem most important or crucial for you to consider right now?

4. Reflect on the best way to use this book (e.g., professional learning communities, teacher workshops) to support SoBL implementation in your district or school. What are your goals for reading this book? Who in your school or district might benefit from reading it with you? What steps are needed to initiate collaborative reading, learning, and application to enhance SoBL implementation?

Further Reading

*   Californians Together, ACTFL, Modern Language Association, National Association for Bilingual Education, National Association of English Language Program Administrators, National Council of State Supervisors for Languages, & TESOL International Association. (2020). *Guidelines for implementing the Seal of Biliteracy* (Joint report). https://www.actfl.org/sites/default/files/resources/SOBL_Updated_Guidelines%20_October_2020.pdf

*   Davin, K. J., & Heineke, A. J. (2017). The Seal of Biliteracy: Variations in policy and outcomes. *Foreign Language Annals, 50,* 486–499. https://doi.org/10.1111/flan.12279

*   Heineke, A. J., & Davin, K. J. (Eds.) (2020b). *The Seal of Biliteracy: Case studies and considerations for policy implementation.* Information Age.

*   Subtirelu, N. C., Borowczyk, M., Hernández, R. T., & Venezia, F. (2019). Recognizing whose bilingualism? A critical policy analysis of the Seal of Biliteracy. *Modern Language Journal, 103,* 371–390. https://doi.org/10.1111/modl.12556

Tool 1.1. Determine State Seal of Biliteracy Requirements

Directions: Each state has a website that lists requirements for the Seal of Biliteracy (SoBL). Navigate to that website and complete the following table.

GUIDING QUESTIONS	NOTES
In what state is your school or district located?	
Is the recognition called a Seal of Biliteracy in your state or does it have a different name (e.g., *Bilingual Seal, Global Languages Endorsement*)?	
Does your state have one tier or multiple tiers of the SoBL?	
What is the minimum required proficiency level in world language (e.g., Intermediate Mid, Intermediate High)?	
What forms of evidence of world language proficiency are accepted (e.g., seat time, approved assessment, portfolio)?	
What forms of evidence of English language proficiency are accepted (e.g., seat time, approved assessment, graduation)?	
Is your school required to register with the state to implement the SoBL?	
How do districts and schools report SoBL recognitions to the state department of education? What must be included in the report?	
Who awards the SoBL (e.g., private schools, charter schools, community organizations)?	
Who is the appropriate contact at the state level and what is their contact information?	

Tool 1.2. Connect with an Exemplar School in Your State

Directions: There are many details to consider when implementing the SoBL. Other schools in your state that have implemented the SoBL can be a wonderful resource. Use the steps and questions below to interview colleagues about SoBL implementation.

1. As you begin to consider implementation, or as you think about how to revise implementation, do an internet search to find out who else in your state is awarding the SoBL. Make a list of schools or districts in your state that implement the SoBL. In some states, a list of schools is provided on the department of education's website. In others, you might need to reach out to the state language supervisor or the language organization (e.g., the Foreign Language Association of North Carolina or the Massachusetts Foreign Language Association) to ask for recommendations of contacts.

2. If the school has a webpage focused specifically on the SoBL, look for the email address of the SoBL contact. Send that person an email to request a telephone call or meeting. If a contact person is not listed, consider reaching out to the world language department chair or the counseling department.

3. During your meeting, you might ask questions such as the following:

   a. How long have you been implementing the SoBL?

   b. In which languages do you award the SoBL?

   c. What are the goals and purposes of your SoBL efforts?

   d. How did you get the program up and running?

   e. How do students earn the SoBL? Through particular assessments?

   f. If students achieve the SoBL through assessments, when are they offered? Where are they offered? Who pays for them? Who proctors them? What technology is necessary?

   g. Who in the school oversees SoBL implementation? If this person is compensated, in what way?

   h. How do you ensure that it is not only the students enrolled in language classes that receive the SoBL? In other words, how do you ensure that students who speak languages not taught in the school have access?

   i. How do you advertise the SoBL opportunity to faculty, students, and parents?

   j. How do you celebrate students' biliteracy?

   k. How do you communicate information about the SoBL to families and the community?

   l. What challenges have you encountered in implementation? How have you handled them?

   m. What impact of SoBL implementation have you observed on programs, teachers, and students?

   n. Could you share a success story or a positive experience in SoBL implementation in your context?

Chapter 2
Purpose: Framing the Work in your School and Community

Hassan grew up in South Africa and spoke both English and Somali when he arrived in the United States. When asked who the SoBL was designed to benefit, Hassan replied that it was designed for "minorities for sure." He stated, "You could see that on award day, the room was filled with people of color." He did not know much about the SoBL but decided to take the SoBL assessment after hearing he could get college credit for his competencies in Somali. But he explained that "even if the main aim wasn't for [minorities], even if the main aim was for everyone, you can see that people of color were taking the test and then getting the seal." Hassan's perspective seemed to align with the stated SoBL policy goals of his school district's administrators, one of which was to promote racial equity. As an assistant superintendent explained, "The opening statement of our racial equity policy talks about [how] a student's ethnic and cultural identity should be a contributor to their learning. Well, what greater way than to have their home language be honored."

Guiding Questions

How and why does implementation vary based on local context?

Why begin implementation with the end goals in mind?

In what ways can implementation goals center on students?

This chapter centers efforts to implement the SoBL around a clearly defined purpose. With this first facet of the framework, we recognize that schools are complex and dynamic settings, and that the SoBL may serve different purposes depending on unique contextual factors (Heineke, 2020). Drawing from the sociocultural paradigm on language education policy, we recognize that policy is not top-down or prescriptive; rather, it yields space and flexibility for local stakeholders to implement the SoBL in ways that respond to the complex and dynamic nature of schools, districts, and communities (Johnson, 2013; Levinson & Sutton, 2001; Ricento, 2000). In this way, SoBL implementation looks mark-edly different depending on the unique context, as stakeholders shape policy design and implementation to match students and schools (McCarty, 2011; Menken & García, 2010).

Defining purpose has been a frequent theme emergent in our research on the SoBL, including state-level stakeholders' intent for enacting legislation (Heineke & Davin, 2020a), district-level administrators' objectives in adopting the initiative (Heineke & Davin, 2021), and school-level educators' targets in implementing the SoBL on the ground (Davin et al., 2018). Whereas having clearly defined goals is important across all education (Wiggins & McTighe, 2007, 2011), the voluntary nature of the SoBL makes such definition an integral step. Like the administrators in the vignette whose goal was to promote racial equity, stakeholders define the *why* to guide overall efforts, as well as to secure the initial buy-in and resources necessary for implementation. In our research across the country, we have found that stakeholders' goals vary but have three important similarities: (a) strategic use of the SoBL as a mechanism to promote biliteracy, (b) focus on unique student demographics and home languages, and (c) prioritization of focal language programs (Heineke & Davin, 2021). Similarly, as illustrated by the story of Hassan in the opening vignette, it is critical that students, as well as other stakeholders, understand and inform the policy's purpose.

This chapter walks through these important steps of defining purpose. We begin by prompting reflection upon the purpose driving your SoBL work and then delve into four steps to define or refine those goals (see Figure 2.1). First, we embrace unique and varied contexts to frame goals around students' language use in homes, communities, and schools. Second, we consider ways to collaboratively define and refine these goals for SoBL implementation. Third, we explore how to situate SoBL goals within larger state policies and district initiatives to extend this work beyond one program or department in the school. Finally, we share how to seek the buy-in of district administrators and school boards with these thoughtfully drafted goals. We suggest that you use Tool 2.1 throughout the chapter to guide exploration, drafting, refining, and sharing of the purpose that drives SoBL implementation in your setting.

Figure 2.1. Steps to Defining Purpose for SoBL Implementation

Probe your school's unique linguistic landscape.

Draft goals to guide SoBL implememntation.

Situate the SoBL within other policies and initiatives.

Seek buy-in and support from relevant stakeholders.

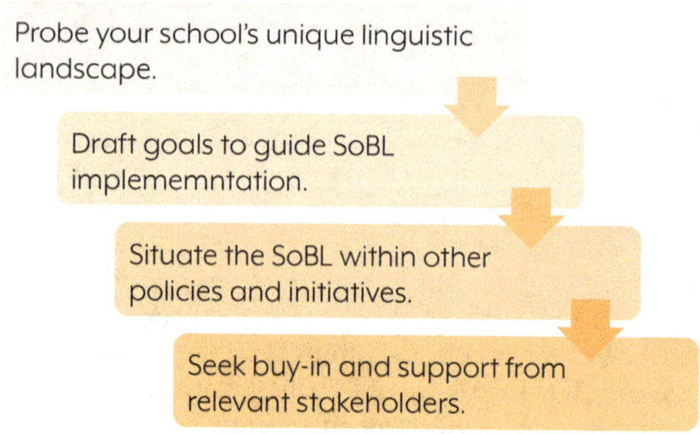

Considering Current Goals and Priorities

Each reader comes to this book with different circumstances. For those initially exploring or starting efforts, this chapter supports you in defining goals for SoBL implementation. For those with existing SoBL efforts, the focus lies in refining goals, whether those have been explicit or implicit in your previous work. All readers can begin by reflecting on what drew you to the SoBL. Why implement this recognition in your school or district? What do you hope to accomplish? If already engaging in implementation, whether initial or extensive, consider the focus of your current efforts. Whose biliteracy do you typ-

ically recognize? What do you hope to accomplish in refining your efforts? Purpose drives your work, whether you have defined that purpose overtly or not. By reflecting on what has inspired and shaped your current efforts, you begin to define what you value and seek to accomplish.

Of course, your roles and contexts shape how and why you embark upon this work. If you coordinate world language programming, then perhaps you envision the potential of the SoBL for increasing enrollment in those programs. If you teach and support ELs in English-medium courses, then perhaps you seek a way to encourage students' biliteracy outside of the formal curriculum. If you teach at a community language school, then perhaps you see this work as crucial to maintaining more children's heritage languages. Reflect upon how your role influences your purpose for this work, both to embrace the rich expertise that you bring and recognize where you might extend your focus to reach more students. Think about the potential purposes that the SoBL might serve, spanning learners, languages, and program models. How might the SoBL nurture the biliteracy of world language learners, heritage language learners, and ELs? Keep these reflections in mind as you work through this chapter on defining purpose.

Probing the School and Community Context

North School District (a pseudonym) houses K-12 schools in a mid-size urban area in the western United States, welcoming students speaking over 100 home languages with Spanish spoken by over a third of students. The district offers K-12 dual-language immersion in Spanish and English, as well as Spanish, Chinese, French, and German as world languages in middle and high schools. Stakeholders initiated the SoBL shortly after the state passed the legislation, hoping to legitimize world language study and strengthen language education in a context where world language existed as an elective rather than a requirement for graduation.

As world language teachers and leaders began to implement the SoBL, they recognized the great potential to expand beyond their initial goals to bolster formal world language study. With the Indigenous language Paiute used in the community, they partnered with the tribal council to create a Paiute language program in select high schools, as well as an assessment tool for students to receive the SoBL. They also responded to other community populations, adding options for students to demonstrate proficiency in heritage languages including Greek, Italian, Japanese, Portuguese, Russian, Tagalog, and Vietnamese.

Marie (a pseudonym), the district's world language director, shared, "The list [of languages] just keeps getting bigger and bigger as students begin to find that they're valuing their own languages that they've spoken at home. We've heard from grandparents who said, 'Did you know that my granddaughter wants to take the test in Cebuano, and so I've been practicing with her.' This is bringing out such joy. It's really legitimizing the [students'] native languages."

All policy plays out in different ways depending on context, but this flexibility is a hallmark of the SoBL. As described in Chapter 1, the SoBL started as a grassroots effort in California and grew into a nationwide initiative with iterations responding to the unique contexts, demographics, and goals within states (Heineke & Davin, 2020a; Olsen, 2020). As the movement enters local settings, the same spirit remains: enacting the SoBL in response to students, families, schools, and communities. This approach stems from two features of this policy. First, districts voluntarily choose to participate in the SoBL without government funding, so stakeholders ground efforts in their unique contexts to justify the use of local resources. Second, state-level policies are markedly flexible, setting the desired outcome of biliteracy without prescription as to how to achieve it (e.g., bilingual education, world language study, home language use).

In this way, SoBL implementation begins locally with clear understanding of the local linguistic landscape. This requires exploration of language use in home, community, and school settings (see Figure 2.2), guided by three questions:

- Whom are we serving?
- How are we facilitating and encouraging biliteracy among our unique population?
- What languages and language programs need attention in our efforts?

The vignette above demonstrates how North School District stakeholders responded to the goals and needs of language programming within the district, as well as the linguistic resources of families and communities. These steps bolster biliteracy efforts by recognizing the rich linguistic assets of heritage language learners and encouraging language study among world language learners. In this section, we explore language use in homes, communities, and schools to frame your SoBL work.

Figure 2.2. The Local Linguistic Landscape

How do students use languages in homes?

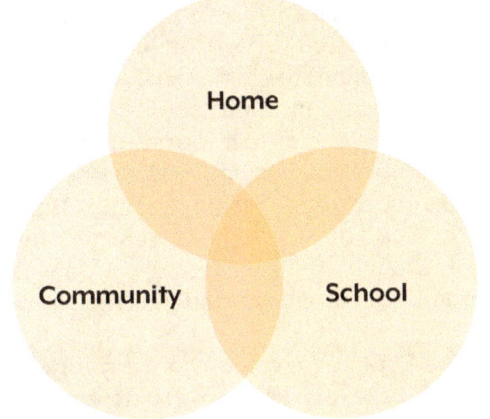

How do students use languages in the community?

How do students use languages in schools?

Language Use in Homes The place to start this exploration is with languages used in homes, specifically focused on students and families. Since students are often the targets of educational policies, ethical decision-making centers on prioritizing their best interests in implementation (Honig, 2006). Copious research confirms the importance of maintaining home and heritage languages (e.g., Cook, 1999; Fishman, 1991; García, 2019; Valdés, 2005; Valdés et al., 2006). Since 20 percent of students use languages other than English at home, with that percentage rising in many communities, the focus on students' home languages comprises an integral component of SoBL implementation (NCES, 2019). Starting with students' home languages: (a) builds educators' awareness of the rich linguistic resources of students and families, (b) brings attention to languages that might not be taught in schools, and (c) centers SoBL implementation on the interests of a school's or district's constituents.

In our research in communities across the country, we have heard multiple stories about the power of the SoBL to validate home and heritage languages (Heineke & Davin, 2021). Take the example above from the North School District, where the SoBL prompted a high-school student to practice Cebuano with her grandfather. In the Walsh School District, students find space to develop their cultural and linguistic identities through Somali heritage language instruction. In the Morton School District, high schools center on family language use, with large bilingual celebrations and reflective videos by students and parents to underscore the value of maintaining Spanish (Heineke & Davin, 2021; these examples are explored in more depth in upcoming chapters). It is easy to reduce the value of bilingualism to economic terms, such as enhancing future job attainment, but the SoBL also supports personal, familial, and related social-emotional development through attention to heritage languages (Subtirelu, 2020). The aim is not to curricularize heritage languages in English-dominant schools, reducing home language competencies to a course or assessment (Valdés, 2020). Instead, school stakeholders offer equitable opportunities for students like Hassan to pursue the SoBL in their home languages, demonstrating the value of those languages alongside that of the traditional languages taught in schools.

The SoBL relies on formal language proficiency assessments to determine biliteracy. But students come to school with an array of language competencies, including various dialects, language varieties, and cross-linguistic capabilities where they flexibly and fluidly tap into multiple languages to communicate. Stakeholders should recognize all language competencies as assets for learning and biliteracy development.

Working to implement the SoBL begins by exploring the languages spoken by students and families (see Tool 2.2 at the end of this chapter). At North, Marie seeks out assessments for languages based on students' requests. When a student or family member indicates interest in earning the SoBL in a particular language, she and her team explore assessment options. Another approach is using existing data from the **Home Language Survey** that parents and guardians complete upon enrolling their children in school. Aligned to federal requirements, the brief three- or four-question instrument asks about the languages used in the home, the first language used by the child, and the language most often used by the child (Goldenberg & Rutherford-Quach, 2012). In addition to having this data available for individual students, schools typically generate reports that list all languages with the number of students using each

one. Stakeholders then use this data to proactively seek out avenues for students to develop and demonstrate their language competencies.

It is important to note that students speak languages other than English in every corner of the United States. This linguistic diversity might be more evident in urban and suburban settings, where children often use a multitude of different languages in addition to English in homes. But even seemingly homogenous small towns and rural communities house families with rich linguistic repertoires and histories. The Home Language Survey often provides eye-opening data for teachers who may not have known that students or family members used other languages at home. However, a family member's occasional heritage language use might not prompt parents to check the box on the survey. For this reason, anecdotal data collection through talking to students and family members to understand the assets that they bring to school deepens understandings of home language use. By identifying the languages used in homes, you might choose to define or refine purpose to recognize all students' biliteracy via SoBL implementation.

Language Use in Communities Another lens to consider is language use in the community. Take the example of Paiute, an Indigenous language used in the North community that stakeholders prioritize and offer as a world language in addition to traditional offerings like Spanish, French, and German. Across the country, localities have embraced the SoBL to maintain Indigenous community languages, with educators partnering with tribal councils to offer both language programming and assessments. Many states prioritize Indigenous languages in SoBL policies. In New Mexico, state legislation provides guidance for local districts to develop avenues in tribal languages such as Navajo. In Hawai'i, the Indigenous language of 'Ōlelo Hawai'i holds the same status as English; to achieve the SoBL, students demonstrate proficiency in either English or 'Ōlelo Hawai'i, as well as another world or heritage language. Indigenous languages play integral roles in communities across the country, and the SoBL provides rich opportunities to partner with tribes to support heritage language maintenance.

Immigrants' languages also mediate daily life and interactions in many communities. As families have immigrated to the United States over generations, they have often settled in communities with others from the same country of origin or cultural background (Suárez-Orozco, 2004). In these enclaves, residents use the languages of their countries of origin to engage in commerce, worship, and regular interactions. This is readily evident in urban areas like Chicago, where Urdu mediates commerce on Devon Avenue, Vietnamese dots signage in Uptown, and Spanish abounds across Little Village. But community language trends also emerge in suburban and rural areas, reflecting historical trends in immigration. For example, some ethnic communities moved to nearby suburbs after initially settling in Chicago, resulting in regular use of Hebrew in Skokie and Polish in Harwood Heights, among others. Some towns across the United States still reflect the linguistic heritage of early immigrant settlers, such as Portuguese in Fall River, Massachusetts, German in Berks County, Pennsylvania, and Norwegian in Blair, Wisconsin.

Whereas some immigrant family groups have resided in the same communities for multiple generations, others have more mobility. In rural areas from California to Iowa to Vermont, *migrant workers* move in and out of different communities depending on seasonal crops and available work. This unique community context provides challenges to nurturing and recognizing students' biliteracy, as children move schools frequently and may not receive longitudinal support for their developing language competencies. When embarking upon SoBL implementation in areas with migrant populations, educators can build awareness about migrants' language usage in communities. These languages enrich the community's linguistic landscape, subsequently shaping stakeholders' decision-making about the *Purpose* of the SoBL, as well as the *Proficiency Assessments, Programs, Partners,* and *Promotion* needed to facilitate migrant students' achievement of biliteracy.

Exploration of a community's linguistic landscape is often as simple as a web search and walk around town (see Tool 2.2). The storied past of the community can often be found in online sources that allow for reading and understanding the historical trajectory and trends of Indigenous, immigrant, and migrant groups in the region. Many cities, towns, and villages have historical societies and museums with information that promotes fascinating discoveries about the community. That history shapes the current context of language use in communities, including the shared value placed on maintaining heritage languages and the daily use of those languages in settings around the community. *Community walks,* an experience where educators walk through the attendance zone of a school, provide rich data on authentic language use outside of schools: How are languages used orally (e.g., personal interactions) and in print (e.g., signage)? Where do other languages mediate daily life (e.g., places of worship)? Are there locations that involve formal education in another language (e.g., Polish Saturday School, Korean Sunday School)? These community assets support SoBL implementation in schools.

Language Use in Schools Language use in schools is often more straightforward to explore, as those implementing the SoBL are typically intimately involved in local language programming. English is the medium of most instruction in U.S. schools, but it is important to document other focal languages, including those developed via: (a) world language study, (b) bilingual education, and (c) student organizations involving language and culture. At North, Marie and her team enacted the SoBL to bolster world language study, which was not required for graduation in their state. In the Wilmot School District, leaders wanted to recognize and strengthen the long-standing Spanish dual-language program. At Stevenson High School, stakeholders responded to languages used in informal clubs like Polish, Hebrew, and Hindi (Fisk, 2020, discussed in detail in Chapter 6). To round out your exploration of linguistic landscapes, document the languages used in your setting (see Tool 2.2). SoBL efforts can tap into these efforts, as well as sustain them over time.

In addition to listing the mediums of instruction at your school, including English and focal languages in world language and bilingual settings, think about those used in schools within your larger district. For example, if you are in the high-school setting, consider the languages of instruction in the elementary and middle schools that your students have attended. If you are in elementary or middle schools, explore the extended trajectories of formal language study that your students will have access to in future years. The shared goal of promoting biliteracy calls for recognition of the need for long-term efforts (Kroll & Dussias, 2017). Despite variance in the level of proficiency needed to achieve the SoBL, stakeholders should apply a longitudinal lens when defining the scope of the SoBL in their schools or districts. SoBL pathway recognitions, described in the first chapter, can involve stakeholders spanning preschool through high school in these efforts to support language development over time.

By surveying language use in homes, communities, and schools, stakeholders develop understandings of the local linguistic landscape that situates the

SoBL (Herrera, 2016). Maintain **asset-based perspectives** during these explorations, which means situating students' diverse and dynamic language competencies as resources rather than detriments (Cook, 1992; Jessner, 2008). Remember that the lived experience of candidates for the SoBL may not reflect strict separation of languages and students' multilingual practices may not fit into English-dominant and monolingual norms in U.S. schools, resulting in deficit-based perspectives on students for whom English is not the primary language (García, 2009). When considering the linguistic landscape of your school and community, push yourself to challenge dominant ideologies that emphasize monolingualism and standard language usage. Embrace the many and varied linguistic assets of students, including oral language abilities in home languages and dynamic translanguaging spanning multiple languages (Creese & Blackledge, 2015; García et al., 2015; Valdés, 2020). Starting with an asset-based lens at this early stage of planning influences all other facets of SoBL implementation and supports equity in biliteracy development and recognition (Heineke & Davin, 2021). Tool 2.2 supports language-focused asset mapping that results in useful data for defining implementation goals that center on equitable access to biliteracy for all students.

Drafting Goals for Implementation

District leaders in Greene Public Schools (a pseudonym), a large urban school district, were overjoyed when state lawmakers passed SoBL legislation and opened the door to recognizing students' biliteracy. In a city where almost half of the 350,000 students were Latinx and 19 percent of students were labeled as ELs, the district embraced the SoBL to showcase students' linguistic resources. The district wanted a collective effort across the city, so central office administrators invited language-focused stakeholders, including school administrators, university educators, and community leaders, to join a steering committee.

Initial conversations among the steering committee members centered on the Spanish-speaking population, particularly current and former ELs, with stakeholders wishing to encourage bilingualism and dual-language education in place of the subtractive approaches more common in schools across the city. The resulting goals promoted significant change in bilingual education in the district, with money and efforts funneled into starting dual-language programs around the city. The steering committee bolstered these efforts through the SoBL Pathway Award, which recognized the biliteracy of fifth through eighth graders in dual-language programs.

The mayor and superintendent joined the conversation to set hard-and-fast goals: 25 percent of students to receive the SoBL by 2020 and 50 percent by 2030. After initially focusing on Spanish speakers, they extended the goals to include speakers of multiple languages to reflect the multilingual urban area. With the goal to foster the biliteracy of a lofty percentage of all students, the district added assessments in languages including Arabic, Bulgarian, Chinese, French, German, Italian, Japanese, Latin, Polish, Portuguese, and Russian.

Educators have long embraced and used backward design to guide various efforts in schools, centering on the foundational tenet to start with the end in mind (Wiggins & McTighe, 2005). In planning instructional units of study, for example, practitioners first define the learning goals and then determine the evidence and design instruction to help students achieve those goals. Policy work and reform efforts in schools also benefit from a backward-design approach. Before embarking upon daily activities, local stakeholders define what they seek to achieve via implementation (Wiggins & McTighe, 2011). Goal setting is especially pertinent with policies that are not mandated but voluntary in nature, as buy-in and commitment are key to securing the resources needed for implementation. By collaboratively discussing and defining goals grounded in the unique school, district, and community context, stakeholders commit to a shared purpose in policy implementation (Datnow, 2006).

Of course, in the case of the SoBL, the end goal is already defined: biliteracy. But biliteracy for whom—all students, world language learners, heritage language learners, ELs? And biliteracy through what means—world language study, bilingual education, home-language usage? And biliteracy in what languages—only those formally offered in schools, or a broader group that includes the languages used in homes and communities? Local stakeholders decide how the SoBL situates within their unique linguistic landscape and how these efforts benefit language programming, as well as the students, families, and communities that they serve. Drafting goals for SoBL implementation involves : (a) determining whom to invite to the table to collaboratively discuss and define SoBL efforts, (b) considering focal priorities for local implementation within the unique linguistic landscape, (c) crafting clear and precise goals to drive work moving forward, and (d) evaluating progress and refining goals over time (see Figure 2.3).

Figure 2.3. Drafting Initial Goals for SoBL Implementation

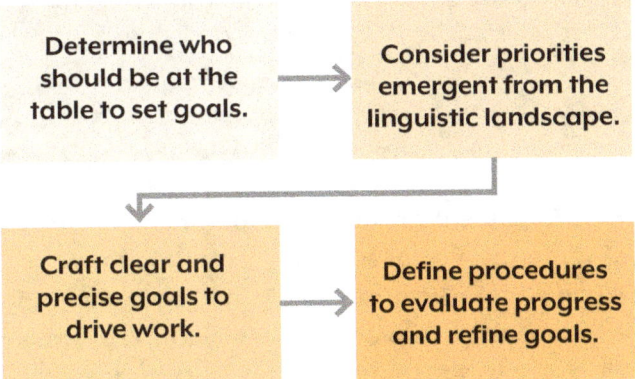

Before initiating discussions around goals, determine whom to invite to the table. As noted in Chapter 1, SoBL implementation requires collaboration. Participants might include administrators, teachers, students, parents, community members, and tribal leaders. To enrich the conversation and ensure that goals respond to a wide array of constituents, discussions should involve a culturally, linguistically, and pedagogically diverse group of stakeholders. Those at the table guide the goal setting, as well as garner initial buy-in for SoBL efforts, so strategic selection of collaborators is key. In the Greene Public Schools vignette above, the district's initial goals centered on Spanish-speaking students in dual-language programming, stemming from the community context and steering committee participants' expertise in Spanish-English bilingual education (e.g., dual-language school principals, bilingual education professors). When considering whom to involve, connect back to exploration of homes, communities, and schools, aiming for equitable representation of roles and perspectives.

With relevant stakeholders at the table, engage in rich discussion about the SoBL as situated in the local linguistic landscape. First, ensure that all participants understand the SoBL initiative and policy.

Next, draw upon findings regarding language use in homes, communities, and schools to ground the conversation in your unique context. Then, based on the shared understanding of the SoBL and the linguistic resources available to support its implementation, allow participants to share their perspectives. Consider using questions to guide the discussion, such as: How can the SoBL strengthen our language programming? How can the SoBL serve students, families, and communities? We recommend using this dual focus on potential benefits both inside and outside of schools. It is often easy to get wrapped up in how the efforts aid the daily work of educators, such as by bolstering world language enrollment or bringing attention to bilingual programming. But ultimately the SoBL should benefit students and those who nurture and support them in homes and communities.

Systemic racism plagues the U.S. educational system, often leading to structures and programs that benefit White, English-dominant students. When seeking to define goals, stakeholders should recognize and grapple with these underlying ideologies and seek to challenge them through SoBL implementation.

Following rich discussion around SoBL efforts broadly, precise goals should emerge to guide implementation efforts moving forward. In the vignette above, stakeholders started with a broad focus on target students and programming and then narrowed to numeric projections for SoBL attainment. A common framework already used in many schools, the SMART goals mnemonic (Doran et al., 1981), supports refining SoBL goals (see Table 2.1). Goals are *specific* and detail the focal purpose for implementation, including target students or programming. Biliteracy is the goal, but biliteracy for whom and through what means? Data sources attach to ensure goals are *measurable* and track progress over time. *Attainability* connects to language programming and assessments; for example, the goal to recognize biliteracy in 50 languages is not attainable if the state only allows students to demonstrate proficiency on approved assessments in 25 languages. *Relevancy* means grounding SoBL efforts in larger contexts, which we explore in the next section. *Timebound* encourages a set timeframe to achieve and reflect upon goals.

Defined collaboratively with grounding in the community, the resultant goals drive SoBL implementation. But it is important to remember that goals

Table 2.1. SMART Goals for the SoBL

CRITERIA	CONSIDERATIONS	EXAMPLES
Specific	What do you wish to achieve with the SoBL?	Language programming Home language maintenance Equity for ELs
Measurable	How will you know you have reached this goal?	Number of recognitions Percentage of recognitions Number of languages
Achievable	Can you realistically achieve these goals?	Language programming Available assessments Community partnerships
Relevant	How do the goals align with the larger context?	District strategic plan School vision and mission Community context
Timebound	When do you seek to achieve these goals?	Annual progress Long-term goal Time for roll-out

evolve and change over time, so returning to your goals annually to evaluate progress and check alignment with dynamic changes in home, community, and school language use is an essential part of the process. For example, in the vignette above, Greene stakeholders initiated the SoBL work with a focus on Spanish-speaking students and dual-language programs. After targeting Spanish to get the initiative off the ground in this urban area, district leaders expanded SoBL recognition to additional languages, using the existing infrastructure for recruitment, assessment, and recognition. Situated in a multilingual city with over 100 languages used in students' homes, leaders recognized that they could expand SoBL languages to meet their goal of 50 percent of students receiving the SoBL by 2030. Data is key in these subsequent conversations, use of recognition numbers, percentages, and languages permits evaluation of progress toward goals and ensures equity in SoBL implementation in the local setting. Tools 2.1, 2.2, and 2.3 can guide you in conducting your goal-setting discussions.

Situating Goals within State and Local Policies

When a new superintendent began at Walsh School District (a pseudonym), she initiated the strategic planning process with community stakeholders to define high-level goals for the district. This mid-sized suburban district in the western United States greatly valued its diversity, with 75 percent of the K-12 population comprised of students of color speaking over 100 languages. When the Director of Language Learning introduced the topic of biliteracy in the strategic plan discussions, other stakeholders identified a pertinent goal: all students graduate bilingual and biliterate.

Not only was this goal inscribed into the district's strategic plan, but stakeholders instituted the state's SoBL as the way to determine students' achievement of biliteracy. Directly integrated into the guiding document for the district's work, the SoBL occupied a central role in regular conversations among upper-level administrators. The superintendent and school board members requested regular updates on SoBL implementation efforts, eager to see the progress toward their goal of universal biliteracy. They also gave significant funding to SoBL implementation and language education to bolster these important efforts.

A district-level team coordinated SoBL efforts and language programming across schools, including K-12 Spanish and Vietnamese dual-language programs and high-school language study in American Sign Language, Arabic, Chinese, Samoan, Somali, and Vietnamese. They

offered the SoBL in 26 languages by partnering with their state language organization to design assessments in less commonly taught languages. In a state requiring world language study for graduation, Walsh leaders used the state's competency-based credit policy so that students could garner high-school credit for their proficiency in other languages without the need to sit through coursework.

As has been emphasized throughout this chapter, SoBL implementation has the potential to push back against the common silo-based approach where educators focus only on initiatives within their areas of expertise (Smith et al., 2020). This is a frequent occurrence with the SoBL: one person maintains sole responsibility for the recognition, which remains relatively unknown to teachers, parents, and even students. Educators can break down such silos by connecting the SoBL to other policies and practices, a linkage that is essential due to the unfunded and voluntary nature of the SoBL. Since biliteracy supports students, schools, and society, the SoBL connects to priorities like equity and diversity, college readiness, global education, social-emotional learning, and school belonging. By couching local implementation within larger goals and initiatives, stakeholders can garner resources, provide coherence, and foster collaboration (Honig & Hatch, 2004).

Since both the SoBL and other educational policies vary by state, we want to highlight the need to dig into your specific context (Davin & Heineke, 2017). Conversations among teams center on how the recognition might connect with other initiatives, seeking to break down silos in practice while bolstering language-focused efforts in districts and schools. As evidenced in the vignette above, Walsh stakeholders have sustained their efforts by situating the SoBL within the district's larger strategic plan, as well as connecting to state policies allowing students to receive competency-based credits in world languages for high-school graduation. These two lenses are integral: consideration of state policies that may reinforce SoBL efforts, and situation within local priorities, such as district and school goals and programming.

State Policies Language education policies provide a good starting point for exploration, including those guiding bilingual and world language education.

State **_world language policies_** center on whether world language is considered an elective or a requirement for graduation. SoBL efforts attach to either, exemplified by North School District's use of the SoBL to bolster interest in world language study as an elective and Walsh's use of SoBL assessments to meet world language graduation requirements. **_Bilingual education policies_** typically involve mandates for the instruction of ELs, such as requiring transitional bilingual education in languages spoken by more than 20 students at the school site. While transitional programs do not typically aim for biliteracy, these policies set the minimum threshold with the potential for districts to enact dual-language programs that develop ELs' home-language competencies in addition to English. In states like Delaware, additional funding is available for districts to implement dual-language immersion programs that seek to foster biliteracy, serving as a boon to unfunded SoBL efforts.

 **Some states' existing education policies do little to serve biliteracy development, particularly where world language policy is absent and subtractive programming prioritizes ELs' English proficiency. The SoBL has the potential to disrupt these policies and promote additive bilingualism and biliteracy development.**

Broad educational policies such as the use of competency-based credits described in the vignette above connect to the SoBL. Situated in a state where world language is required for graduation, Walsh School District facilitates proficiency assessments so that students earn high-school credit and the SoBL in their home languages. The state's competency-based credit policy, which is synonymous with credit-by-exam policies in other states, allows students to demonstrate competency and receive high-school credit in place of taking coursework. These state policies are particularly valuable for heritage speakers and ELs. In the case of Walsh, district leaders assert the necessity to value students' existing multiliteracies rather than require them to take an additional world language. Similarly, across the country in the Villa School District, educators use the state's credit-by-exam policy to promote equity for ELs, allowing them to use their home language abilities to become eligible for the advanced diploma that requires world language study. As you investigate your context in more depth, explore whether your state allows the SoBL to attach to high-school or college credit.

Policies in areas beyond education, such as those seeking to maintain language and culture, also play a role in SoBL implementation. Federal law prioritizes the maintenance of Indigenous languages, with millions of dollars in grant funding available for efforts to revitalize languages through education and other efforts. Originating in 1990 and reauthorized in 2019, the Esther Martinez Native American Language Programs Act (§101-477) supports states and municipalities with Indigenous language programming. Various states have enacted their own related legislation to prioritize educational efforts, such as those to preserve tribal languages and cultures in New Mexico (§22-23A-1, 2009) and the 'Ōlelo Hawai'i language in Hawai'i (302H§1-7, 2009). In Utah, legislation focuses more broadly on critical languages, providing funds for immersion education in Indigenous, immigrant, and high-priority languages including Navajo, Spanish, Chinese, Arabic, and Russian (SB41, 2008). Since state statutes like these often come with funding, aligning unfunded SoBL efforts with them can be helpful.

Local Priorities Situating SoBL efforts within local priorities is also a valuable strategy for breaking down silos, garnering resources, and promoting biliteracy more broadly. In the Walsh School District, the district-level strategic plan pinpoints the goal for all students to graduate bilingual and biliterate, one of six overall priorities that drive efforts and resources in that community. With stakeholders elevating biliteracy and the SoBL across the district, the commitment to the work expands beyond the language department. This commitment comes with funds to support three district-level team members and multiple language programs, including initiation of Samoan, Somali, and Vietnamese as heritage languages. Even with biliteracy not stated directly in district goals, other districts have successfully attached the SoBL as a measure of related goals, such as those related to 21st century learning, global education, and college and career readiness. Overall, the aim is to work within the unique local context to elevate biliteracy, the SoBL, and language education as central initiatives within district work.

The same consideration of local priorities needs to occur within individual schools. Our research has found that even high-awarding districts have large discrepancies in SoBL recipients by school (Heineke & Davin, 2021). In schools that recognize biliteracy with greater frequency, two factors have emerged to explain why certain schools engage more actively in implementation. First, schools benefit from having at least one educator who is passionate about the SoBL and willing to initiate and lead the efforts on the ground. Even if efforts center at the district level, school-level leadership is integral to promoting awareness among students, families, and colleagues. Second, school-based educators tend to embrace the SoBL when they see clear alignment with existing programming, such as dual-language, family engagement, and International Baccalaureate programs. By demonstrating how the SoBL bolsters current practice, such as celebrating the biliteracy of two-way immersion students and engaging bilingual families around students' achievements, stakeholders build the buy-in that is needed to connect directly with students and families.

In summary, the SoBL and its pertinent focus on biliteracy should not be kept in a silo for the language-focused educators in districts and schools. SoBL implementation can be eased and enhanced by connecting goals with other policies, initiatives, and priorities in your state, district, and school. In the next section, we discuss ways to cultivate buy-in and awareness by sharing these interconnections with administrators and school boards.

Seeking Buy-in from Local Stakeholders

Jason (a pseudonym) stood in front of the school board for its annual budget meeting in the Elmwood School District (a pseudonym). He came to engage with board members once a year to share the suburban district's progress in implementing the SoBL and make the case for maintaining his budget for language proficiency testing. He started with a brief explanation of the SoBL, centering on the benefits of learning another language and valuing students' languages and cultures. In a district with 55 percent Latinx students and over 100 languages spoken by students, as well as a strong K-12 Spanish dual-language program and world language study in Chinese, French, German, Japanese, and Spanish, the SoBL was a natural fit.

But to seek the buy-in of what Jason described as a largely White and conservative board, he emphasized the cost-benefit analysis. Board members latched onto the tremendous value of the initiative, so Jason focused on how spending 20 dollars on one language proficiency test could yield one student up to 8,000 dollars in college credit at a state university. Each year, he shared the number of kids who took exams to get the SoBL, the money spent by the district on these exams, the number of credits the exams generated for college, and the amount of cost-saving for students attending state universities. Situated in a state where the SoBL was attached to credit at public colleges and universities, this was the key selling point.

At the district level, administrators and school board members lead educational efforts in communities with decision-making roles and responsibilities spanning personnel, programs, curriculum, and budget. These stakeholders play important roles in SoBL implementation, serving as gatekeepers for enacting the policy in schools and providing resources to implement the initiative on the ground. Without national and state funding, districts typically sustain SoBL efforts with both human resources (i.e., district and school educators with dedicated time to focus on the SoBL) and monetary resources for testing, programming, professional development, and other related efforts. With budgetary decisions housed at the district level, it is important to connect with these stakeholders to seek initial and continued buy-in and support. As depicted in the vignette, communication with administrators and school board members includes framing the work, sharing goals, pinpointing costs, and highlighting results.

Framing the work centers on two key components: the linguistic landscape of the district and the research bolstering the need for multiliteracy. Remember that superintendents and school board members have ties and commitments to the community but not necessarily expertise and experience linked to language education. It is important to ensure their prior knowledge on the scope of language use in homes, communities, and schools, drawing from the linguistic explorations described earlier in this chapter. Then the goal emerges to solidify the district's focus on developing and maintaining students' languages, drawing from the multitude of research studies on the benefits of bilingualism and biliteracy (see Chapter 1). Knowing your audience and recognizing the backgrounds and potential orientations of district leaders is key to obtaining their buy-in. For example, Jason described the board as "conservative" and centered his pitch around

economic benefits. Other districts have prioritized discussion of the research related to developing cultural identity, communicating with family, and enriching worldviews.

After grounding the work in the community context and related research, the next step is to define the SoBL goals and attach them to larger initiatives within the district. Whether you are seeking initial or ongoing approval, stakeholders benefit from a brief overview that helps them recollect key details of the initiative, including (a) the definition of the SoBL, (b) a brief overview of its history and origins, and (c) key details of the state policy. This backdrop provides the context for outlining the specific goals that you have defined for implementation, demonstrating both the time and effort that has gone into these deliberations and the ultimate value for district programming and constituents. Earlier, we walked through defining goals and attaching them to larger priorities and initiatives in districts. This latter point emerges as critical when seeking the buy-in of district stakeholders, as you want to demonstrate how the SoBL contributes to achievement of the broader goals of the district. Think back to the vignette of the Walsh School District, where the superintendent and school board had intense commitment to the SoBL because of the district's strategic plan goal for all students to achieve biliteracy. Visions, missions, and strategic plans drive the work of districts, and the SoBL gets a much-needed boost if it attaches to those larger priorities.

 Currently, the SoBL comes with no direct funding from federal or state government, leaving the onus on districts and opening the potential for equity concerns. In addition to allocating local funds, such as those generated from property taxes, districts can tap into federal and state funds in their budget (e.g., Title IV funds) if the SoBL connects to larger efforts, such as supporting ELs' and low-income students' learning (e.g., Title I).

With buy-in secured for the SoBL, the next step is to request funds to support these efforts. In districts with demonstrated success with the SoBL, educators have described budget requests that (a) outline specific line items covered by the budget, (b) provide rationales as to how these line items contribute to larger goals, and (c) include a cost-benefit analysis of how line items support the bigger picture for students and programming. Proficiency assessments typically usurp the bulk of SoBL budgets, which is a key consideration when it comes to equity: if districts cover the cost of language proficiency tests, all students then have opportunities to demonstrate biliteracy regardless of socioeconomic status, given the existence of a test in the target language. Other funding requests might tie to awards and ceremonies to celebrate the SoBL with families and communities or resources to expand language offerings, which we discuss in more depth in later chapters. In Elmwood, the allocated SoBL budget largely covered testing, and Jason wisely juxtaposed the minimal cost of one language test to what one student might save in college tuition. Leaders in other contexts have taken similar approaches to emphasize the value of these funds for individual students in line with state policies, such as earning competency-based credits toward high school graduation or receipt of an advanced diploma.

Data is the final component to incorporate in communication with district stakeholders. Data-driven decision-making is what propels the world of education, meaning that data bolsters efforts to seek buy-in and funding from administrators. Even after initial approval to enact the SoBL, school boards typically reconvene to approve the annual budget, which may mean a return visit to make your case for the continued need for funding. This is why maintaining data to show the efficacy of the SoBL is essential. Data points often center on current students, including numbers of students tested, numbers of recognitions, languages offered, or students enrolled in language study. It is also valuable to highlight data in line with district goals, such as number of ELs recognized or amount of competency-based language credits bestowed toward graduation. In addition to formal data, anecdotal stories about the value of the SoBL told by students, parents, families, and alumni also provide powerful narratives. In the Morton School District, students and parents are invited to make videos about what the SoBL means to them, yielding emotional tributes to biliteracy that provide an integral personal lens to the larger policy. By merging formal and anecdotal data, you deepen buy-in of district stakeholders by demonstrating the impact of the policy in practice.

In sum, district-level administrators and board members play an integral role in SoBL implementation. Interaction with these stakeholders typically comes once per year in the context of a school board meeting, where the formal request for funding is made to support SoBL efforts (see Table 2.2). But in addition to presenting at an annual board meeting, it is valuable to maintain visibility and communication across the school year. For example, you might invite district leadership and school board members to SoBL celebrations or send quarterly updates via email detailing progress toward district goals. These open lines of communication go a long way toward securing long-term buy-in and commitment to sustain SoBL implementation over time.

Table 2.2. Making the Case for Biliteracy to Administrators and School Boards

✓ Build background knowledge regarding the linguistic landscape, including languages formally taught in schools and languages used in homes and communities.

✓ Discuss the value of bilingualism and biliteracy. Draw from research to emphasize the multitude of ways that multilingualism serves to benefit students and schools.

✓ Describe the SoBL initiative, both broadly in the state and in the context of the local district. Share specific goals for the initiative in the local setting.

✓ Attach these SoBL goals to the larger goals of the district, such as the strategic plan. Consider related initiatives, such as college readiness and equity.

✓ Propose a budget to support this work with specific line items and rationales, such as paying for all students' testing or purchasing items to celebrate SoBL recipients.

✓ Provide a cost-benefit analysis to demonstrate how the district's funds contribute to the bigger picture, such as students' achievement of high-school or college credit.

✓ Provide data from previous years to show efficacy of implementation over time, such as numbers of students recognized or enrolled in language study.

Chapter Summary

Defining the **Purpose** for the SoBL is the first step in initiating efforts to implement it. Local goals provide clarity, collaboration, and buy-in among stakeholders, as well as initiate a roadmap for action in schools and districts. But the SoBL looks different across contexts, and the initiative should respond to unique community, district, and school settings. To make the SoBL both valuable and attractive to various stakeholders, the work begins by responding to the linguistic landscape, including languages used in homes, communities, and schools. Stakeholders then collaboratively define goals for implementation, considering how the SoBL supports students and programs. The SoBL does not have to be a standalone initiative, and implementational efforts are enhanced by attaching the recognition to other state or local priorities, such as diversity and equity, college readiness, and global education. In the spirit of backward design, implementation begins with these end goals in mind. The remainder of this book charts paths to measuring biliteracy goals (Chapter 3), achieving goals through language programming (Chapter 4), building mutually beneficial partnerships (Chapter 5), and extending reach through thoughtful promotion (Chapter 6).

Questions for Discussion and Reflection

1. In collaboration with other stakeholders in your school or district, reflect upon what drives your work with the SoBL. What are your aspirations for your students' language development? How do you wish to expand and grow your school's world language, bilingual, and EL programming? Use Tool 2.1 to move from general brainstorming about your unique context to setting specific, measurable goals to guide SoBL implementation.

2. Use Tool 2.2 to assess the linguistic landscape of your district and answer the question: What languages are used in homes, communities, and schools? Amass relevant data from available sources, such as the Home Language Survey. Organize a community walk and use web searches to learn more about potential sources of multilingualism and multiliteracies. Survey or interview students, families, and colleagues to learn more about language assets available in homes, communities, and schools.

3. Who can support your efforts in SoBL implementation in the larger school or district? Use Tool 2.3 to enlist the support of district-level stakeholders, such as administrators and school board members.

Further Reading

- Anya, U. (2020). African Americans in world language study: The forged path and future directions. *Annual Review of Applied Linguistics, 40*, 97–112. https://doi.org/10.1017/S0267190520000070

- Flores, N., & Chaparro, S. (2018). What counts as language education policy? Developing a materialist Anti-racist approach to language activism. *Language Policy 17*, 365–384 (2018). https://doi.org/10.1007/s10993-017-9433-7

- Hancock, C., & Davin, K. J. (2020). A comparative case study: Administrators' and students' perceptions of the Seal of Biliteracy. *Foreign Language Annals, 53*(3), 458–477. http://doi.org/10.1111/flan.12479

- Heineke, A. J., Davin, K. J., & Dávila, A. (2019). Promoting multilingual communities, schools, and students: A closer look at the Seal of Biliteracy in Washington state. *TESOL Journal, 10*, 1–5. https://doi.org/10.1002/tesj.451

Tool 2.1. Defining Purpose for the Seal of Biliteracy

Directions: Use these four steps and related prompts to collaboratively define Seal of Biliteracy (SoBL) goals.

1. PROBE YOUR UNIQUE CONTEXT	2. DRAFT GOALS FOR IMPLEMENTATION
Reflect and discuss the following: Whom do we serve? What characterizes our students, families, and communities? Who should achieve biliteracy and through what pathways? What dreams and aspirations do we have for students and programs?	After initial brainstorming around the SoBL's potential in your context, define goals: Who is the target audience? What are the focal programs? What is the specific objective? How will we measure success? When do we aim to achieve this?
Notes:	Notes:

3. ATTACH TO OTHER POLICIES	4. SEEK BUY-IN FROM STAKEHOLDERS
Research related state and local policies: Can SoBL goals be couched in broader district initiatives, such as college readiness or global education? How do SoBL efforts connect to other state policies or offerings, such as competency-based or college credit?	List the people from whom you need buy-in to start, strengthen, and sustain efforts. Who needs to approve the SoBL? What might strengthen your case for the SoBL to the focal audience? Are there potential points of pushback for which you can prepare?
Notes:	Notes:

Tool 2.2. Mapping the Linguistic Landscape

Directions: Use this tool to guide your exploration of language use in homes, communities, and schools.

SETTING AND DIRECTIONS	YOUR RESPONSES
Home How do students use languages in homes? Directions: Use *Home Language Survey* data to list languages spoken in homes, as well as number of students using each language.	
Community How do students engage with languages in the community? Directions: Explore community sites where various languages are used, such as businesses, churches, and organizations. Star those that offer language programming.	
School How do students use languages in school settings? Directions: List programs in your school or district that promote biliteracy, including world language, bilingual, and EL education. Note the involved grade ranges.	

Tool 2.3. Seek Support for the Seal of Biliteracy

Directions: Use this tool to guide your exploration of language use in homes, communities, and schools.

TALKING POINTS	NOTES
Introduction to the SoBL What is the SoBL? What is the state's SoBL policy? What is biliteracy? How does biliteracy value students?	
Grounding in SoBL Implementation Goals What is the district's linguistic landscape? What are the district's SoBL goals? What has been the progress toward goals? How have previous funds supported efforts?	
Connecting to Larger District Goals How does the SoBL attach to district goals (e.g., equity, college readiness)? Have you seen larger shifts in outcomes or practices related to the SoBL?	
Financial Considerations What funds do you need for the SoBL? How will the funds be utilized? How will these funds benefit students in the long run (e.g., credits, advanced diplomas)?	
Next Steps for Communication Will you invite stakeholders to celebratory and other SoBL events? How and when will you report outcomes?	
Other Considerations What else is important to consider given the specific audience? What might sway their buy-in and eagerness to support the SoBL?	

Chapter 3
Proficiency Assessments: Ensuring Access for All Students

Anas grew up in Tunisia where he used Derja at home and Arabic at school. Around sixth grade, he also began to learn French. His family moved to the United States around ninth grade, at which time Anas entered school and began to learn English. He had few opportunities to use Derja, Arabic, or French in school until his 12th grade year, when his ESL teacher told him about the SoBL. Anas wasn't sure what to expect from what he called "the Seal test" and he wasn't sure if he would pass, but he decided to take the test in Arabic anyway because he wanted "proof" of his language proficiency. He knew he had forgotten French and was not sure if he had also forgotten Arabic, because he had not read in Arabic since arriving to the United States. After the test, he was worried because he had difficulties with the keyboard during the assessment. Regardless, Anas earned the required scores and received a SoBL. He called the assessment "refreshing" and told us that it "refreshed my mind and [made me realize] what I actually remember about the language."

Guiding Questions

What language proficiency assessments and resources are needed for SoBL implementation?

How can one assess languages for which no assessments are available?

What logistics factor into planning for proficiency assessment?

How can classroom assessment prepare students for proficiency assessments?

This chapter focuses on the second facet of the 5Ps framework, *Proficiency Assessments*. As explained in Chapter 1, language proficiency refers to "what individuals can do with language in terms of speaking, writing, listening, and reading in real-world situations in a spontaneous and non-rehearsed context" (ACTFL 2012b, p. 3). Therefore, *language proficiency assessments* measure how well an individual can use language to communicate in real-life contexts, unlike achievement tests that measure what an individual knows (Language Testing International, 2021). As described in Chapter 1, all states' SoBL policies allow for students to demonstrate world language proficiency through assessment. The number of states that require students to demonstrate English proficiency via assessment is also growing. These assessments typically include measures of the four domains (listening, reading, speaking, writing) or three modes of communication (interpersonal communication, interpretive communication, presentational communication).

Proficiency assessment is one of the most complex and challenging aspects of SoBL implementation, further complicated by the fact that states' policies vary in small yet significant ways. Familiarity with state policies for acceptable evidence of biliteracy is the first step in planning for proficiency assessment. In states like Minnesota and Washington, legislation provides options for assessment development in languages where commercial assessments do not exist. In these contexts, local educators alert the state to the need for language assessments and then work with language organizations, institutions, or private companies to develop them. In states like Arizona and Illinois, legislation allows for the use of ***alternative assessments*** such as portfolios of language abilities spanning listening, speaking, reading, and writing. Development of such assessments often involves partnerships between the school and community stakeholders who have the needed language resources. As you explore your need for assessments beyond those offered via commercial providers, consider how to work strategically and flexibly with state policy guidelines and think creatively about various assessment options. To get started, complete Tool 3.1 to determine your state's assessment guidelines.

Our research has revealed benefits and barriers to the use of assessments in SoBL implementation. At the program level, language proficiency assessments provide detailed data that coordinators and teachers can analyze to determine strengths and weaknesses of curricula and instruction (Davin et al., 2018). For students, like Anas in the vignette, language assessments can boost confidence in language abilities and provide external proof of language proficiency (Davin & Heineke, 2018; Davin, 2021a). But language assessments are often a gatekeeper to recognizing biliteracy, especially in less commonly taught and tested languages. Most state governments do not yet fund the SoBL, resulting in some schools passing the cost of proficiency assessments to students. Moreover, many students in the United States are proficient in languages for which appropriate and affordable language assessments are not readily available. Most states offer ***alternative assessment protocols*** for these languages—methods other than commercial assessments through which students can demonstrate proficiency—but those can be challenging to carry out. In states that

do not allow alternatives to assessments, advocacy efforts become integral, as state policies are not static and unchangeable.

This chapter details how to plan for proficiency assessment (see Figure 3.1). We begin by describing the various commercial assessments of world languages and English and provide steps to take when students use languages for which commercial assessments do not exist. We outline the logistics to consider, such as when to offer language assessments, how often, and necessary resources. The chapter concludes by connecting language assessments to classroom instruction and program evaluation, explaining the importance of regularly assessing students using proficiency-focused assessments and rubrics.

Considering Your Current Language Assessments

Readers, even those within the same district or school, may begin this chapter with very different understandings of language assessment, which differs from assessment in other content areas. Start by reflecting on the assessments already in place in your context. What assessments measure world language proficiency, heritage language proficiency, and English proficiency? What additional assessments are needed? For those who have not yet implemented the SoBL, perhaps your school already administers assessments such as AP exams, the WIDA ACCESS 2.0 for ELs, or Logramos for students in Spanish-English bilingual programs. For those who have experience with the SoBL, you might be familiar with administering the proficiency assessments described in this chapter. However, we

Figure 3.1. Steps in Planning for Assessment

Determine the assessment requirements in your state's SoBL policy.

Poll students to determine the languages for which you need assesssments.

Choose the commercial assessments that you will use for each language.

For languages without commercial assessments, create or follow an existing alternative assessment protocol.

Develop an assessment implementation plan.

challenge all readers to expand access to the SoBL beyond the low-hanging fruit (e.g., students in AP world language courses) to heritage language learners, including those who use less commonly taught and tested languages.

Your role in SoBL implementation shapes the lens through which you approach this chapter. State or district language coordinators might think about how to streamline the proficiency assessment process across schools to get bulk assessment pricing or how to set up alternative assessment processes for languages without available assessments. School administrators and counselors might seek to structure the logistics of assessments to ensure high levels of student participation. Language teachers might focus on how best to prepare students for proficiency assessments like the ones we describe. Teachers across the school might be helpful in identifying potential SoBL participants who are not enrolled in a world language but may be proficient, such as those who have exited EL programs, learned another language at home, or taken language classes at community sites. And those working at community language schools or institutions of higher education might think about how they could offer proficiency assessments for the SoBL in their space, providing users of that language with pathways to the recognition. Across all roles, remember to maintain a focus on equity as you read, thinking about how to structure assessments so that all biliterate students have access to the SoBL.

Procuring the Tools: What Tests and Resources Are Needed

Villa School District (a pseudonym) set a clear priority in its SoBL implementation: equity for ELs. In a suburban district in the eastern United States where students spoke over 100 languages, district leaders recognized that the EL label often resulted in students not being able to take a world language. Not only did high-school ELs have required ESL coursework dominating their schedules, but many of their heritage languages were not formally taught in schools. The state did not require world language study for graduation, but students successfully completing coursework became eligible to receive an advanced diploma. Since ELs lacked space in their schedules for world languages, they were not eligible for the advanced diploma. Villa leaders decided to tie the SoBL to competency-based credits, allowing ELs to demonstrate proficiency on approved assessments and get credit for home language competencies. In this way, ELs had equitable access to the advanced diploma.

Stakeholders evaluated programs and assessments to ensure alignment with their goals. They analyzed programming to develop biliteracy, including K-12 Spanish world, heritage, and dual-language as well as Arabic, American Sign Language, French, German, Japanese, Latin, and Mandarin world language study in middle and high schools. They then looked at the primary languages used by ELs to ensure options for assessments, subsequently expanding to use various proficiency tests in 36 languages. Using a database of every middle- and high-school student currently or formerly labeled as an EL, district leaders sent information on the SoBL testing opportunities in multiple languages to students and families. They collected data annually to monitor progress toward their goals for EL equity, finding that 72 percent of kids who took SoBL exams were ELs and 195 students gained eligibility for the advanced diploma by sitting for these exams.

Starting with Students: Who Needs Tests in What Languages After building familiarity with state-specific requirements for assessments (see Tool 3.1), consider your linguistic landscape to determine which languages need assessing (see Tool 2.2). This should be done several months before test administration to allow time to find and purchase all necessary tests and materials and set up administration procedures. Some schools use an application process, where students indicate intent to pursue the SoBL in particular languages. Another common approach is to consult results of the **Home Language Survey** and reach out individually to students using other languages in homes. However, because parents may fear discrimination or not want institutional labels affixed to their children, this data may be incomplete or inaccurate. Thus, a combination of several approaches may be required for a school to determine its language assessment needs.

Some districts and schools, particularly those that cover the cost of assessments, implement a pre-screening process to ensure students' readiness. For example, in the Walsh School District, the coordinator asks each student interested in taking a SoBL assessment to complete a self-assessment of language proficiency using the NCSSFL-ACTFL Can-Do statements (NCSSFL & ACTFL, 2017a). Coordinators and teachers can use data from self-assessments to advise students on how to improve proficiency. Appendix 2 offers an example self-assessment based on the NCSSFL-ACTFL Can-Do statements for Intermediate Mid proficiency, which is the minimum required level for SoBL attainment in the majority of states.

An additional consideration in determining who takes world language assessments relates to timeframe. Teams should discuss which grades or levels of world language coursework provide the best opportunity for taking the assessment. Ideally, if resources permit, students should have more than one opportunity to take SoBL assessments. Some states have a statute of limitations on the length of time for which test results are valid. For example, in Minnesota, a student can earn college credit for the SoBL, but the student must have passed the test within three years of requesting the credit. We recommend using your state's SoBL requirements to think through when students should take a SoBL assessment to maximize potential.

Choosing Appropriate World Language Proficiency Assessments Once you determine the languages for which you require assessments, the next step is to choose which assessments to administer (see Figure 3.2). Various factors influence this decision, including state policy requirements, cost, and test format. Return to your findings from Tool 3.1 regarding acceptable evidence for world and heritage language proficiency, which can serve as a starting place to explore available language assessments for your student population.

When considering assessments for world and heritage languages, districts typically turn to commercial assessments. In some world language programs, students already take AP and IB language assessments, making this the most convenient option for students to demonstrate biliteracy in available languages. Many other external assessments are available, and the list of languages available grows each year (See Appendix 1). It is important to note that the four domains (listening, reading, speaking, writing) may not all be applicable to languages

Figure 3.2. Steps to Determine Appropriate Language Assessment

Determine if an assessment of the four domains or three modes of communication exists for the language.

If no assessment of the four domains exists, determine if an assessment of productive skills (i.e., speaking, writing) exists. Ensure that assessments of productive skills only are acceptable evidence of world language proficiency in your state.

If no assessment of productive skills exists or your state does not accept evidence of productive skills only, reach out to your state's world language supervisor or SoBL representative to verify your next best option.

such as American Sign Language, Latin, and some Indigenous languages. States' SoBL policies take this into account and only require evidence of applicable domains. In the Villa School District, stakeholders tapped into several of these assessments to provide testing opportunities in less commonly taught languages.

 Languages tested in AP and IB programs are those commonly taught in U.S. high schools. Relying solely on AP or IB testing presents an equity issue, as students proficient in additional languages may not enroll in these courses. AP and IB assessments require preparation beyond language proficiency, such as content knowledge related to a language's culture and literature.

Because it can be difficult to find assessments of all four domains for some languages, some states' policies allow students to demonstrate proficiency with assessments that measure only the productive skills of speaking and writing (See Table 3.1). As of July 2021, policies in 16 states included provisions for using assessments of productive skills only, with three additional states allowing their use only when no assessment of the four domains exists. An analysis of scores from individuals who took an assessment in seven different languages and in all four domains found speaking and writing scores to be reliable indicators of listening and reading scores for that assessment (Egnatz & Santos, in press). Because pol-

Table 3.1. States that Permit Assessments of Productive Skills Only

ACCEPTED EVIDENCE	STATES
Assessments of productive skills only (e.g., ALTA Language Tests, STAMP WS, ACTFL OPI & WPT for the Seal of Biliteracy)	Arizona, Arkansas, Connecticut, Indiana, Iowa, Kansas, Maine, Maryland, Michigan, Mississippi, New Hampshire, New Mexico, North Carolina, Oregon, Utah, Virginia
Assessments of productive skills only when no assessment of four domains exists	Massachusetts, New Jersey, Ohio

Table 3.2. Questions to Consider in Assessment Selection

Is this assessment appropriate for my population?

How long does the assessment typically take for students to complete?

Are the prompts on the assessment in English or the target language?

Does a student have to complete all portions of the assessment on the same day or can they be broken up into different administration days (e.g., reading portion on one day, speaking portion on another day)?

If a student scores too low on one portion of the assessment, can the student retake that portion without having to retake and pay for the other portions?

If a student retakes a portion of the assessment, is it still a valid measure of their proficiency?

What are the technology requirements of the assessment?

If the assessment requires keyboarding, is there practice available?

Can students handwrite their responses for the written assessment? If so, does this entail an additional cost?

icies change frequently, we encourage you to reach out to your state's SoBL administrator for guidance.

In addition to cost and availability of assessments, it is important to consider various nuances, including (a) the test's target population, (b) linguistic medium (target language or English) of test prompts, (c) technology requirements, and (d) available retake options. For example, some language tests are created for adults in professional fields, so these are more appropriate for older students. Prompts and questions on some tests are in the target language, meaning that the writing test inherently assesses students' ability to read and understand the prompt. Some tests allow students to complete the writing assessment by hand, which may be appropriate for students not familiar with a computer or for districts or schools that do not have the resources to purchase keyboards or keyboard overlays in different scripts. Some assessments allow for students to retake singular portions of the assessment at a lower cost. When evaluating the suitability of an assessment, consider the questions presented in Table 3.2.

We recommend discussing how to pave as many pathways as possible for SoBL attainment, and how to make those pathways as wide and maneuverable as possible. Consult your state's SoBL guidelines and consider areas of flexibility in the policy. For example, in Washington, if a student scores unusually low on a speaking test, perhaps due to anxiety or lack of experience recording themselves speaking, and the student's scores would otherwise qualify them for the SoBL, they might take the speaking section of a different assessment. Similarly, if a newcomer student struggles with reading proficiency in English, the student might take a language test on which

writing prompts are in the target language. We encourage you to remain focused on your students, using assessment tools flexibly to allow demonstration of rich language competencies.

Choosing Appropriate World Language Assessments for Pathway Recognitions Readers in contexts that offer or would like to offer pathway recognitions (see Chapter 1) need to consider assessments for younger students. Many of the assessments used for SoBL testing are not appropriate for students in elementary school, but testing companies often have versions designed for younger students (see Appendix 1).

If you have the resources and these assessments are available in languages used by your students, it is advantageous to administer them as evidence for pathway recognition. They allow students to become familiar with the format of proficiency assessments and can provide ongoing snapshots of students' proficiency growth through school. However, because pathway recognitions are typically not part of official SoBL legislation, you may choose to create your own proficiency assessments to measure students' performance along the path to biliteracy. We provide guidance on creating these types of assessments later in this chapter.

Determining the Need for English Language Proficiency Assessments As mentioned in Chapter 1, some state SoBL policies require educators to procure assessments for demonstrating English proficiency. Begin by checking your state's requirements.

- If you work in a state that has adopted or revised SoBL policies so that all students who fulfill the high-school graduation requirements are considered proficient in English, you **do not need** to procure any English assessments.

- If you work in a state that requires students to earn a minimum GPA in a course of study to demonstrate English proficiency, **you may still need** to procure English assessments, but only for ELs. This depends on whether your state allows alternative measures of proficiency for this student population.

- Finally, if you work in a state that requires students to earn a minimum score on an assessment to demonstrate English proficiency, you **may need** to procure English assessments. This depends on whether your state allows alternatives to end-of-year ELA, ACT, or SAT assessments for ELs and non-ELs.

 ELs should have equitable opportunities to develop and demonstrate biliteracy. Take a critical look at your state's policy and district's practice to determine if ELs have equitable paths to receive the SoBL. Collecting and analyzing data on ELs' SoBL attainment in your context can support advocacy efforts.

In many states that require a minimum GPA in a course of study or an assessment, ELs can instead demonstrate English proficiency with minimum required scores on the assessments given by the state to determine eligibility for EL services. The most common assessment to determine EL services across states is the WIDA ACCESS for ELLs 2.0 test, although some states have their own tests, such as the Arizona English Language Learning Assessment (AZELLA) and the English Language Proficiency Assessment in California (ELPAC). Five states (Arkansas, Illinois, Kansas, Nebraska, Utah) allow the option of demonstrating proficiency via another English proficiency assessment outside the federally

mandated EL identification process, such as AAPPL, STAMP 4S, or TOEFL. Figure 3.3 displays a process for determining whether you should procure such English assessments.

In the 13 states in which English proficiency tests are not permitted, evidence of English proficiency comes from scores on end-of-year ELA assessments or tests like the ACT or SAT, resulting in numerous issues. In some states, these tests are offered in 10th or 11th grade, shortening the timeline for students to develop English proficiency. In addition to timeline issues, these tests are being used in ways inconsistent with their original purpose. Remember that language proficiency assessments are meant to measure what one can do with a language, unlike achievement tests that measure what one knows. Unlike the AAPPL or STAMP, which are designed to measure language proficiency, the SAT and ACT seek to predict college readiness and require content knowledge and reasoning skills. Assessments such as these are achievement tests rather than proficiency assessments and do not show attainment of or proficiency in English.

Consider this example of SoBL implementation in Massachusetts. While piloting implementation in preparation for the official SoBL, stakeholders discovered inequities that pertained specifically to ELs, as fulfilment of the English proficiency requirement for the SoBL was determined by an ELA exam given in 10th grade. Not only did this take away two critical years of language development, but the requirement also appeared markedly inequitable because non-ELs had until the 12th grade to demonstrate world language proficiency (Sherf et al., 2020). Led by state NABE, TESOL, and ACTFL affiliates, stakeholders advocated for change to this policy, so that students labeled as ELs could demonstrate proficiency on the annually proctored ACCESS for ELLs 2.0 rather than the state ELA assessment.

As this example shows, states that require assessment evidence of English proficiency for SoBL attainment should allow English proficiency assessments in place of achievement tests like the SAT, ACT, or end-of-year ELA assessments. If your state accepts scores from English proficiency assessments as evidence, we recommend that you offer them to students who do not, or may not, fulfill the English requirements of the SoBL through the other allowable forms of evidence. A student unable to achieve the minimum required score on a test such as the ACT or SAT might have more success on an assessment that measures language proficiency. If

Figure 3.3. Process for Determining Assessment Needs

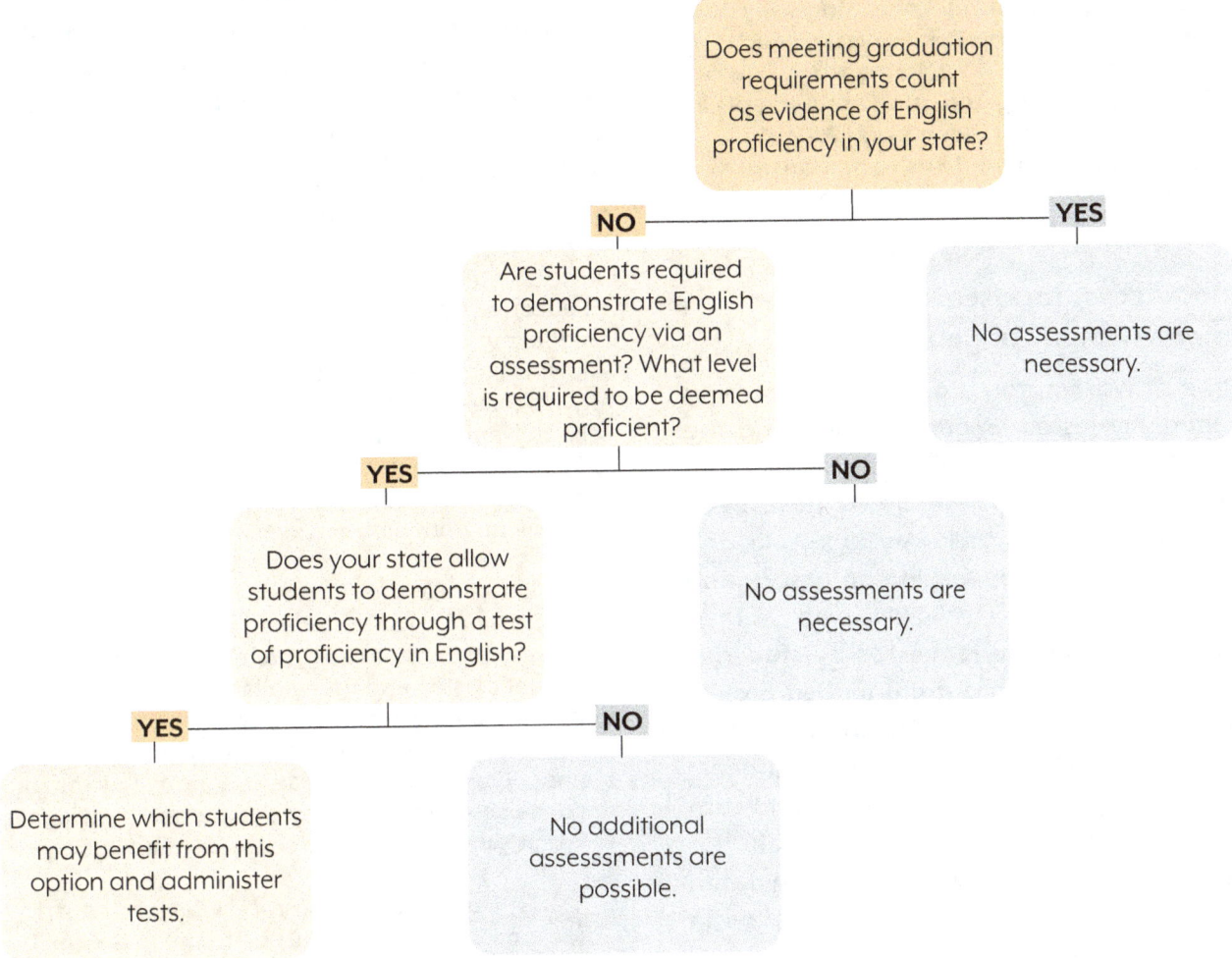

your state requires students to pass an ELA content exam (e.g., ACT or SAT) for the SoBL, consider advocating for change as those in Massachusetts did.

Building Awareness Prior to Proficiency Assessments Before students sit down to take a language proficiency assessment, teachers and counselors can discuss and build understandings about the test, including its purpose and format, as well as potential biases to recognizing students' language competencies. In our research across the country, students have stated that they had no idea what to expect on the exam, such as not realizing that all four language domains would be assessed (Davin & Heineke, 2018; Davin, 2021a). Many tests offer free demonstrations with sample questions and tasks on their websites. Students should have opportunities to explore these resources, which may help them to decide if they want to take the test to pursue the SoBL.

In addition to providing students with information about the test, educators can promote students' **critical testing literacy**, that is, the understanding that such tests are fallible (Davin, 2021a). Students, parents, and educators should understand that language proficiency tests define language and language use in specific ways (de Bot et al., 2007; Larsen-Freeman, 2010; Larsen-Freeman & Cameron, 2008; Ortega, 2011; Valdés, 2020); that they penalize students for switching between languages even though people often combine languages when speaking in real life (Grosjean, 2008; Rothman & Iverson, 2010); and that they validate only particular dialects or languages while failing to recognize others (Makoni & Pennycook, 2015; Valdés, 2020). Because of the potential impact on identity development, students, especially heritage language learners and ELs, should understand that such tests are imperfect and not always valid.

Standardized tests perpetuate a number of inequities in the educational system. The SoBL recognition relies rather staunchly on formal language proficiency tests, which should cause scrutiny with regard to equity. Consider selecting and using assessments in ways that benefit students and widen opportunities for students to demonstrate their abilities.

Ensuring Access for Users of Less Commonly Tested Languages

The state of Washington is a leader in assessing less commonly tested languages, awarding the SoBL in 69 languages in 2019, which was more than any other state. These efforts have been spearheaded by Dr. Michele Anciaux Aoki and her colleagues with the Washington Association for Language Teaching (WAFLT), who worked to assess any language requested by students. Their work evolved from a grant-funded project through the State Office of Superintendent of Public Instruction (OSPI), which allowed students proficient in languages other than English to earn high-school elective world language credits for their proficiency. After passing the Washington State Legislature in 2014 and becoming law in 2015, the SoBL became an additional incentive for students to pursue this competency-based credit option.

The state team decided on specific external assessments to use, selecting a variety of options to cover as many languages as possible. When a language was not covered by any of these, OSPI made Custom Tests with speaking and writing tasks.

While chair of the ACTFL Special Interest Group on Less Commonly Taught languages, Dr. Aoki met Monique Roske of M2 Language Consultants, LLC. In Monique, she found a language colleague who knew, or was willing to find, fluent adult speakers of many languages around the world. WAFLT worked with the Center for Applied Second Language Studies (CASLS) at the University of Oregon to

develop presentational writing and speaking prompts with Avant Assessment as a platform for assessment delivery. Their prompts were designed to target Intermediate Mid to Intermediate High levels of proficiency. For almost ten years, Monique used her connections to find and train evaluators for each language, while WAFLT worked with the districts to order and administer the tests.

To effectively promote and expand the SoBL, stakeholders must work toward equitable access by allowing students to demonstrate proficiency in any language, including languages not taught at the school. Nonetheless, one of the biggest challenges to SoBL implementation is the lack of assessments in many languages. Some states, like Minnesota and Washington, have engaged in efforts to create a wider array of language assessments. For example, administrators at the Minnesota Department of Education compiled a list of the most commonly used languages in the state for which no appropriate assessment existed and then collaborated with several districts to create proficiency tests for those languages. They gathered users of languages including Hmong, Karen, Lakota-Dakota, Oromo, and Somali to create assessments. They also trained individuals in larger school districts to score assessments.

One of the most common ways that districts and schools propagate inequity is by taking a low-hanging fruit approach, testing only languages offered in the school and only students enrolled in world language. This approach provides access only to students who have the space in their schedules to study a world language in school and excludes students who use another language at home or in the community. Schools must strive to offer SoBL access to all students, recognizing all languages that students use.

As described in the vignette, Washington state administrators tapped into grant funds and partnered with a national assessment company to develop tests of less commonly tested languages. The Custom Tests consist of three presentational writing prompts to which students respond by handwriting and three presentational speaking prompts to which students respond using LinguaFolio Online, an online portfolio tool. The Custom Tests are evaluated by native speakers or linguists who determine whether the samples meet the proficiency levels that correspond to competency-based credits. The OSPI covers the cost of the assessments for these less commonly tested languages, making them available to any district in the state. Dr. Aoki, the WAFLT Testing team, and Veronica Trapani, the current World Languages Program Supervisor at OSPI, are working with local Indigenous groups to adapt this process to award credit in Indigenous languages. In Washington, local tribes determine the level of proficiency for their languages and the assessment process to qualify students for the state SoBL.

 **Critical to implementing the SoBL with an equity lens, alternative assessments allow students to demonstrate biliteracy when formal language assessments are not available. States should include options for alternative assessment protocols in SoBL policies, and local educators should work to provide them for all students' home languages.**

Many readers likely do not have state resources to assess less commonly tested languages and instead need to consider a ***language portfolio process***. In this approach, students submit portfolios with samples of skills in all four domains (listening, reading, speaking, writing) or three modes of communication (interpersonal, interpretive, presentational). For example, in New Hampshire, a portfolio must include the following language samples (New Hampshire Department of Education, 2021):

1. Listening: Written summary (150-200 words) from an authentic audio or video that is at least one minute in length. The source must be included.

2. Speaking: Recorded presentation on any academic topic of interest (4-5 minutes).

3. Interpersonal Communication: Recorded interview (2-3 minutes) of a conversation with a native speaker (e.g., a family member) on the topic, What are your future goals and how can bilingualism be a benefit?

4. Reading/Writing: Written summary (200-300 words) of a current event taken from an authentic, written news article from the home country.

Other states, such as Massachusetts, Mississippi, and New York, have similar guidelines for portfolio creation and include rubrics for scoring those portfolios. If your state does not have explicit guidelines, you might consult Mississippi's SoBL guidelines, which include detailed procedures for portfolio creation.

 **Many existing proficiency scales were developed for individuals learning commonly used languages for employment or travel and may not be applicable for Indigenous languages that are no longer widely spoken (Kahakalau, 2017). When creating an assessment or portfolio option for Indigenous languages, we recommend flexibility rather than strict conformity to existing notions of proficiency and proficiency levels.**

Remember that while portfolios provide equitable access for students who use less commonly tested languages, they also present several logistical challenges. Educators need to provide students with guidance to understand how to independently develop portfolios, and they must secure individuals who can score the portfolio, who may require payment and training. Refer back to Tool 1.2 and reach out to high-awarding districts in your state to determine how they have confronted this challenge. Chapters 2 and 5 also support you in brainstorming potential community partners for finding proficient users of various languages, particularly community language schools and organizations. You can provide individuals with the NCSSFL-ACTFL Can-Do statements (NCSSFL & ACTFL, 2017a) to determine if students have the required proficiency level to achieve the SoBL.

It is our hope that federal resources may someday support the assessment of less commonly tested languages, but in the meantime, we encourage creativity. If you cannot find existing assessments for a particular language, consider creating your own. We have created Tool 3.1 to support you in crafting assessment prompts based on the minimum proficiency level students must meet in your state. You might create three interpersonal speaking and three presentational writing prompts. Or, due to difficulties in training and preparing individuals to conduct interviews for interpersonal assessments, you might instead assess presentational speaking, similar to Washington's model. In Appendices 3 through 6, we offer several examples that others can use or adapt. You might consider using online tools such as Extempore or LinguaFolio Online (available through CASLS), which allow students to record speaking and submit writing samples to create these portfolios.

Improving Logistics of Language Assessment Processes

Administrators at Bolton School District (a pseudonym) learned a lot from their first two years of SoBL implementation. In the first year, they discovered that just awarding the SoBL to students enrolled in AP courses was inequitable and excluded many biliterate students. In the second year, they expanded language testing, offering SoBL assessments to all seniors on a Saturday in February. When a blizzard hit that day and the test had to be cancelled, they realized the pitfalls of a one-shot approach to language testing.

The following summer, administrators planned a series of workdays during which they committed to carefully thinking through the logistics of the SoBL. They dedicated one of these days solely to figuring out the logistics of the language assessment process. Their initial goal was for 20 percent of their graduates to earn the SoBL. The team decided that the best approach was to coordinate assessments at the district level rather than asking each school to coordinate its own assessments. This way, they could get better pricing on tests and could streamline the process, easing the burden on schools.

Leaders decided to have designated testing days for specific languages, thinking that students might be more willing to come if others in their community were also going. They enlisted the support of community language organizations to help advertise and proctor on these days. For example, they chose one weekday morning in February to offer the Somali test, and an individual from the Somali community organization was invited to proctor. The team reached out to a university to use its large computer lab with wired internet connection and headsets. After testing

the most common languages, the district offered two more testing days for students who had missed their test day or who needed a test in a language not previously offered

In addition to securing assessments, SoBL coordinators and teams need to determine various logistics related to offering these assessments in ways that maximize access and participation. Content areas like science and mathematics often have strict rules and procedures related to when such tests occur, who must take them, and how they are administered. Because the SoBL is voluntary, districts and schools often coordinate these assessments on their own. Such coordination requires educators to think through methods for administering assessments, incorporating technology, and tracking data. An inequitable approach in even one of these aspects can derail accessibility. For example, a school might offer a wide variety of assessments in less commonly taught and tested languages, but if the tests are only offered one Saturday a semester, some students may be unable to participate. We turn now to considerations for each of these aspects of the assessment process. Use Tool 3.3 to create your own assessment plan.

Deciding When to Offer Assessments One important but challenging aspect of SoBL implementation is decisions about when to offer language assessments, which can determine which and how many students participate. Some districts offer tests once a semester on a Saturday, which might (a) exclude students without transportation, who work, or who care for their siblings on weekends, (b) disregard students whose religious practices forbid schooling on a Saturday, and (c) require staff to work on the weekend to proctor the assessments. Other districts offer SoBL assessments after school. With this approach, students do not have to find transportation to school, but the school must arrange transportation home following test administration. Tests can take up to four hours, which is a stretch for students after a long school day. Additionally, students may not sign up for testing if they have work, childcare duties, or sports after school.

Another common approach for test administration is to offer SoBL assessments during the school day, similar to required end-of-year assessments of math and literacy. In schools with large populations of biliterate students, stakeholders might set aside one calendar date per year when everyone in the school has the option to take the assessment. Those not interested in taking a SoBL assessment might be given study hall or a reading day. In schools with smaller populations of biliterate students, we have seen a *field trip* approach, in which students who wish to take the assessment are released from their regularly-scheduled classes for the assessment. However, there can be many distractions during the school day, and students may not perform at their best or may be reluctant to opt in for a lengthy assessment.

We recommend offering multiple testing days and times throughout the year, as well as allowing students to take assessments more than once. For example, Seattle Public Schools offers monthly testing on a Saturday and encourages high schools to offer several testing dates after school, on early-release days, or during the summer before the school year begins. Inevitably, some students miss the test due to illness or other reasons, so scheduling at least one make-up day is important.

In most states, students must earn the minimum required proficiency level (e.g., Intermediate Mid) in all four domains. Therefore, if a student scored an Intermediate Mid in reading, writing, and listening, but an Intermediate Low in speaking, the student would not qualify for the SoBL. Determine whether the test you are using allows students who require a higher score in a particular domain to retake portions of the assessment rather than retaking the entire test. Something as simple as allowing a student another opportunity to take a portion of the assessment before graduation could be the difference in obtaining the SoBL and subsequently earning high-school or college credit.

Due to the cost of tests, some districts only allow seniors to take the test. This practice makes the test high stakes in that students have only one opportunity to pass. If both juniors and seniors take assessments, then those who did not pass in junior year can practice for an additional year and try again. In an ideal scenario, districts provide students with access to tests throughout their schooling, perhaps in fifth grade, eighth grade, and several times in high school. As described in Chapter 1, this approach provides pathways for students to assess their progress and teachers to analyze data and adjust instruction accordingly.

Determining Where to Administer Assessments
Frequency of test administration influences location. Most tests require students to be on devices connected to the internet. For this reason, the internet connection must be strong enough for many students to be connected simultaneously, making an ethernet connection preferable to wireless, especially if the test falls during the regular school day with large quantities of students already online. Because SoBL assessments measure listening and speaking, students require headsets. Students can take assessments of many different languages in the same room, but this may provide challenges to concentration. Additionally, some students may be reluctant to speak loudly enough to produce audible recordings when surrounded by peers. Therefore, another option is to test reading, writing, and listening in a large group, but have students come in before or after school to take the speaking component in a quiet location.

Some districts choose to cluster assessment sites by language to aid in coordination and control group sizes. For example, everyone in a district who speaks Somali might be invited to one school to take the assessment on a particular day while everyone who speaks Hmong is invited to a different school for the assessment on the same day. For students, this configuration may provide comfort in having others who speak the same language present. Additionally, for languages such as Arabic that require a keyboard overlay with Arabic script, this approach can ensure that the correct materials are in the correct location.

Schools do not have to be the sole sites that administer assessments. Community language schools can be helpful partners, such as the Tamil Saturday School in Minnesota that offers the Tamil SoBL assessment and provides results to the local school district. Universities often have the capacity to support more languages and writing systems. WAFLT, described in the vignette, has offered assessment days in the language learning labs of local universities. This approach streamlines the resources needed for test administration, reduces the cost through the purchase of assessments in bulk, and brings students to local universities to provide a real-world backdrop for demonstrating biliteracy. We discuss partnerships with community language schools and universities in more depth in Chapter 5.

Collaboration can allow for greater flexibility. In the Walsh School District, stakeholders spent the early months of the COVID pandemic coordinating who would meet individual students for masked and distanced test proctoring outside on picnic tables. At-home testing is also a growing trend, yielding more flexibility while maintaining assessment validity. Many assessments allow students to test remotely and securely via artificial intelligence and remote human proctoring. When logistics are both collaborative and flexible, more students have access to the SoBL.

Obtaining the Necessary Technology Another key step in working through assessment logistics is determining the technology needed to facilitate the various language tests. Test proctors should be aware that certain languages may present challenges to the writing portion of the assessments. Cyrillic-based languages (e.g., Russian), Devanagari-based languages (e.g., Hindi), and character-based languages (e.g., Chinese) require language-specific keyboards or keyboard overlays. Before assessment administration, coordinators should review the proctoring guides available online from the test companies to ensure that the necessary technology is downloaded. Technology support should also be on hand during testing that requires different writing systems. The Input Method Editor (IME) often has to be configured on each computer for students to access the correct script.

Alternatively, some tests offer a booklet option so that students can handwrite rather than type written portions. The handwritten option is critical for many Indigenous languages for which no keyboard option exists. In Chapter 5, we suggest that districts and schools with restricted resources consider partnering with universities or community language organizations.

Designing Procedures to Efficiently Track Data
Finally, teams should consider how to manage, input, and track data. Bolton School District, presented in the vignette, entered testing data into Infinite Campus, which was coded to detect whether a student had met all requirements for the SoBL. However, not all districts have automated procedures, making data tracking laborious. For example, in the Walsh School District, students who receive the SoBL also earn high-school credit, including for languages not taught in the district. When SoBL assessment scores arrive, the testing coordinator enters the results on a spreadsheet to indicate students' eligibility for credit. If any scores were rated *Not Gradable,* she determines whether a problem such as a technology failure warrants another opportunity to take the test. Using her spreadsheet, she reviews qualifying students' transcripts to ensure no duplication of credits earned through coursework and then sends the spreadsheet to each school for the registrar to enter the credits. Next, she compiles a list of seniors eligible for the SoBL, many of whom may have passed the SoBL assessment earlier in their

schooling. After ensuring students' clearance for graduation from school counselors, she updates the spreadsheet, prints award letters and score sheets, and sends those to each school for distribution.

Each district needs to find the approach to data management that works given its human and technological resources. Start by exploring the state's data management system for SoBL recognition. For example, North Carolina uses a system called PowerSchool that codes students who have met SoBL requirements, significantly streamlining local data management. In states where such structures do not exist, administrators might explore how SoBL data management can be tackled within their existing systems. Some districts like Walsh are fortunate to have a full-time district staff member dedicated to data management who can commit a significant portion of her workload to SoBL assessment work. In other contexts, this level of support may not be possible. SoBL implementation teams should explore reasonable ways to approach data management in their contexts and provide time and space in the coordinator's workload to tackle this pertinent but potentially time-consuming task.

Attaching Assessments to Instruction and Program Efficacy

At Elmwood School District (a pseudonym), the world language department has worked to establish an equitable language assessment program that provides useful data for teachers. The district pays for SoBL assessments for all students, regardless of income strata. Students have many opportunities to take assessments, including options during the school day or after school if they do not want to miss class time. Unlike schools that require students to wait until their junior year to take the test, Elmwood encourages students to take the tests as early and as often as possible. While teachers initially had concerns about this policy, worrying that students would pass the test and no longer enroll in world languages, they came to embrace the resulting data to inform instruction. Some teachers even encourage students to take assessments after passing so that they can use the data for programmatic evaluation.

Faculty in the French department use SoBL assessment data as one of their two required student learning outcome data points to measure student growth. When test results arrive, faculty analyze each student's performance to create personalized student learning plans. The data allow the teachers to tell students about their strengths and where they need to improve to reach the next proficiency level. As a result, students' proficiency growth in French has greatly improved, as has enrollment in French courses.

The washback of the SoBL assessments on instruction at Elmwood has been positive. Analysis of test data has led teachers in the department to rewrite their curriculum to focus on the three modes of communication. Additionally, teachers have revised their scoring rubrics, drawing language from the ACTFL Performance Guidelines (ACTFL, 2012a).

Uses of language assessments such as those described in this chapter go far beyond determining who achieves the SoBL. In our work across the country, the connection between the SoBL and language programming has been one of the most powerful outcomes of the SoBL movement. Not only are students being recognized for their biliteracy, but educators are looking critically at their language programs, curricula, and instruction as they seek to enhance students' language competencies (Heineke & Davin, 2021). SoBL assessment scores (i.e., proficiency levels by language domain) allow teachers to provide targeted language instruction and supports, potentially enhancing students' biliteracy and subsequent performance on SoBL assessments. While alignment between SoBL assessments and instruction might seem commonsensical, teaching toward proficiency may represent a departure from historical methods of language teaching for many educators, potentially requiring support to push beyond teaching in the ways that they were taught (Davin et al., 2018; Donato & Davin, 2018).

Designing Classroom-Based Performance Assessments Although tests to achieve the SoBL might only be taken once per year, teachers should engage students in interpretive, interpersonal, and presentational tasks on a regular basis. While teachers might occasionally use less cognitively demanding

assessments, such as vocabulary or verb conjugation quizzes, classroom assessments of the three modes of communication should typify classroom practice. **_Performance assessments_** involve language-rich, authentic tasks that capture data to inform students' developing proficiency (Abedi, 2010). Distinct from proficiency, **_performance_** refers to students' ability to use language learned and practiced in an instructional setting; that is, in familiar contexts and content areas (ACTFL, 2012a, p. 4). Like proficiency tests, performance assessments prompt students to use language for real-world tasks. One example is the Integrated Performance Assessment (IPA; Adair-Hauck et al., 2013), which assesses the three modes of communication around the same topic. For example, in a unit on the Caribbean Sea taught in a fifth-grade Spanish classroom, the teacher assesses students' _Interpretive_ communication by showing a video about a trip to the beach and posing questions to students. After providing students with feedback, she assesses _Interpersonal_ communication through a paired, picture-difference task in which students identify differences in two beach scenes. Following feedback, she concludes by assessing _Presentational_ communication, asking students to write a magazine article about what to do at the beach (Davin et al., 2011). Students communicate in all three modes while the teacher collects data to inform subsequent instruction.

 When designed in response to the unique students in the classroom, performance assessments allow teachers to observe students' dynamic language use in authentic and relevant situations. To promote equity, teachers can select assessment topics that tap into students' background knowledge and tasks with scaffolds (e.g., graphic organizers, visuals, sentence stems) to support students at varying proficiency levels.

To develop students' proficiency and prepare them for SoBL assessments, teachers can provide targeted feedback using performance-based and proficiency-based rubrics. Teachers can use **_performance-based rubrics_** throughout the year to measure performance related to the units studied. Some refer to these as **_performance-toward-proficiency rubrics_** (Jefferson County Public Schools, 2021a). **_Proficiency-based rubrics_** measure content not yet studied to provide pre- and post-measures on student learning outcomes, similar to what one might encounter if suddenly living in a country where the target language is spoken. Both rubrics allow for

Figure 3.4. Aligning Assessments to Support Language Learning

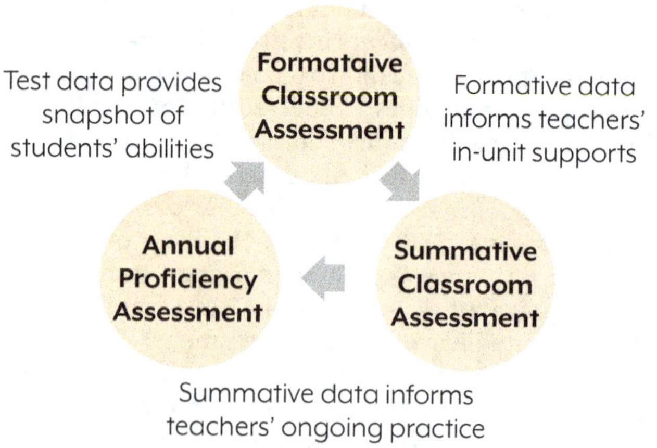

Test data provides snapshot of students' abilities

Formataive Classroom Assessment

Formative data informs teachers' in-unit supports

Annual Proficiency Assessment

Summative Classroom Assessment

Summative data informs teachers' ongoing practice

targeted feedback on the components of proficiency, such as language function, vocabulary, comprehensibility, and language control. They describe the characteristics of proficiency, provide learners with concrete understandings of how to improve proficiency, and identify strategies for improvement. We recommend that teachers unfamiliar with rubric creation draw from strong examples online, such as the *Jefferson County Public Schools World Languages Rubrics* (Jefferson County Public Schools, 2021b), the *Ohio Rubrics for World Languages* (Ohio Department of Education, 2021), or the *Shelby County Schools World Languages Performance Feedback Tools* (Shelby County Schools, 2021).

While performance assessments have been a growing trend in the field, replacing traditional tools such as multiple-choice and cloze-task assessments, their use also directly connects to efficacy with SoBL implementation. Programs that graduate a high number of SoBL recipients use performance assessments that approximate SoBL assessments (Kissau & Adams, 2016). This means that students should have opportunities throughout the school year to demonstrate and receive proficiency-focused feedback on their developing language within the modes of communication, and teachers should use the resulting data to inform their supports for students' language development. In this way, all facets of assessment align: formative unit assessments align with the summative unit assessments which align with formal proficiency assessments (see Figure 3.4). This alignment is valuable to consider in world language, bilingual, and EL classrooms. Just as world language teachers can gather data on students' language use in various communication modes, as aligned with world language assessments, bilingual and EL teachers can capture language use across domains (listening, reading, speaking, writing), as aligned with results from English proficiency assessments. In between annual tests, teachers can glean valuable data on language development while engaging students in meaningful communicative tasks.

Using Data from Classroom-Based Assessments for Program Evaluation In addition to data-driven instructional practices in classrooms, SoBL assess-

Table 3.3. Potential Questions for SoBL Assessment Data Analysis

LENS	POTENTIAL QUESTIONS	PROGRAM IMPLICATIONS
Program Availability and Duration	**Across languages, consider:** In which languages is the highest percentage of students earning the SoBL? In which languages is the lowest percentage of students earning the SoBL?	Potential extensions to sequences of language study or additional offerings by level or language
Program Access and Equity	**Within and across languages, consider:** How are students performing in particular demographic groups (e.g., race)? How are students performing in particular institutional labels (e.g., ELs)?	Revisions to institutional structures and tracks, as well as discussions with faculty to disrupt potential biases
Curriculum and Instruction	**In each language, consider:** In which modes of communication or domains are students scoring the lowest? In which modes of communication or domains are students scoring the highest? How do students' scores compare across teachers of the same level?	Focused refinements to curriculum and instruction, such as attention to particular communication modes, while also maintaining support in areas of strength

ments can inform larger program evaluation and subsequent revisions to allow equitable access to high-quality language instruction and biliteracy development. Following receipt of all test results, stakeholders can analyze the data, similar to the educators in the vignette. In Elmwood, stakeholders not only use test results to award the SoBL, but continually analyze and reflect upon the data to enhance their language programs. Table 3.3 presents examples of ways that teams might look holistically at SoBL assessment scores. This list is not exhaustive, and schools and districts can analyze data through various lenses as aligned with the specific goals defined for SoBL implementation. Overall, it is important to remember that SoBL assessments offer powerful data that can inform evaluations of whether programs, curricula, and instruction are producing their desired results. We discuss how to evaluate SoBL implementation in Chapter 7.

Whether you are just starting to establish SoBL implementation in your setting or working to refine it, use Tool 3.4 to evaluate assessment practices in your language programs. Consider how often students can take SoBL assessments. Think about the extent to which summative and formative assessments align with the three modes of communication and whether students receive feedback on language proficiency and development. You might convene language teachers to analyze and code each assignment in their gradebooks based on the focal communication mode (interpretive, interpersonal, presentational) or language domain (oral language, reading, writing). Using these codes, teachers can discuss balancing assessment practices and providing students with sufficient practice in each mode depending on various factors. For example, heritage language learners at intermediate levels might benefit from presentational writing and interpretive reading tasks, whereas world language learners at beginning levels might benefit from interpersonal and presentational speaking tasks.

Chapter Summary

In this chapter, we have explored the second facet of the 5Ps framework, *Proficiency Assessments*. Creation of an assessment plan is an important and challenging aspect of SoBL implementation. The process is time- and resource-intensive and presents a wide variety of potential equity pitfalls. In this chapter, we have outlined different options for assessing students' world language and English proficiency and discussed options for situations where no assessment exists, underscoring that schools must ensure that all biliterate students have opportunities to demonstrate their home language skills. We have provided information to inform decisions related to when and where to offer language assessments along with needed resources. Finally, we have discussed the importance of attaching assessments to program efficacy, connecting to classroom language assessments and using the data from commercial assessments in program evaluation.

Questions for Discussion and Reflection

1. How does your state's SoBL policy inform the use of proficiency assessments in your context? What types of assessment are accepted as evidence for world language and English proficiency? What assessment procedures are in place for less commonly taught and tested languages? Use Tool 3.1 to guide your analysis of assessment requirements. The information that you gather guides the creation of your assessment plan.

2. Select one language used by students at your school or district. As a team, use Tool 3.2 to compose leveled assessment prompts that approximate those on SoBL assessments. If the language is already taught and tested in your setting, you can use these prompts for students to practice for the SoBL assessment. If the language does not correspond with an existing commercial assessment, these prompts can be the start of an alternative assessment to expand access to the SoBL.

3. As a team, use Tool 3.3 to think through the details of your assessment plan. Discuss how to determine which languages to test and how to address the logistics of the process.

4. Use Tool 3.4 to consider how your classroom assessments align with proficiency testing data. Do most graded classroom assignments assess a mode of communication? What tools measure proficiency? Do average scores on proficiency assessments point toward a mode of communication in need of increased attention in the language classroom?

Further Reading

- Adair-Hauck, B., Glisan, E. W., & Troyan, F. J. (2013). *Implementing integrated performance assessment.* ACTFL.

- McTighe, J., Doubet, K. J., & Carbaugh, E. M. (2020). *Designing authentic performance tasks and projects: Tools for meaningful learning and assessment.* ASCD.

- Sandrock, P. (2010). *The keys to assessing language performance: A teacher's manual for measuring student progress.* ACTFL.

- Shohamy, E. (2007). Language tests as language policy tools. *Assessment in Education: Principles, Policy & Practice, 14*(1), 117–130. https://doi.org/10.1080/09695940701272948

Tool 3.1. SoBL Assessment Requirements in Your State

Directions: Before you create your assessment plan, complete this tool by consulting your state's SoBL guidelines to understand the requirements for demonstrating world language and English language proficiency.

GUIDING QUESTIONS	NOTES
What forms of evidence of world language proficiency (e.g., seat time, approved assessment, portfolio) are accepted?	
Which assessments can be used to demonstrate world language proficiency? List assessments or note the website where they can be found. Note the minimum required score on each assessment.	
When (e.g., sophomore, junior, senior year) are students allowed to take the assessments required to demonstrate their world language and/or English language proficiency?	
Which language domains (listening, reading, speaking, writing) must be assessed in the world language?	
What is the procedure for awarding the SoBL to students proficient in a language that is not taught in school or for which there is not an approved assessment?	
What forms of evidence of English language proficiency (e.g., seat time, approved assessment, graduation) are accepted? What is the minimum requirement for attainment?	
Are there alternative or additional forms of evidence for ELs? If so, what are they?	

Tool 3.2 Creating Assessment Prompts

Directions: When writing assessment prompts, it is important to consult the NCSSFL-ACTFL Can-Do statements (NCSSFL & ACTFL, 2017a) to ensure your prompt elicits language at the proficiency level required by the SoBL in your state. Use the following steps to guide your prompt creation. You might first compose the prompts in English so that they can be translated into other languages by your raters. Additional example prompts are included in Appendices 3 through 6.

Step 1. Review SoBL requirements. Review your state's SoBL policy. Note the minimum required level of proficiency and the required evidence (e.g., evidence of all three modes of communication or all four domains). If your state has multiple tiers of the recognition, list each one.

Step 2. Download or print the NCSSFL-ACTFL Can-Do statements. Via the ACTFL website or through an internet search, locate the freely-available NCSSFL-ACTFL Can-Do statements (NCSSFL & ACTFL, 2017a). Choose the appropriate proficiency level, typically Intermediate Mid or Intermediate High in most states.

Step 3. Find the appropriate performance indicators. Highlight, circle, or write down (in the third column) the performance indicator for each mode of communication, based on your state's requirement. (Page 59)

Step 4. Choose a language function for each mode. For each of the three modes of communication, choose a language function to target with your prompt (i.e., the middle column of the table in Step 3). Review the performance indicator (i.e., the third column of the table in Step 3) to reflect on what type of prompts might elicit a sample of whether students can fulfill the requirements of the proficiency level you chose.

Step 5. Write your prompt. Use the GRASPS format (Wiggins & McTighe, 2005) to write a prompt, including the Goal, Role, Audience, Situation, Product/Performance, Purpose, and Standards and Criteria for Success, as exemplified in this sample based on the Intermediate Mid level of proficiency.

Example Presentational prompt for narration:

You are the student body president and you are responsible for taking a group of students visiting from Beijing on a tour of your school. Your goal is to show them the different parts of the school (e.g., gym, cafeteria, language lab) and describe what types of activities occur in each part. The principal has requested that you prepare by writing a script for your tour. She wants you to write five paragraphs, identifying one location in each paragraph and describing who uses the space, what activity occurs in the space, and when the space is typically used.

Step 6. Assess students' performance. Via the ACTFL website or through an internet search, locate the freely-available ACTFL Proficiency Guidelines (ACTFL, 2012b). Find the description for the level and mode that corresponds to your prompt. In the case of the example prompt in Step 5, you would find the Intermediate Mid description for Writing, which says:

> Writers at the Intermediate Mid sublevel are able to meet a number of practical writing needs. They can write short, simple communications, compositions, and requests for information in loosely connected texts about personal preferences, daily routines, common events, and other personal topics. Their writing is framed in present time but may contain references to other time frames. The writing style closely resembles oral discourse. Writers at the Intermediate Mid sublevel show evidence of control of basic sentence structure and verb forms. This writing is best defined as a collection of discrete sentences and/or questions loosely strung together. There is little evidence of deliberate organization. Intermediate Mid writers can be understood readily by natives used to the writing of non-natives. When Intermediate Mid writers attempt Advanced-level writing tasks, the quality and/or quantity of their writing declines and the message may be unclear. (ACTFL, 2012b, p. 13)

Analyze the student's performance using the description provided in the ACTFL Proficiency Guidelines. Consider consulting the description of a lower sublevel (e.g., Intermediate Low) as well to help you determine whether the student has met that proficiency requirement.

For Step 3, based on your state's requirements, record the performance indicator for each mode of communication in the third column of the table.

MODE	LANGUAGE FUNCTION	PERFORMANCE INDICATOR
Interpretive Communication		
	What can I understand, interpret or analyze in authentic informational texts that I hear, read, or view?	Example for Intermediate Mid: I can understand the main idea and key information in short straightforward informational texts.
	What can I understand, interpret or analyze in authentic fictional texts that I hear, read, or view?	
	What can I understand, interpret or analyze in conversations and discussions that I hear, read, or view, in which I am not a participant?	
Interpersonal Communication		
	How can I exchange information and ideas in conversations?	Example for Intermediate Mid: I can exchange information in conversations on familiar topics and some researched topics, creating sentences and series of sentences and asking a variety of follow-up questions.
	How can I meet my needs or address situations in conversations?	
	How can I express, react to, and support preferences and opinions in conversations?	
Presentational Communication		
	How can I present information to narrate about my life, experiences and events?	Example for Intermediate Mid: I can tell a story about my life, activities, events and other social experiences, using sentences and series of connected sentences.
	How can I present information to give a preference, opinion or persuasive argument?	
	How can I present information to inform, describe, or explain?	

Tool 3.3. Assessment Plan

Directions: Follow the steps below to develop your assessment plan. Consider who should be involved in planning and how tasks can be shared.

Step 1. Determine grade levels in which you offer the assessment. Within your context, consider the grade levels to which you open up the test option. Do all high-school students have access, regardless of grade? Or do you target 11th and 12th graders?

Step 2. Determine which language tests are necessary. Based on the grade levels in which you will offer the SoBL assessments, determine which languages require a test. Potential options:

Review data from the Home Language Survey. Reach out to every student whose parents/guardians indicated that another language was spoken in the home.

Administer a short survey in homeroom or advisory period to all students. Include the self-assessment in Appendix 2 to determine whether students should sign up for a test.

Send a text message and email, on multiple occasions and in multiple languages, to all students and families about the opportunity to take the SoBL assessments. Provide a link where they can sign up.

Step 3. Compile list and determine tests. Create a list of all languages for which students require a test.

Check the websites for testing organizations to determine which languages are available from each.

For those languages not available, consider calling organizations' customer service departments to inquire about other options that might not yet be posted on their website (or widely available), or determine whether there are options from other companies. Consult colleagues in other districts and via the internet to see if they have found a test for the language.

For cases in which no language test exists, consider using the tools in Appendices 3 through 8 to create your own. Consult community members to locate an individual proficient in the language who might be able to score assessments.

Step 4. Determine the approximate cost of assessments and seek funding. Based on the results of Steps 2 and 3, calculate an approximate cost of the assessments themselves. Add in the cost of technology needs (e.g., headsets, keyboard overlays, human resources). Consult administration, the Parent-Teacher Association, and community organizations regarding ideas on how to fund or subsidize the assessments. Based on how much funding you obtain, consider how much students will be charged.

Step 5. Determine logistics.

Create a committee of individuals who oversee SoBL implementation. Within the committee, determine who leads advertising, testing, data analysis and entry, social media campaigns, and the recognition and celebration of SoBL attainment.

Determine when and where to offer assessments. Consider issues of proctors, technology support, and transportation.

Tool 3.4. Evaluate Assessment Procedures

Directions: Begin by gathering your students' proficiency assessment scores. Look for patterns in the data, including strengths and areas of need. Next, analyze the prevalence of performance-toward-proficiency assessments in language programming. Consider how classroom-based assessments might be revised to better prepare students for SoBL assessments.

Program Assessment Gather data from your assessment to indicate the proficiency ratings available at all levels (grade levels for bilingual and EL programs, course levels for world language) and language offerings (e.g., Spanish world language, Vietnamese dual-language, ESL). Respond to the following questions for each language at each level.

1. In which modes of communication or domains are students scoring the lowest?
2. In which modes of communication or domains are students scoring the highest?

Classroom Assessment Pick one grading period (e.g., quarter, semester). For each entry in your gradebook, label the assignment as Interpretive (reading or listening), Interpersonal, Presentational (speaking or writing), or Not Communicative, based on which mode of communication was assessed (Kissau & Adams, 2016). For example, an assignment in which students write an essay would be labeled as Presentational. A vocabulary quiz in which students translated a list of words would be labeled as Not Communicative. Then, divide the number of each type of assignment by the total number of assignments for the grading period to calculate the percentage. The goal is to phase out non-communicative assignments and achieve balance across modes.

MODE	NUMBER OF ASSIGNMENTS	PERCENT OF TOTAL
Interpretive Reading		
Interpretive Listening		
Interpersonal Speaking		
Presentational Speaking		
Presentational Writing		
Not Communicative		

Assessment Discussion Questions

1. Which mode of communication is the most frequently assessed? Which mode of communication is the least frequently assessed? What percentage of the graded assignments are not communicative?

2. How do average scores on proficiency assessments correspond to the frequency of graded assignments for each mode of communication?

3. What changes are necessary to ensure that more graded assignments are communicative?

4. What changes are necessary to the distribution of classroom graded assignments to target areas of weakness on proficiency assessment at the programmatic level?

Chapter 4
Programs: Enhancing Pathways to Developing Biliteracy

Anna grew up in rural Illinois in a home where only English was spoken. She attended schools in a local public school district and began studying Spanish in eighth grade. Reflecting on her learning, she told us, "I have not been the best Spanish student." Despite her struggles, Anna loved Spanish class and adored her teacher. In talking about the courses, she explained that "[the teachers] don't just integrate grammar and all the textbook stuff, they bring in culture, they bring in your personal life." She elaborated, "I can't tell you how many times we've done a speaking [assignment] about us or a writing [assignment] about us and that really helps you connect with it. And I feel like that's what makes learning [Spanish] so much easier and so much more fun." As a high-school junior in Spanish IV, she took a test of language proficiency and told us that she "did awful" but decided to move on to Spanish V and take the test again as a senior. She told us, "I got the Seal of Biliteracy, and my Señora cried because she was so happy...It made me cry. I was so happy." She said, "And it's just things like [passing the test on the second try], you see yourself grow, that really motivates you".

Guiding Questions

In what ways do classroom instruction and assessment support biliteracy?

What are common characteristics of curricula in language programs that graduate a high number of SoBL recipients?

How can language programs be designed to foster bilingualism and biliteracy?

In this chapter, we present the third facet of our framework: *Programs.* The SoBL recognizes students who read, write, speak, and understand in two or more languages. To achieve biliteracy, students need programs that target language proficiency. As described in Chapter 1, various programs target language in schools, including world language and bilingual education, as well as various programs serving ELs (e.g., ESL, sheltered instruction). Of course, we know that myriad factors impact learners' language development, with research confirming that two learners may engage with the same language for the same number of years and reach different levels of proficiency (Collier, 1989; Hakuta et al., 2000; Zhang et al., 2020). While no two individuals learn and develop language in the same way, this chapter describes factors common across programs that successfully nurture language and biliteracy development.

Through our research on SoBL implementation across the United States, we have discovered many creative and effective ways in which districts and schools use the SoBL to enhance language programming and vice versa (Davin et al., 2018; Hancock & Davin, 2020; Heineke & Davin, 2021). Leaders have utilized the SoBL in ways that garner attention for language programs, such as elevating the status of bilingual programming for ELs in the community or attracting new families to the district through extensive world language programming. In many settings, SoBL efforts have prompted extensions to language study to better nurture students' biliteracy, including expansion of elementary and middle-school world language education and high-school dual-language coursework in the content areas. Others have leveraged the SoBL to develop new program offerings, such as heritage language coursework in less commonly taught languages such as Somali and Samoan. In addition to larger programmatic revisions and additions, stakeholders in districts with well-established SoBL initiatives consistently describe using SoBL assessment data to enhance classroom instruction and pedagogy, often transforming teachers' practice to center on meaningful student interaction and authentic language use.

This chapter prompts consideration of actionable ways to develop and enhance language instruction, curricula, and programs as a part of larger SoBL implementation efforts (see Figure 4.1). We see this link between language programming and SoBL efforts as integral, going beyond the conception of a one-time recognition for those who have been given the opportunity to become biliterate and using the initiative to prompt meaningful change in schools (Schwedhelm & King, 2020; Valdés, 2020). We begin with the micro level of *instruction*, exploring classroom approaches that promote language development, including high-leverage practices that span world language, bilingual, and EL settings. We then turn to the meso level of *curriculum*, including approaches and tools to create and revise longitudinal trajectories of study. We close with the macro level of *programs*, discussing characteristics of effective language programs that enhance biliteracy. Of course, this chapter cannot fully capture the extensive research and details about effective programming for all types of language education. Instead, we present overarching themes to consider with suggestions for additional texts and resources that allow you to go deeper depending on focal areas of need in your context.

Figure 4.1. Levels of Language Programming

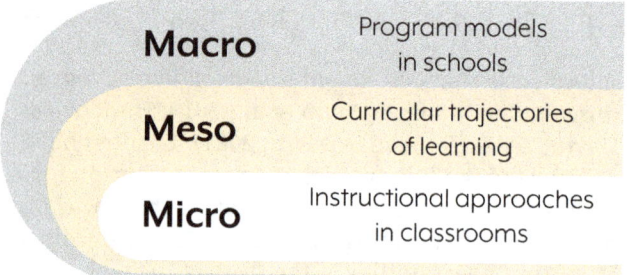

Macro	Program models in schools
Meso	Curricular trajectories of learning
Micro	Instructional approaches in classrooms

Considering Your Current Language Programs

Whether just getting started or fully engaged in SoBL implementation, you can find common ground with this chapter's focus on programming. You no doubt already have language programs in your school or district, including world language programs that facilitate learning languages like Spanish, French, and Mandarin Chinese and programs that facilitate learning English, potentially alongside home languages, for students labeled as ELs. So start there: In your setting, what programs support world, heritage, and English language development? Now return to the definition of the purpose of SoBL implementation that you developed in Chapter 2. How do your programs align with your goals? Which programs yield biliteracy? How might programs, curriculum, and instruction be enhanced to bolster biliteracy? For those in initial implementation, you might focus on refining current programs while getting assessment logistics off the ground. For those refining SoBL efforts, perhaps you explore the potential for new programs, such as heritage language offerings for languages commonly used by students but not currently offered in schools.

This chapter allows for ample flexibility, from adding new strategies to your teaching repertoire, to integrating existing tools such as Can-do descriptors, to designing programs that increase access to biliteracy development in schools. Reflect upon your locus of control and embrace your agency to enact change—whether that be in your classroom, your school, your district, or your community. Teachers might focus on classroom instruction, noting ideas for collaborative applications with colleagues in professional learning communities. Department chairs and school leaders might consider tools and approaches to support longitudinal curricular design for language development. District administrators might tackle ways to refine programs and curricula across the K-12 trajectory. Find your entry point, recognizing that many actions widen students' access to high-quality language programming in support of biliteracy. In the next section, we start with steps for refining instruction in classroom practice.

Providing High-Leverage Language Instruction

The 2020 Georgia Foreign Language Teacher of the Year, Meredith White, is a high-school Spanish teacher recognized for her creative instructional practices that motivate students and promote communicative proficiency. After attending a professional development workshop, she adopted Norah Jones' philosophy that "Every day is an IPA" (Integrated Performance Assessment; Adair-Hauck et al., 2013). This means that Ms. White uses backward design to ensure that her daily instruction aligns with her assessment practices and desired proficiency results.

On a typical day in Ms. White's classroom, students read or listen to an authentic written or aural text that relates to the unit theme and meaningful cultural context of the lesson. In choosing the text, she subscribes to the aphorism, Lead with culture, and language will follow. Next, students discuss the text in pairs using an oral interpersonal communication task. They then prepare a written or oral text, such as a social media post, to tell others about what they learned in the interpretive and interpersonal tasks.

Throughout these activities, Ms. White speaks in the target language and requires students to use the target language. Rather than complete textbook grammar drills, she focuses students' attention on form in context; that is, providing grammar instruction when required by students to understand how a form in the text is used to make meaning or to use a form themselves to make meaning.

Language and biliteracy development, and hence the number of students earning the SoBL, depends on practices that take place in classrooms—that is, how teachers engage students in learning. In classrooms like Ms. White's, teachers use language in meaningful ways, both as the vehicle for and the content of instruction. In world language, bilingual, and EL classrooms (i.e., any classroom with ELs), students learn *about* and *through* language, requir-

ing a unique set of pedagogical skills from general education or other content-area teachers. In this section, we draw from experts in the fields of world language, bilingual, and EL education to describe a set of core practices, also referred to as **high-leverage teaching practices**, that characterize strong language instruction (Ball & Forzani, 2009; Howard et al., 2018; Glisan & Donato, 2017, 2021). These practices, which are a selection of those proposed by Glisan and Donato (2017, 2021), are displayed in Figure 4.2. They are research-based, span program models, target languages and proficiency levels, and are characteristic of classrooms where students attain high levels of proficiency in support of biliteracy development (Vyn et al., 2019; Zhai, 2019). As you read this section, reflect on which of these practices are prevalent in your world language, bilingual, and EL programming and which might potentially require development.

Figure 4.2. High-Leverage Language Teaching Practices

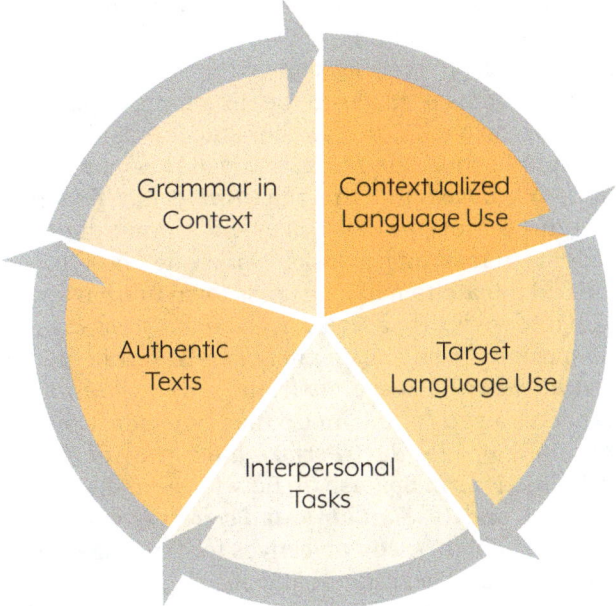

Establishing Meaningful and Purposeful Contexts for Language Learning High-quality language instruction centers on establishing meaningful and purposeful contexts for learning like the ones that students encounter on assessments of language proficiency. **Context** refers to "the interrelated conditions within which a communication takes place that renders the communicative event comprehensible, meaningful, appropriate, and memorable" (Glisan & Donato, 2021, p. 17). Scholars initially designed language immersion programs on the premise that students learn through meaningful interaction and academic learning, with recent research confirming the need for students to engage with authentic language with purposeful scaffolds and strategies supporting language development (Ballinger, 2013; Swain & Lapkin, 2013). Across settings, meaningful contexts for language learning ask students to use language for authentic purposes, see connections with background knowledge and experiences, and receive appropriate scaffolds based on language proficiency level (Herrera, 2016; Moll et al., 1992). In this approach, teachers design learning experiences that establish context for instructional activities, building students' understanding of why they are learning the language and how that learning extends beyond the classroom.

Take for example a world language lesson where teachers design a meaningful and purposeful context for students to engage in authentic language use. Ms. White might prompt students to use a map of Madrid's mass transit system to explain to a friend how to get from one place to another in time for a job interview. She watches as students excitedly get into pairs and use the map along with sentence frames to engage in this real-world simulation of language use. In contrast to a textbook exercise in which students write down the directions to places shown on a map, she and her students find this lesson to be more engaging, motivating, and interesting. We have found that the **GRASPS task format** (Wiggins & McTighe, 2005) is useful for engaging students in meaningful tasks. Ms. White's task defines (a) a **Goal** (to make it across town in time for a job interview), (b) a **Role** for students (your Spanish-speaking friend desperately needs your help), (c) an **Audience** (the desperate friend), (d) a **Situation** (you have a copy of the metro map but your friend does not), (e) a **Product/Performance** (providing oral directions in Spanish on how to get to the location), and (f) **Standards and criteria for success** (alignment with lesson objectives for language use). Through these meaningful, purposeful, and interesting tasks, students engage and learn at higher levels.

 All students bring background knowledge to classrooms, though classroom curriculum may reflect only that of White, English-dominant, middle-class students (Anya, 2020). By discerning and tapping into all students' rich sources of background knowledge in classroom instruction, teachers can better engage students, build their confidence and self-efficacy, encourage active participation and language use, and springboard equitable access to learning.

Prioritizing Target Language Use Students are expected to use and understand the target language to earn the SoBL; thus, it is no surprise that classroom instruction must support these skills. When the goal for language classrooms is to develop proficiency in another language in service of biliteracy, then the target language must be prioritized among both teachers and learners to encourage language development. Specific to world language classrooms, ACTFL recommends "that language educators and their students use the target language as exclusively as possible (90% plus) at all levels of instruction during instructional time and, when feasible, beyond the classroom" (ACTFL, 2010, n.p.). Whereas some teachers believe that 90% target language use in novice-level courses is too difficult (McMillan & Rivers, 2011), research has found that higher percentages of teachers' target-language use correspond to higher proficiency outcomes, especially for learners in early levels of language study (Vyn et al., 2019).

In bilingual education, program models vary by language allocation, and classroom language use corresponds with the percentage designated by the school's program (e.g., 80% Urdu, 20% English). But it is important to note the growing pushback against rigid separation of languages in bilingual settings, which has implications for instruction in bilingual classrooms (García, 2012). As teachers seek to maintain the overall language allocations, prioritizing target language use in line with the research-based program model, they should also remember the complexity and dynamism of the bilingual brain. Scholars have been saying for decades that the bilingual individual is not the sum of two monolinguals, but rather a holistic being who taps into multiple languages simultaneously when thinking, learning, and engaging with others (Grosjean, 1989). In bilingual and EL classrooms, this means allowing space for multilingual students to **translanguage**; that is, to use all of their cognitive, cultural, and linguistic resources to access academic content, tapping into their multilingual repertoires as resources for learning (García, 2012; García & Wei, 2014).

High-leverage practices in world language, bilingual, and EL classrooms converge around the need for comprehensibility. In the fields of world language (e.g., Glisan & Donato, 2017) and bilingual education (e.g., Larsen-Freeman & Tedick, 2016), scholars draw from Krashen's (1981, 1982) input hypothesis and research on the importance of interaction (Long, 1983; Swain, 1985, 1993; Vygotsky, 1978) to articulate ways that teachers engage learners in interaction that is comprehensible. Glisan and Donato (2017) describe three practices for supporting comprehensibility. First, teachers create comprehensible language, using vocabulary and structures familiar to students, slowing down the rate of speech when necessary, and repeating new words and expressions frequently. Second, teachers create contexts for comprehension by designing lessons relevant to students' lives, using gestures and visuals to support comprehension, and making sure students understand lesson objectives. Third, going beyond comprehensible input to focus also on interaction (Vygotsky, 1978), teachers foster comprehensible interactions among students by engaging them through strategic lesson and task design, as well as through questioning strategies that prompt language use.

Engaging Learners in Oral Interpersonal Communication Beyond the teacher's use of comprehensible language, students require opportunities to engage in oral interpersonal communication where they must speak spontaneously and negotiate meaning (Long, 1983; Swain, 1985; Vygotsky, 1978), similar to those found on many proficiency assessments. Nonetheless, interpersonal communication does not often receive sufficient attention in language classroom instruction or assessment (Kissau & Adams, 2016; Lyster, 2007). Research has found that interpersonal communication might be confused with presentational communication, where students speak to each other in pairs but read scripts or prefabricated texts rather than speaking spontaneously (Adair-Hauck et al., 2006). We have also found that teachers might avoid interpersonal communication tasks due to difficulties in monitoring large classrooms of students conversing simultaneously. But interpersonal communication is integral to language development and use in homes, schools, and communities, requiring explicit attention in classroom practice to eventually allow conversations with new people in new contexts.

Interpersonal communication tasks provide learners with the opportunity to engage in spontaneous (i.e., not scripted or memorized) conversation in which each participant must listen to the other, interpret meaning, and respond accordingly. Ms. White frequently uses information gap tasks, in which she pairs students and gives each a particular set of information, to promote oral interpersonal communication. Because each learner is missing important information to solve the problem or tackle the situation, partners must ask questions and respond to one another to collaboratively obtain the missing information. In one lesson targeting her customized Novice Mid Can-Do statement *I can tell the location of a place relative to another on a map*, Ms. White uses a **picture-difference task** where each partner has the same picture but with different items missing. One student has a map of a town with a grocery store and library, whereas another has the same map but with the post office and park. To construct a complete map, students must ask and answer each other's questions to describe where places are located. Through this strategically designed task, students engage in meaningful interpersonal oral communication to push forward language development.

Using Authentic Texts in Language Learning
High-quality instruction for language learners uses authentic texts to promote interpretive communication, including listening and reading comprehension. **Texts** include any object that can be interpreted—including videos, audio recordings, or written artifacts such as blogs, street signs, novels, or text messages. Texts serve as both mirrors and windows for students (Sims Bishop, 1990). In bilingual education, teachers often use texts as **mirrors** to tap into students' background knowledge and experiences in support of reading engagement and comprehension (Rodríguez, 2019). In language-focused classes like world language and ESL, teachers often use texts as **windows** to show learners how members of the target culture use language for authentic purposes (Glisan & Donato, 2017). Regardless of setting (e.g., world language, bilingual, ESL) and text use with students (e.g., window, mirror), this high-leverage practice involves strategic selection of texts with explicit lenses on authentic language and culture.

In world language, consideration of **text authenticity** centers on language. With this lens, authentic texts are written or signed by members of a language group for members of the same language group, such as emails written between friends, billboards advertising products, or commercials on television. Inauthentic texts are those contrived for use in language classrooms, such as an email written by an author in a textbook for students to interpret, a billboard made by a German teacher for class, or a commercial in Russian created by American students. Authentic texts should appear in their original form, rather than being edited for the purposes of instruction, so that learners examine language as it is used to make meaning in the target culture and thus become able to use language in similar ways themselves (Glisan & Donato, 2017, 2021). Further, by interpreting authentic texts potentially above their proficiency level, students learn that they do not have to know every word to understand the meaning, which is important for proficiency assessments and using language in a real situation such as in a local community, for a project, or traveling abroad. While authenticity requires maintaining the text in its original form, teachers differentiate text-related tasks based on learners' proficiency level (Shrum & Glisan, 2016).

In bilingual and EL education, educators center text selection on *cultural authenticity*, seeking to provide learners with texts that accurately reflect their and others' experiences in homes, communities, and schools (Rodríguez, 2019). Within this lens, authentic texts are typically written by members of the target culture, yielding authentic nuances that stem from their experiences and sentiments (Cai, 2003). Texts with cultural authenticity include accurate and purposeful details to capture the lived realities of individuals, families, and communities. In contrast, inauthentic texts might include inaccurate or surface-level details, as well as perpetuate stereotypes about the target culture. Culturally authentic texts have been shown to support bilingual students' language and literacy development (Martínez-Álvarez & Ghiso, 2017; Medina & Martínez-Roldán, 2011). Students tap into their rich sets of cultural and linguistic background knowledge to engage deeply with and make meaning of these texts, as well as to connect with the nuanced characters, settings, and storylines to engage in interactive literature discussions and bilingual writing. Students see themselves in texts, which reinforces cultural and linguistic identities and promotes deeper engagement with reading and subsequent biliteracy development (Al-Hazza & Bucher, 2008; López-Robertson, 2012).

Teaching Grammar in Context As students develop proficiency in pursuit of the SoBL, they require greater knowledge and skills with grammar. Any discussion of language education, whether world language, bilingual, ESL, or ELA, yields consideration of how to approach teaching grammar. A focus on form is pertinent to second language learning for individuals to develop linguistic understandings and support pathways to language proficiency (Lyster, 2004). Whereas individuals acquire their first language naturally through everyday experiences, differences emerge when learning an additional language in school contexts with limited instructional time (Vygotsky, 1986). Across settings, the research is clear: grammar must be taught in context (Glisan & Donato, 2017; Fortune et al., 2008; Lyster, 2007). This high-leverage practice lies in stark contrast

to the traditional, decontextualized approaches still used in some classrooms. Think of the world language classroom where students create verb conjugation charts or study a grammar point of the day, or the ESL classroom where students complete daily drills on discrete grammatical skills with the insistence on using only English without connections to home languages (Auerbach, 2016; Gebhard et al., 2019). Instead, students need the opportunity to analyze how language forms or concepts are used in aural, visual, and written texts to fulfill various language functions.

In world language classrooms, teachers guide learners in manipulating grammatical forms or concepts across various contexts to make meaning. For example, in one approach called *PACE* (Adair-Hauck & Donato, 2016), the teacher first *Presents* an authentic text in which a particular form is used frequently. The teacher next guides learners' *Attention* to the use of the form throughout the text. The teacher and learners examine how the form is manipulated to make meaning and *Co-construct* an explanation or rules for the form. Once an accurate explanation has been developed, the teacher provides learners with *Extension* activities in which they must use the new form to make meaning. For example, Ms. White might first present students with a recipe for arepas, a Colombian staple. She would guide learners through interpreting the recipe before drawing their attention to the commands in each step of the recipe. Next, she would engage learners in an instructional conversation through which she would ask questions and encourage students to hypothesize how the verb endings are manipulated to form commands. Finally, once Ms. White and her students had co-constructed a grammatically accurate explanation, students would compose their own recipes using commands.

In bilingual and EL classrooms, teaching grammar in context involves connecting students' languages to develop *metalinguistic awareness* regarding how language works (Bialystok, 1986). Whereas a lesson may be facilitated in one language depending on the program model and language allocation, *bridging* is the instructional moment when the teacher brings languages together to compare linguistic nuances and encourage transfer of content learning between languages (Beeman & Urow, 2012). For example, in a second grade Spanish-English dual language classroom, the teacher closes each lesson with a bridge to support students in developing biliteracy. In one lesson, she uses the bilingual picture book *Liliana's Grandmothers* (Torres, 2005) to begin a writing mini-lesson. She reads the text and facilitates the lesson in English, but before sending children to work independently on their writing in both languages, she writes the text's title in both languages on the whiteboard: "Liliana's Grandmothers" and "Las abuelas de Liliana." She prompts students to explore and discuss the differences between languages, specifically that English uses possessive nouns whereas Spanish does not. By teaching grammar in context, including the guided exploration of both languages, children develop metalinguistic awareness in support of biliteracy.

Designing Longitudinal Curricular Trajectories

Glastonbury Public Schools in Connecticut has a nationally recognized world language program that graduates one of the highest numbers of SoBL recipients in its state. All students begin studying Spanish in first grade with options to study Spanish, French, Chinese, or Russian in middle school. In sixth grade, students new to the district who have not previously studied Spanish are placed in an Introductory Spanish course, rather than in the same course as students who have studied the language for five years. At the high-school level, students can continue studying these four languages or begin the study of Latin or Ancient Greek. As with middle school, course offerings are differentiated so that students are learning alongside others with similar language exposure. Additionally, students studying Chinese, French, or Spanish can elect to take the Level 6: Advanced Placement/UConn Early College Experience language course. These courses are taught at the high school campus by teachers who are certified as adjunct faculty members by the University of Connecticut.

Students also have the option of enrolling in world language camps in the summer. Glastonbury offers STARTALK programs (a U.S. Department of Defense grant-funded program) for students and teachers of Chinese and Russian as well as summer camps in Spanish and French.

Glastonbury Public Schools' world language department sets a proficiency level outcome goal for each course. The department has created units of study for all languages and grade levels along with essential questions for each language. For example, in fifth grade, the proficiency target is Novice. The essential questions that guide the fifth-grade Spanish curriculum are: "Who am I? Who are the people of the Americas?" Students engage in six units of study on topics related to Central and South America with a focus on Peru. Because educators use the curriculum across the district, students can change schools and continue language instruction where they left off. Additionally, teachers share resources and collaborate rather than creating units independently (Glastonbury Public Schools, 2021).

Language programs play an integral role in developing biliteracy by targeting world, heritage, and English language development. Whereas teachers use approaches and strategies in individual classrooms, as described in the last section, curriculum ties together instruction across programs to nurture students' progress toward long-term goals for learning. Glastonbury Public Schools provides an example of extended sequences of world language study spanning K-12 that prioritize key features of high-quality language curricula, including (a) using standards to tailor curriculum, (b) articulating goals for language proficiency, and (c) crafting learning trajectories with backward design (McTighe & Willis, 2019; Menken et al., 2014).

Various tools guide curricular design, including standards and language proficiency level descriptors. A common feature in 21st century education across disciplines and programs, standards provide practitioners with roadmaps for designing curriculum. Drafted by experts in their respective fields, standards break down larger bodies of knowledge and skills into categories that spiral across years and developmental levels. When programs target language development, proficiency levels also factor into curricular design. As described in previous chapters, students pass through stages of language proficiency, which provide valuable information for teachers to use when scaffolding and crafting curriculum. In world language, bilingual, and EL education, *proficiency level descriptors* accompany standards, providing valuable tools to craft curriculum that promotes language development and ultimately biliteracy. Remember that these proficiency levels align with the assessments described in the previous chapter, providing an integral connection between the targeted supports provided in classroom curriculum and SoBL implementation.

Backward design is an approach to planning curriculum which emphasizes the need to start with the end in mind. Understanding by Design is one widely used iteration of backward design that breaks down planning into three stages (Wiggins & McTighe, 2005). In Stage 1, practitioners flesh out goals for learning, including how students transfer and use language outside of the classroom, pertinent understandings about language and its related cultural components, and specific linguistic knowledge and skills. Stage 2 prompts design of assessments that capture data on students' progress toward learning goals, centering on authentic performance tasks with meaningful language use (Heineke & McTighe, 2018). Finally, Stage 3 entails designing trajectories of instruction to support students in attaining the defined goals. When used in conjunction with standards and proficiency levels, backward design guides lesson and unit design, as well as longitudinal curricular design across a given language program, such as the K-12 trajectory in the Glastonbury Public Schools. We explore the use of standards, proficiency levels, and backward design in world language education next.

Curricular Design in World Language World language curricula stem from the World-Readiness Standards for Learning Languages, the national content standards for world language education (National Standards Collaborative Board, 2015). These standards offer "a roadmap to guide learners to develop competence to communicate effectively and interact with cultural understanding" (National Standards Collaborative Board, 2015, p. 11). First developed in 1996, the standards outline five goal areas of world language instruction: ***Communications, Cultures, Connections, Comparisons,*** and ***Communities*** (see Table 4.1). Within the five Cs, 11 standards guide curricular design for pre-kindergarten through post-secondary world language programs, spanning languages and applying to coursework for world and heritage language learners.

Many world language teachers write their own curriculum. The 11 standards guide this process, informing the planning and delivery of curriculum, instruction, and assessment. At the unit level, teachers should work to address all 11 standards. At the lesson level, teachers should endeavor to address all three standards in the *Communication* goal area to nurture proficiency and prepare students for SoBL assessments. The remaining goal areas, while not directly assessed for the SoBL, make instruction relevant and engaging. As teacher educators, we encourage candidates to address at least one of the four other goal areas in every lesson. Unlike the Common Core or Next Generation Science Standards, the ACTFL World-Readiness Standards are not grade-level, proficiency-level, or language specific but provide a powerful framework for curricular design and delivery.

Proficiency-based curricula prompt learners to communicate in meaningful and real-life contexts, just as they are asked to do on the SoBL assessments. Rather than creating a conjugation chart of the verb *to go* or translating a list of vocabulary words related to places around town, proficiency-based programs might require students to direct a classmate on how to get to a location on a map or to create an audio guide for a city tour. As illustrated by Anna in the opening vignette, the use of language for real-world communication engages 21st century learners. ***Proficiency-based programs*** recognize that knowledge of grammatical rules or structures does not equate to using language for meaningful communication. While such metalinguistic knowledge contributes to one's ability to use the language (Negueruela-Azarola, 2013; Vygotsky, 1986), learners require iterative opportunities to practice communicating across the three modes of communication (see Table 4.2). For example, teachers might involve students in tasks that prompt (a) spontaneous conversation in the target language (interpersonal communication), (b) reading, listening to, or viewing authentic texts such as movies, literature, or podcasts (interpretive communication), and (c) composing oral, written, or signed texts such as speeches, essays, or articles (presentational communication).

In addition to teachers' curricular design, district and school leaders use backward design at the macro level to design curriculum spanning extended sequences of language study. Like Glastonbury Public Schools in the vignette above, programs can attach proficiency goals to backward design curricula across grade levels and programs (refer to Chapter 1 and Figure 1.1 for a description of the proficiency levels). This allows students to follow the same curriculum as they move across schools in the district, purposefully promoting proficiency in the target language each year. For example, Table 4.3 illustrates the minimum exit proficiency levels

Table 4.1. World-Readiness Standards for Learning Languages

GOAL AREA	STANDARD	DESCRIPTION
Communication: Communicate effectively in more than one language in order to function in a variety of situations and for multiple purposes	1.1 Interpersonal Communication	Learners interact and negotiate meaning in spoken, signed, or written conversations to share information, reactions, feelings, and opinions.
	1.2 Interpretive Communication	Learners understand, interpret, and analyze what is heard, read, signed, or viewed on a variety of topics.
	1.3 Presentational Communication	Learners present information, concepts, and ideas to inform, explain, persuade, and narrate on a variety of topics using appropriate media and adapting to various audiences of listeners, readers, or viewers.
Cultures: Interact with cultural competence and understanding	2.1 Relating Cultural Practices to Perspectives	Learners use the language to investigate, explain, and reflect on the relationship between the practices and perspectives of the cultures studied.
	2.2 Relating Cultural Products to Perspectives	Learners use the language to investigate, explain, and reflect on the relationship between the products and perspectives of the cultures studied.
Connections: Connect with other disciplines and acquire information and diverse perspectives in order to use the language to function in academic and career-related situations	3.1 Making Connections	Learners build, reinforce, and expand their knowledge of other disciplines while using the language to develop critical thinking and to solve problems creatively.
	3.2 Acquiring Information and Diverse Perspectives	Learners access and evaluate information and diverse perspectives that are available through the language and its cultures.
Comparisons: Develop insight into the nature of language and culture in order to interact with cultural competence	4.1 Language Comparisons	Learners use the language to investigate, explain, and reflect on the nature of language through comparisons of the language studied and their own.
	4.2 Cultural Comparisons	Learners use the language to investigate, explain, and reflect on the concept of culture through comparisons of the cultures studied and their own.
Communities: Communicate and interact with cultural competence in order to participate in multilingual communities at home and around the world	5.1 School and Global Communities	Learners use the language both within and beyond the classroom to interact and collaborate in their community and the globalized world.
	5.2 Lifelong Learning	Learners set goals and reflect on their progress in using languages for enjoyment, enrichment, and advancement.

Source: National Standards Collaborative Board, 2015

Table 4.2. Three Modes of Communication

MODE OF COMMUNICATION	DOMAIN	CHARACTERISTICS	EXAMPLE
Interpersonal Communication	Listening & Speaking; Reading & Writing Viewing & Signing	Two-way spontaneous exchange of information; Allows for clarification requests, negotiation of meaning, and adjustments for understanding	Unrehearsed conversation with a partner about plans for the weekend
Interpretive Communication	Reading Listening Viewing	One-way reading, listening, or viewing a text; No allowance for negotiation of meaning or requests for clarification	Completing a graphic organizer to show the relation of the key information and ideas in a video or text in the world language
Presentational Communication	Speaking Signing Writing	One-way creation of a spoken, written, or signed text; No allowance for negotiation of meaning	Writing a story or delivering a speech

Source: World-Readiness Standards and NCSSFL-ACTFL Can-Do Statements

Table 4.3. Minimum and Target Proficiency Levels for Category I Languages in Charlotte Mecklenburg Schools

COURSE LEVEL	MINIMUM EXIT PROFICIENCY LEVEL	TARGET PROFICIENCY LEVEL
Level I	Novice Mid	Novice High
Level II	Novice High	Intermediate Low
Honors Level III	Intermediate Low	Intermediate Mid
Honors Level IV	Intermediate Mid	Intermediate High
Honors Level V or AP Level V	Intermediate High	Advanced Low
Honors Level VI or AP Spanish Literature VI	Advanced Low	Advanced Mid

Source: Mara Cobe, CMS World Language Coordinator, personal communication, August 2020

Table 4.4. Novice Low, Interpersonal Communication, Exchanging Information and Ideas

Proficiency Benchmark	I can communicate in spontaneous spoken, written, or signed conversations on both very familiar and everyday topics, using a variety of practiced or memorized words, phrases, simple sentences, and questions.
Performance Indicator for Exchange Information & Ideas	I can provide information by answering a few simple questions on very familiar topics, using practiced or memorized words and phrases, with the help of gestures or visuals.
Examples	I can... (customize with specific content). I can introduce myself when I meet people. I can answer questions about who is in my family. I can answer questions about my favorite weekend activities.

Source: NCSSFL & ACTFL, 2017a, p. 9

and the target proficiency levels for students studying Western European languages such as French and Spanish in Charlotte Mecklenburg Schools in North Carolina. For languages more difficult for English speakers to learn, such as Chinese and Japanese, the target proficiency level is typically set at one sublevel lower for reading and writing only. For heritage language courses, the department sets the expectation at one sub-level higher than world language courses. In addition to high school courses, **feeder-school analyses** examine patterns from elementary to middle to high school to ensure that students at one level of schooling have access to the same world language at the next level.

Once proficiency targets are set for each level or course, practitioners use the detailed *NCSSFL-ACTFL Can-Do Statements* (2017a) to backward design the curriculum. Can-Do statements inform the desired outcomes (Stage 1), assessments (Stage 2), and learning experiences (Stage 3; Wiggins & McTighe, 2005). They also identify and set learning goals for teachers to plan communication learning targets and for students to chart their progress (NCSSFL & ACTFL, 2017a). Organized according to the three modes of communication, the statements align with the ACTFL Proficiency Guidelines (ACTFL, 2012b) and Performance Descriptors (ACTFL, 2012a). For each proficiency benchmark, statements include performance indicators that deconstruct the benchmark with examples that illustrate language performance in various contexts. Table 4.4 shows an example from the Novice level for Interpersonal communication. Once students consistently perform Novice Low Can-Do statements, for example, they begin working toward Novice Mid statements. The Novice Mid performance indicator for the same language function as the one in Table 4.4 states that students request information by "*asking and* answering a few simple questions on very familiar *and everyday* topics" (NCSSFL & ACTFL, 2017a, p. 3).

An additional tool for designing meaningful and engaging curricula is the *Can-Do Statements for Intercultural Communication* (NCSSFL & ACTFL, 2017a). **Intercultural competence** is the "ability to interact effectively and appropriately with people from other language and cultural backgrounds" (ACTFL, 2020). These Can-Do statements, along with the accompanying reflection tool (NCSSFL & ACTFL, 2017b), clarify and support the *Cultures* goal area and guide students' development of intercultural competence. They consist of two **Global Proficiency Benchmarks**: *Investigation* of products and practices to understand perspectives, and *Interaction* with others in and from another culture. The Global Proficiency Benchmarks are broken down into performance indicators at each level of proficiency that have corresponding examples. For example, a Novice-level example for *Investigate* is: "In my own and other cultures I can identify locations to buy something and how culture affects where people shop." The corresponding example for *Interact* is: "I can use rehearsed behaviors when shopping in a familiar type of store" (NCSSFL & ACTFL, 2017a, p. 5). Regardless of language proficiency level, every curriculum should promote students' intercultural competence, raising the cognitive demand of instruction and dispelling stereotypes or misconceptions about other cultures.

Curricular Design in Bilingual and EL Programs
Whereas world language education teaches the target language, bilingual and EL programs center on academic learning through language. In other words, the language is not the primary focus but the medium of instruction, with academic content areas serving as the vehicle to develop language (Escamilla, 2010). While language and content should intersect in all bilingual and EL programming, this balance manifests differently by program. In self-contained bilingual and general education classrooms, as well as **sheltered instruction** and **Integrated English Language Development** (ELD) where ELs learn content in English, curriculum emerges from grade-level content standards, with teachers using language standards and proficiency levels to scaffold disciplinary learning. In contexts that use pull-out or self-contained ESL, also referred to in some contexts as **English as a New Language** (ENL) or **Designated ELD**, curriculum aligns with content standards but focuses explicitly on language development, using language standards targeting focal proficiency levels. Regardless of context, standards and proficiency levels help educators design curriculum that supports language development and scaffolds content learning, whether that be in English or another language.

In the context of EL education in the United States, language standards typically imply English Language Development standards. With the reauthorization of the Elementary and Secondary Education Act in 2001, states had to adopt ELD standards, resulting in two consortiums banding together to create these tools. WIDA provides standards and tools to two-thirds of the nation, including 35 states, the District of Columbia, and various territories. ELPA21 has 11 member states, whereas Arizona, California, New York, and Texas use their own standards. Despite variances in organization, these six sets of standards

Table 4.5. Sample Proficiency Descriptors from California ELD Standards

LEVEL	EMERGING	EXPANDING	BRIDGING
Grade 5, Offering Opinions (G5.1A3)	Negotiate with or persuade others in conversations using basic learned phrases (e.g., I think...), as well as open responses, to gain and/or hold the floor.	Negotiate with or persuade others in conversations using an expanded set of learned phrases (e.g., I agree with X, but...), as well as open responses, to gain and/or hold the floor, provide counterarguments, and so on.	Negotiate with or persuade others in conversations using a variety of learned phrases (e.g., That's an interesting idea. However,...), as well as open responses, to gain and/or hold the floor, provide counterarguments, elaborate on an idea, and so on.

Source: California State Board of Education, 2014, p. 78

share a focus on developing language while learning academic content. For example, WIDA (2020) uses five standards: (a) social and instructional language, (b) the language of language arts, (c) the language of mathematics, (d) the language of science, and (e) the language of social studies. ELPA21 (2013) has 10 standards centered on language functions that span content areas, such as constructing meaning from oral presentations and analyzing and critiquing others' arguments. Some contexts offer standards in other languages, such as WIDA's Spanish Language Development Standards or New York's Native Language Arts Standards, which serve as excellent tools to bolster biliteracy as connected to SoBL efforts.

In addition to their common focus on language development during academic instruction, ELD standards share in their organization by proficiency level. Within each standard strand (e.g., the language of math, connecting and condensing ideas), *proficiency level descriptors* provide detailed expectations on what a student at each proficiency level can do with language. Table 4.5 shows a sub-strand from California's ELD Standards (California State Board of Education, 2014), providing an example of how expectations expand with each level. While proficiency levels vary in name and number, such as WIDA's six levels (Entering, Beginning, Developing, Expanding, Bridging, Reaching) and New York's five levels (Entering, Emerging, Transitioning, Expanding, Commanding), they share grounding in second language acquisition theory and expanding expectations for language use. In each state, ELD standards (e.g., WIDA) and related assessments (e.g., ACCESS) align with the same proficiency levels, meaning assessments yield data to inform curriculum and instruction.

Language standards and proficiency level descriptors serve as tools to facilitate backward design that attends to language development simultaneously with disciplinary learning (Heineke & McTighe, 2018). Stage 1 involves defining goals for learning, using content standards to inform content-specific goals and language standards to pinpoint the language functions and features needed to engage with the content. ELD standards support curriculum designers in recognizing the language demands in a given discipline and prioritizing the development of that language in instruction. Stage 2 prompts the design of authentic and culturally relevant classroom assessments that glean data on students' language development, giving teachers snapshots of students' language proficiency across units of study. Stage 3 yields language-rich learning trajectories where students listen, speak, read, and write to engage with disciplinary topics, tasks, and texts. Since teachers typically have ELs of varying proficiency levels, proficiency level descriptors provide actionable ways to scaffold language, provide access to grade-level content, and support ongoing language development.

In addition to bilingual and EL teachers, content area and general education teachers can approach curricular design with dual lenses on disciplinary learning and language development. In this way, students' language development receives attention and support across the school day, rather than just in periods or blocks designated as bilingual, ESL, or ELD. In the earlier sub-section on world language curriculum, we explored how to define proficiency goals longitudinally across K-12 programming. But in curricular design for ELs, where multilingual students with varying levels of language proficiency learn language *and* grade-level content, it is not feasible to set grade-by-grade proficiency goals. Instead, the goal is for all teachers across grade levels and content areas to plan with a language lens to pinpoint language demands, engage students in meaningful and scaffolded experiences with language, and capture rich and nuanced data on students' language development. In this way, students develop and use language across the school day and year, subsequently bolstering language development in service of biliteracy. Schools can encourage this all-hands-on-deck approach with a common planning template that includes the language lens (e.g., Echevarria et al., 2013; Heineke & McTighe, 2018), as well as space to share language-rich instructional strategies, approaches, and materials.

Developing Programs That Foster Biliteracy

The St. Paul Public Schools (SPPS) in Minnesota offer dual-language immersion programs to support children in becoming bilingual, biliterate, and bicultural. They offer one-way immersion programs in Spanish, Mandarin, and French, which give English-dominant students the opportunity to become bilingual, and two-way immersion programs in Spanish and Hmong, where English- and Hmong-dominant speakers are placed in the same classroom to learn academic content and develop literacy in both languages (SPPS, 2021b).

The development of the Hmong dual-language program involved district leaders responding to the context of the community. With over 9,000 Hmong students, stakeholders recognized the need to offer bilingual instruction tailored to this student population. SPPS began dual-language programs at two elementary schools, with academic content taught in Hmong and literacy in English. Following completion of elementary school, students can attend one of two middle schools that offer Hmong heritage language classes. They continue these courses at two high schools in the district. While only two levels of Hmong for Hmong speakers are offered in high school, students can serve as teaching assistants in subsequent years.

These efforts to prioritize dual-language education for the Hmong population are not without challenges. Due to years of conflict and persecution, the Hmong people are spread across countries that include China, Vietnam, Laos, Thailand, and Myanmar. As a result of enduring conflict, many Hmong refugees arrive in the United

States without literacy instruction in Hmong, and print resources are almost impossible to find. SPPS pays community members to create dictionaries, alphabet strips, and books in Hmong, which they sell on their district website (SPPS, 2021a). They use proceeds from sales of these materials to develop and train scorers for the Hmong SoBL assessment, which allows more Hmong students to be recognized for developing biliteracy.

In addition to micro-level instruction within classrooms and meso-level curriculum across classrooms, stakeholders can consider refinements and additions to macro-level programming. This macro-level lens emerges as pertinent in expanding SoBL efforts, given that students first require access to language programs to subsequently benefit from the high-quality curriculum and instruction within them. In other words, even if your SoBL efforts involve clear purpose, wide access to proficiency assessments, and research-based classroom practice, you cannot promote biliteracy widely without strong programs of study. Individuals' opportunities to develop biliteracy in school rest upon larger programmatic decisions, such as which languages are taught, for how long, and who has access. In the example of the St. Paul Public Schools, district administrators' decision to prioritize and build Hmong language programming across K-12 settings continues to enhance their ability to support and recognize biliteracy.

Whether working to initiate or refine SoBL implementation, larger programmatic changes might be possible to facilitate students' long-term progress toward biliteracy. We recognize that programmatic decisions might fall outside of some readers' locus of control. Even if this is the case, your expertise and well-informed conversations with administrators and coordinators might be a catalyst for change. The idea is to consider all potential actions in line with your defined purpose, so allow yourself to think big during this section as we explore ideas for world language, bilingual, and EL programs. This macro-level lens seeks to nurture more students' biliteracy by (a) shifting the ideological orientation to language teaching, (b) increasing access among marginalized groups, and (c) extending the duration of language study.

World Language Programs Many of you reading this text may be the most familiar with world language programs. They are common in U.S. schools, particularly in contexts with English-dominant student populations or such linguistic diversity that no one language has enough users to sustain an immersion program. In this sub-section, we consider how world language educators can work to increase access, shift orientation, and extend duration of programs to nurture language development and subsequently recognize more students' resulting biliteracy. Tool 4.3 provides questions for reflection and discussion among colleagues.

Strong world language programming is inclusive, ensuring that students across races, socioeconomic strata, and linguistic backgrounds have opportunities to develop biliteracy. Research has shown that world language programs are more common in schools with predominantly White students, as well as students from higher socioeconomic backgrounds (Baggett, 2016; Finn, 1998; Pufahl & Rhodes, 2011). African American and Latinx students, students with *individualized education plans*, and ELs are often underrepresented in world language courses (Anya, 2020; Finn; 1998; Ritz & Sherf, 2021; Schoener & McKenzie, 2016). Use Tool 4.4 to analyze access in your programs, keeping in mind how historical inequities and institutional racism in U.S. schools might impact world language enrollment (Anya, 2020).

African American students are typically underrepresented in world language study (see Anya, 2020). Research attributes this underrepresentation to negative classroom experiences (Moore, 2005; Pratt, 2012) and the institutional practice of tracking that disproportionately impacts students of color (McCardle, 2020; Schoener & McKenzie, 2016). World language courses beyond Level Two are often considered honors or college-preparatory courses; however, many African American students have been tracked into programs where such courses are unavailable (Finn, 1998; Schoener & McKenzie, 2016). When analyzing your existing programs and efforts, be sure to examine the percentage of African American students earning the SoBL as well as the representation of African American students in your district or school's language programming.

In districts and schools with large populations of students who use heritage languages at home, heritage language programs are essential. U.S. schools most commonly offer Spanish (46 percent of programs), French (21 percent), German (8.7 percent), Latin (8.1 percent), and Chinese (6.4 percent; American Councils for International Education, 2017). In our work across the country, we have seen stakeholders make great strides with the SoBL when they add to existing world language offerings and subsequently provide opportunities for heritage language learners to develop biliteracy in schools. Consider the work in the St. Paul Public Schools with middle- and high-school courses for Hmong heritage learners, or the Paiute heritage language program developed with tribal leaders in the North School District. In reflecting on your own world language programming, consider how you might expand language offerings based on student backgrounds, interests, and potential benefits to the community (Lead with Languages, 2021). We explore potential collaborations with community organizations to offer these programs in the next chapter.

Development or revision of existing heritage language programs may require a shift in orientation. Heritage language learners have backgrounds that are distinct from those of world language learners, coming to school with previous competencies in literacy, speaking, and listening. They also have various experiences with heritage languages in homes, communities, and schools and are influenced by other sociocultural variables such as immigration and schooling history (Montrul, 2016; Zyzik, 2016). For this reason, it is not enough to allow heritage language learners access to world language coursework (see Burgo, 2017; Carreira & Kagan, 2018; Goulette, 2020; Randolph, 2017), instead the orientation to world language instruction needs to change to effectively facilitate language learning. For example, with a core mass of students who use Spanish in homes, you can offer heritage language programming rather than providing access to world language courses that target English-dominant students' Spanish proficiency. Schools with small populations of heritage learners might consider online virtual course options shared across schools or a multi-level differentiated class with students at different years of study grouped together. In St. Paul, students who use Hmong as a heritage language take two years of study and can subsequently serve as teaching assistants. If not already doing so, schools might weigh the potential of offering programs of study with coursework designed for heritage language learners.

 **LIke most facets of U.S. education, language programs were often designed to serve White, English-dominant students. When considering programming for heritage language learners and ELs, stakeholders should tap into the research on these specific populations to design curricula that embrace students' rich backgrounds and resources for learning.**

With equitable access to world language coursework that targets students' unique language backgrounds and competencies, stakeholders can tackle ways to extend the duration of language study for all students. Research consistently confirms the need for extended sequences of language study to develop proficiency in the target language (Collins & White, 2011; Donato & Tucker, 2010; Freed et al., 2004). In high school settings, this prompts consideration of world languages as either required or elective coursework. When world language coursework is framed as elective, students might opt out, not realizing that many colleges and universities prefer or even require two or more years of language study. Even if state policy does not require world language coursework, you might weigh the value of all students taking language coursework, both to promote biliteracy in line with goals for SoBL implementation and to ensure all students' eligibility for the postsecondary institution of their choosing.

However, research suggests that four years of high school study is often not sufficient for students to reach the proficiency required for the SoBL (Avant Assessment, 2017). This finding suggests that world language instruction should begin in elementary or middle school to tap into the longitudinal nature of language development. Nonetheless, according to the most recent data collected in 2007-2008, just 25 percent of public elementary schools and 58 percent of middle schools offered world language programming, in contrast to 91 percent of high schools (American Academy of Arts and Sciences, 2017). To achieve goals for biliteracy, consider how language study can be extended across elementary and secondary settings in your context.

Bilingual Programs Although SoBL efforts are often housed in world language departments, it is imperative to span out and consider bilingual programming. Research has shown that certain bilingual programs result in stronger proficiency outcomes than world language programs due to language use across the school day as a part of academic learning starting in kindergarten (Genesee, 1987; Lind-holm-Leary, 2001; Turnbull, Lapkin, & Hart, 2001). But no one approach to bilingual education is the silver bullet to promote biliteracy. In this subsection we explore additive orientations to language learning, longitudinal duration of programming, and equitable access to biliteracy in classrooms and schools. As you read, continue to use Tool 4.3 to reflect upon your context.

Bilingual programs fall into two categories. Those with additive orientation seek to add to students' existing language repertoires and develop biliteracy, whereas those with subtractive orientation result in subtracting home languages in service of English proficiency (Sugarman, 2018). Dual language program models typify the additive orientation, often heralded as the gold standard in bilingual education due to consistent outcomes in biliteracy, cognition, and academic achievement (e.g., Estrada et al., 2019; Thomas & Collier, 2002; Umansky & Reardon, 2014). *One-way* dual language programs involve one group of language speakers, such as the English-dominant students developing French in St. Paul. *Two-way* programs integrate two groups of language speakers, such as a classroom with half Spanish-dominant students and half English-dominant students (Escamilla, 2010). These additive models rely upon *language allocations* to guide language use in classrooms, such as the 50/50 model, which uses an equal balance between languages for all instruction starting in kindergarten, and the 90/10 model, which starts with focused language use in one language and then weaves in the other language over time.

With explicitly defined goals that children become biliterate, dual language programs typically yield the level of language proficiency required to earn the SoBL by the end of elementary school or beginning of middle school (Watzinger-Tharp et al., 2018). Nonetheless, students enrolled in dual language programs often see proficiency slow or decline following elementary school when less time is dedicated to the target language (Burkhauser et al., 2016; Fortune & Tedick, 2015). For this reason, language instruction should ideally continue into middle and high school, the latter of which is when most students demonstrate their biliteracy to earn the SoBL. One option is to extend dual language education into secondary settings, such as in Elmwood where teachers and students use Spanish as the medium of instruction in focal content areas. Another option is to shift from dual language education in the elementary setting to heritage language coursework in middle and high schools, such as the Hmong-language programming in the St. Paul Public Schools.

Table 4.6. Sample Language Allocations in Transitional and Maintenance Bilingual Programs

MODEL	KINDERGARTEN	GRADE 1	GRADE 2	GRADE 3	GRADES 4 & UP
Transitional (Early Exit)	80% Spanish 20% English	60% Spanish 40% English	40% Spanish 60% English	20% Spanish 80% English	0% Spanish 100% English
Maintenance (Late Exit)	80% Spanish 20% English	60% Spanish 40% English	40% Spanish 60% English	20% Spanish 80% English	20% Spanish 80% English

Both approaches extend biliteracy development across K-12 settings but necessitate different human and material resources. Stakeholders must weigh factors like the availability of bilingual teachers and resources, as well as the number of students, when determining which approach to take.

Dual language programs are not the only way to promote biliteracy, however, and other program models also maintain ELs' home languages and foster biliteracy over time. Many districts across the country use the subtractive approach of **transitional bilingual education**, also referred to as **early-exit bilingual programs**, which often correspond to the minimum threshold of bilingual programming required by state policy for ELs. Teachers use the home language in initial years to facilitate English development, quickly phasing out its use to prioritize English (Sugarman, 2018). These districts might instead offer **maintenance bilingual education**, also referred to as **developmental** or **late-exit bilingual** programs. This means changing the goals of the program from English proficiency to biliteracy, as well as extending the duration of home-language use in classrooms beyond early elementary school (see Table 4.6). Thus, students continue to use their home language in school to maintain and deepen their proficiency, rather than discontinuing its use once they achieve English proficiency. If dual language programming is not an option in your setting, consider shifting from transitional to maintenance bilingual programming so that ELs develop their home language over time to become biliterate.

Regardless of the orientation and duration of bilingual programs, stakeholders need to turn a critical eye toward access. Even if your district uses the gold standard of two-way immersion, it is imperative to consider who has the opportunity to enroll in the program and whose needs the program serves. In contexts across the United States, some two-way programs seek to attract White, English-privileged families to districts (Cervantes-Soon et al., 2017;

Flores et al., 2021; Valdés, 1997; Valdez et al., 2016). In this way, heritage language learners and ELs *might* receive access to dual language programming, but only to meet the 50/50 enrollment requirement of the program model that prioritizes the learning of White, elite-bilingual students. Research has shown the detriments of some two-way immersion programs for ELs, including the predominance of English across schools, teachers' lack of preparation to provide ELs access to curriculum, and frequent bullying and discrimination based on cultural and linguistic identities (Cervantes-Soon et al., 2017). We encourage critical analysis of bilingual education to enhance heritage language learners' and ELs' access to additive programming that embraces and sustains their cultural and linguistic identities and practices (Alim & Paris, 2018).

All language programs in U.S. schools operate within a society where monolingual ideologies are entrenched and schooling is typified by systemic racism. Regardless of the model or approach, any program can propagate monolingualism and assimilation if stakeholders do not take deliberate actions to elevate students' home languages and cultures.

English Programs Bilingual programming is not always viable, whether due to restrictive policies, lack of bilingual teachers, or highly diverse multilingual populations. ESL, ENL, and ELD programs emerge under these circumstances, where English serves as the common language mediating instruction (Sugarman, 2018). Despite being monolingual by name and design, English-medium programs can approach teaching and learning with an asset-based orientation that values cultural and linguistic practices as resources for learning (Alim & Paris, 2018; Moll et al., 1992). With a common philosophy across the EL program, faculty collectively enact instructional practices like those discussed in the first section of this chapter. Teachers nurture interconnections between languages by encouraging students to use their entire linguistic repertoires to communicate and make meaning, as well as make cross-linguistic connections between English and home languages (Beeman & Urow, 2012; García, 2012). Teachers integrate culturally relevant *topics* (e.g., history of focal countries of origin), *texts* (e.g., those written by and for individuals in the target culture), and *tasks* (e.g., oral storytelling aligned with cultural traditions). Asset-based orientations open the door for these pluralist practices in classrooms.

However, deficit-based orientations pervade the U.S. educational system, particularly in ESL and ELD programs predicated on deficit-based assumptions about students labeled as ELs (Callahan, 2005; Souto-Manning, 2009). If you recognize the existence of deficit-based presumptions about ELs in your school or district, we encourage deeper ideological reflections and discussions prior to exploring singular instructional strategies or approaches to curricular design. Even the high-leverage practices and language-focused curricular design described in previous sections can be implemented in deficit-based ways if educators unknowingly espouse deficit-based perspectives toward students. Book studies serve as valuable mediums to expose educators to asset-based theories and practices, allowing for in-depth exploration of topics such as *culturally responsive teaching* (Hammond, 2014), *culturally sustaining pedagogy* (Paris & Alim, 2018), *asset-based language teaching* (Calderón et al., 2019), and *translanguaging* (García et al., 2017). We discuss how to engage stakeholders across schools in professional learning opportunities to enhance SoBL implementation in the next chapter.

 **Students labeled as ELs are often framed with deficit-based perspectives. But children and adolescents ascribed this institutional label come to school with rich and varied cultural and linguistic practices that should be embraced and utilized as resources to develop biliteracy across school-based programming.**

Chapter Summary

In this chapter, we delved into the third facet of the framework by focusing on *Programs* that enhance biliteracy. Grounded in work in the fields of world language, bilingual, and EL education, we shared key features of instruction, curricula, and programs that influence biliteracy development. We delved into the features of high-leverage practices in language classrooms, as well as ways to promote data-driven instruction and programming aligned with SoBL efforts in schools. We discussed characteristics of curricula that promote language development, including the use of backward design, articulated sequences of study, and an emphasis on content standards and proficiency. We explored ways to design programs that immerse students in extended sequences of language study typified by meaningful and authentic communication. Central to the points discussed and explored throughout this chapter is that the SoBL is not a standalone initiative where students take tests and earn recognitions. The SoBL plays an integral role in enhancing language programming to prioritize students' developing biliteracy.

Questions for Discussion and Reflection

1. Use Tool 4.1 to reflect on each of the high-leverage teaching practices. Rate expertise on the topic and the frequency with which you use the high-leverage practice in classrooms.

2. In collaboration with members of your team, preferably with representation across language programs and grade levels, use Tool 4.2 to evaluate each language program offered in your school or district. Consider the overall program details, curricular alignment across the program, and instructional practices within the program. For each program, discuss: Do current practices align and support students' biliteracy development? Are teachers aligned in their expectations and philosophies regarding students' language development and use? What professional learning and collaboration might be needed?

3. Use Tool 4.3 to prompt critical discussions about your school's or district's language programming. Based on responses, what strengths emerge? What needs emerge? How might you work toward improving areas of need to enhance students' biliteracy development and progress toward your defined goals for SoBL implementation?

4. Access is integral when implementing the SoBL with an equity lens. Use Tool 4.4 to gather and analyze data related to program enrollment. What programs support students developing world, heritage, and English languages? Who has access to programming that promotes biliteracy? What actions can be taken to expand access to more students?

Further Reading

- Beeman, K., & Urow, C. (2012). *Teaching for biliteracy*. Caslon.

- Glisan, E., & Donato, R. (2017). *Enacting the work of language teaching: High leverage teaching practices*. ACTFL.

- Howard, E. R., Lindholm-Leary, K. J., Rogers, D., Olague, N., Medina, J., Kennedy, B., Sugarman, J., & Christian, D. (2018). *Guiding principles for dual language education* (3rd ed.). Center for Applied Linguistics.

- Shrum, J., & Glisan, E. (2015). *Teacher's handbook: Contextualized language instruction* (5th ed.). Cengage.

- Valdés, G. (2018). Analyzing the curricularization of language in two-way immersion education: Restating two cautionary notes. *Bilingual Research Journal, 41*(4), 388–412. https://doi.org/10.1080/15235882.2018.1539886

Tool 4.1. Self-Assess on High-Leverage Practices

Directions: The table below lists the five high-leverage teaching practices described in this chapter as well as two practices related to curriculum design. For each practice, reflect upon the prompt and rate your expertise on the topic, as well as the frequency with which you use the practice in your classroom.

HIGH-LEVERAGE PRACTICE Prompt for Reflection	RATE EXPERTISE ON TOPIC [5 = expert, 1 = novice]	RATE FREQUENCY OF USE [5 = consistently, 1 = never]
PLANNING WITH BACKWARD DESIGN Do you set goals for students' learning, determine appropriate evidence, and then plan instruction to reach goals?	5 4 3 2 1	5 4 3 2 1
ASSESSING LEARNERS' PERFORMANCE Do you design classroom assessments that engage students in authentic language use and performance? [Refer also to Chapter 3]	5 4 3 2 1	5 4 3 2 1
ESTABLISHING MEANINGFUL CONTEXT Do you engage students in using language in meaningful and purposeful ways in classroom practice?	5 4 3 2 1	5 4 3 2 1
ENCOURAGING TARGET LANGUAGE USE Do you and your students use the target language in line with programmatic expectations and allocations?	5 4 3 2 1	5 4 3 2 1
USING INTERPERSONAL ORAL TASKS Do you incorporate opportunities for students to engage in authentic interaction with one another?	5 4 3 2 1	5 4 3 2 1
INCORPORATING AUTHENTIC TEXTS Do you strategically select and use texts that are both culturally and linguistically authentic?	5 4 3 2 1	5 4 3 2 1
TEACHING GRAMMAR IN CONTEXT Do you teach students about language forms in meaningful context in ways that tap into students' background knowledge and assets?	5 4 3 2 1	5 4 3 2 1

Tool 4.2. Evaluate Language Programming

Directions: For each language program in your school or district, use the table below to consider current practices as a means to determine potential areas to build or refine. Reproduce this chart for use in all program types and languages spanning K-12 in your context, including world language, heritage language, bilingual, and EL programming.

	PROMPTS	NOTES
MACRO: PROGRAM DESIGN	Program type and language	
	Total program duration	
	Sequence/allocation of language	
	Longitudinal program trajectory	
	Student enrollment	
MESO: PROGRAM DETAILS	Framed by appropriate standards?	
	Aligned with proficiency levels?	
	Backward-designed curricula?	
	Data-driven instructional practice?	
	Highly-qualified teachers?	
MICRO: PROGRAM IN PRACTICE	Meaningful language use?	
	Target language use?	
	Oral language interpersonal tasks?	
	Use of authentic texts?	
	Grammar taught in context?	

Tool 4.3. Consider Macro-Level Programs

Directions: To consider how your language programs can nurture more students' biliteracy, reflect upon your existing programs with lenses on orientation, access, and duration. Think about your existing offerings in world language, bilingual, and EL education, using the provided questions to reflect and discuss your thoughts with colleagues. Use these discussions to springboard conversations of potential changes to existing programming.

PROGRAM TYPE	QUESTIONS FOR REFLECTION & DISCUSSION
World Language	How can you ensure access to world language education spanning race, class, and language background? How might you expand language offerings in response to language needs in the community and the world? Do you have significant numbers of heritage language learners that could warrant separate heritage language sections of existing languages (e.g., Spanish) or new programs (e.g., Somali)? Can world language coursework be required or reframed to emphasize its importance in postsecondary settings? How do you expose elementary and middle-school students to world languages to extend offerings across K-12?
Bilingual	What is the primary goal of your bilingual programming—biliteracy or English proficiency? After children develop bilingualism in early elementary school, how do they deepen and maintain biliteracy over time? Whose interests do your bilingual programs primarily serve (e.g., elite bilinguals, heritage language learners, ELs)? What are the experiences of heritage language learners and ELs in your bilingual programs? How do bilingual programs seek to sustain the cultural and linguistic identities and practices of heritage language learners and ELs?
English/ESL	Does your program's approach to teaching and learning English stem from an asset- or deficit-based perspective? What implicit or explicit policies guide teachers' language use in classrooms? Can students use languages other than English? How do you recognize and incorporate students' linguistic resources from homes and communities? Do students have opportunities to develop metalinguistic awareness to understand connections between English and other languages? When do students receive language-specific instructional supports – solely during ESL/ELD time or across content areas?

Tool 4.4: Probing Program Access

Directions: First, use data provided by administrators, school report cards, or the National Center for Education Statistics (https://nces.ed.gov/ccd/schoolsearch/) to compile demographic data for your school. Use this data to complete the School column. Second, gather data within your school related to students enrolled in language programming. Use this data to complete the Language Program column. Third, divide the number of students for each category in the Language Program column by the number of students for each category in the School column. Enter this number under Percent Enrolled.

Expanded Option: Repeat this process for upper-level, honors, and college preparatory language courses, which research suggests are typically more homogenous (Anya, 2020).

Modified Option: If you are currently unable to gather data on the demographics of your entire language program, choose one or two classes and analyze enrollment in those courses. Even a modified analysis provides useful information.

	SCHOOL	LANGUAGE PROGRAM	PERCENT ENROLLED
Total number of students			
Males			
Females			
American Indian/ Alaska Native			
Asian			
Black			
Hispanic			
Native Hawaiian/ Pacific Islander			
White			
Students with Individualized Education Plans			
English Learners			

Chapter 5
Partners: Involving Multiple Stakeholders in Implementation

Aadalarasi grew up speaking Tamil at home with her family, but the suburban school that she attended did not offer any instruction in the language, so she studied French. On the weekends, she attended Tamil classes at the Minnesota Tamil School (MNTS). Typically, enrollment drops at MNTS when students enter high school because students' schedules fill with extracurricular activities to strengthen college applications. However, that has changed since MNTS partnered with public schools to award the SoBL. When Aadalarasi's parents learned of the SoBL, they encouraged her to continue to study Tamil on Saturdays to improve her literacy skills. At MNTS, she took a test of her Tamil proficiency and scored high enough for a SoBL. MNTS educators reported her results to her public school, where she was awarded the SoBL and recognized alongside her peers. Although Aadalarasi attended a university that did not offer credit for the SoBL, she explained that her "hard work paid off." Earning the SoBL made her parents "super happy," and she listed the achievement on her college applications.

Guiding Questions

Who plays a role in SoBL implementation?

In what ways can teachers across schools support students' biliteracy?

How can school-community partnerships promote students' biliteracy?

What can external organizations, colleges, and businesses contribute to SoBL efforts?

This chapter explores the pertinent role of partnerships within and across schools and communities. To achieve the defined *Purpose* of SoBL implementation (described in Chapter 2), including expansive *Proficiency Assessments* (described in Chapter 3) and inclusive *Programs* (described in Chapter 4), you need an all-hands-on-deck approach that welcomes the contributions of *Partners* from inside and outside of schools. Like the one described between the language and public schools in the above vignette, partnerships facilitate and extend SoBL recognition to a wider array of students and languages in the community. Drawing from the sociocultural perspective, we recognize that policy implementation is not top-down and linear but rather co-constructed by actors spanning classrooms, schools, and communities (Datnow, 2006; Levinson & Sutton, 2001). Not only do various stakeholders contribute to implementation, they draw upon their own interests, backgrounds, and experiences to shape decisions and practices (Spillane et al., 2006). With this fourth facet of our framework, we emphasize the collaborative nature of implementing the SoBL to maximize its reach for students, families, and communities.

Partnerships have emerged frequently in our research as a key lever for SoBL implementation (Heineke & Davin, 2020a, 2021). Successful efforts to implement the SoBL include engagement with various stakeholders both inside and outside of schools, including administrators, counselors, teachers, and community partners. In this way, the effort moves from being the sole responsibility of one person to being shared across schools, districts, and communities. By extending beyond one person or department, the SoBL becomes a communal initiative that prioritizes biliteracy outside of world language and bilingual classrooms. With awareness and requisite expertise, educators can encourage students to pursue the SoBL, as well as support and promote biliteracy in classrooms. Partnerships with community organizations and universities can enhance equity in SoBL implementation, as stakeholders can collaboratively develop additional paths for students to develop and demonstrate biliteracy in less common languages. In short, collaboration across stakeholders enhances SoBL implementation.

This chapter prompts consideration of ways to extend SoBL work beyond the confines of world language or bilingual departments to promote biliteracy for all students. Our goal with this facet of the framework is to elevate this focus on language development in schools, which ultimately widens the reach of the SoBL and the many social, cognitive, economic, and societal benefits that come with achieving bilingualism and biliteracy (e.g., Bialystok, 2007; Byram, 1997; Fan et al., 2015; Kroll & Dussias, 2017; Morales et al., 2013). Drawing from research-based vignettes in settings that have successfully forged partnerships to promote biliteracy, we walk through considerations to engage with (a) educators in schools, (b) community organizations, (c) language education organizations, (d) colleges and universities, and (e) businesses and future workplaces for biliterate employees (see Figure 5.1).

Considering Current Partners

Before embarking upon this chapter, stop and reflect on your SoBL work. As we have noted throughout this book, collaboration is key to these efforts. Who have been your partners in implementation to date? What support do you have? What support do you need? Ground this reflection in the goals that you have defined for SoBL implementation. Where might partners support your ongoing efforts to achieve the purpose of this initiative? Throughout this chapter, we explore various avenues for partnerships to bolster different facets of SoBL work. For those just getting started, you might explore partners within your school, as well as networks and resources from world language, bilingual, and EL professional organizations. For those refining implementation, you might look outside of schools to community organizations, universities, and businesses to extend biliteracy to more students in your schools.

Partnerships, particularly those that center on the premise of mutual benefit, involve two-way commu-

Figure 5.1. Layers to Consider When Forging Partnerships

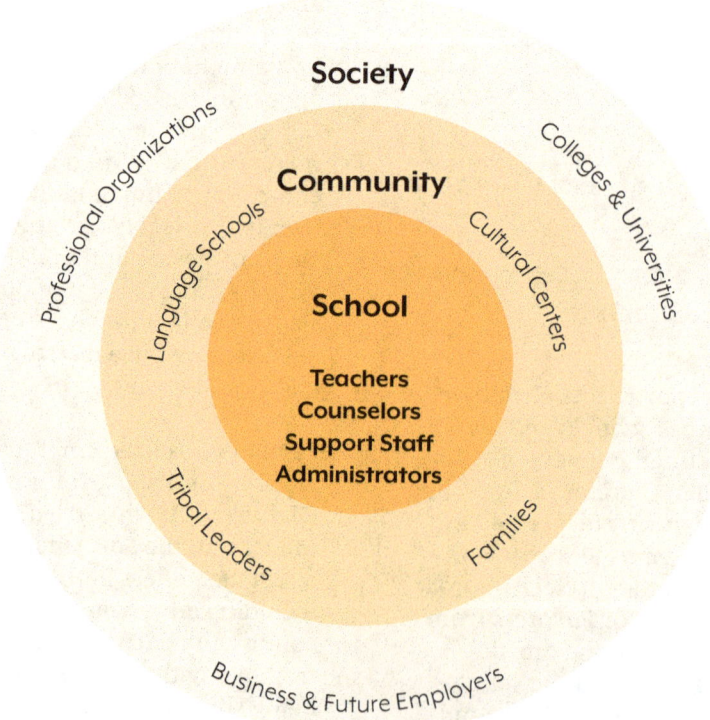

nication and contribution (Kruger et al., 2008). In addition to thinking about the support that you need from others, reflect upon the expertise and resources that you bring to the table that you can share with others. As a school-based educator or administrator, think about how your background and daily work can shape the efforts in your building. If you work outside of schools in community organizations or universities, consider where and how you see the SoBL as complementary to both your work and the biliteracy attainment of students in schools. Overall, the goal is to create meaningful partnerships to support biliteracy, so center your reflections on the best interests of the children and adolescents in your school and community. In the sections to come, we dive into different ways that you and others can collaborate to achieve the purpose of this initiative within, outside, and beyond K-12 schools.

Building Capacity to Support Students' Language Development

In the J. Sterling Morton High School District in Illinois, educators serve a population where approximately 90 percent of students are Latinx, with most speaking Spanish in homes. The district embraced the state's SoBL as a mechanism to recognize and celebrate students' Spanish-English bilingualism, as well as the 18 other languages used by students in homes. Melody Becker leads the district's efforts related to bilingual and world language education, and she coordinates a team of biliteracy coaches who support schools in promoting students' language development, which includes efforts related to the SoBL.

Melody and her biliteracy coaches collaborate frequently with world language teachers, including those teaching Chinese, French, and Spanish, as well as English, ESL, and journalism teachers. All language-focused teachers demonstrate buy-in and commitment to the SoBL, finding space in their classrooms to promote biliteracy development and offer SoBL assessments when needed. Biliteracy coaches work with teachers regularly to support best practices and individual student supports, with the goal of supporting students' biliteracy attainment.

Recently, Melody and her team have expanded beyond language-focused classrooms to build all teachers' capacity to support language development. Because the district uses Understanding by Design to plan curriculum and instruction (Heineke & McTighe, 2018), they have initiated professional development with teachers across content areas to add a language lens to their disciplinary teaching. Partnering with a state organization specializing in ELs, they support content-area teachers in planning content units that support students' language and biliteracy. The human resources director has also fostered partnerships with local universities to prioritize the hiring of teachers with ESL and bilingual endorsements to maintain the language lens across schools.

In schools, educators have different roles to carry out the various functions of schooling. Administrators, clerks, counselors, school psychologists, social workers, classroom teachers, resource teachers, instructional coaches, paraprofessionals, and family liaisons comprise the larger school faculty with distinct responsibilities to nurture students' learning and development. We have found that teachers play an integral role in SoBL implementation due to daily interactions with learners (Davin & Heineke, 2018; Davin et al., 2018; Heineke & Davin, 2021). Partnerships with teachers serve to widen the reach of the SoBL across schools, as well as to deepen the impact of these efforts on students' biliteracy. By building capacity among teachers and instructional support staff, the SoBL becomes a mechanism for meaningful pedagogical change spanning classroom contexts. Surface-level implementation recognizes students who demonstrate biliteracy on approved assessments. In-depth implementation utilizes this initiative to springboard programs and practices that nurture dynamic language competencies. Building on our discussion of programming in the last chapter, this section probes teachers as partners in supporting biliteracy. In Morton, Melody and her team of biliteracy coaches have situated the SoBL within larger efforts to promote biliteracy in language- and content-focused classrooms. Their work to engage and equip teachers involves pinpointing the expertise needed by teachers, as well as determining how to structure professional development and learning opportunities.

Developing Language Expertise As the population grows more linguistically diverse across the United States, teacher education has focused more on preparing the teaching force for language, language development, and language learners. Various resources have emerged in attempts to define needed expertise, including understandings of how language functions and develops and related practices to support language development in classrooms (Adger et al., 2018; Bailey, 2007; Commins & Miramontes, 2006; Glisan & Donato, 2017, 2021; Heritage et al., 2015; Lucas et al., 2008; TESOL International, 2018). These approaches center on the recognition that every teacher is a teacher of language and therefore needs targeted preparation to thoughtfully use and scaffold language in their classrooms in support of students' learning.

World language and bilingual teachers bring a language lens to their work every day, charged to promote students' biliteracy development through context-appropriate methods. Because of licensure requirements, we assume that language teachers come with understandings of language development and practices to promote learning target languages. But teachers' preparation varies depending on when and where they received their training, meaning teachers may need updates to their pedagogical repertoires. Schools might use the high-leverage practices discussed in Chapter 4 to have teachers reflect and pinpoint areas for professional development. For example, world language teachers might recognize use of rigid, grammar-based teaching and look for strategies to facilitate authentic, performance-based language learning (Glisan & Donato, 2017, 2021). Bilingual teachers might seek to understand the interconnections between languages to build from students' strengths, foster metalinguistic awareness, and embrace dynamic language competencies, in contrast to the traditional practice of situating languages as static and separate entities (Beeman & Urow, 2012; Valdés, 2020). With targeted professional learning to boost pedagogy in line with current research, language teachers can dynamically develop students' biliteracy with specific attention to target languages in classrooms.

English-focused language teachers, such as those teaching ESL and ELA, facilitate English-language development, including oral language, reading, and writing with lenses on grammar, vocabulary, literature, comprehension, and composition. Teachers' existing expertise centers on the English language, such as knowledge of English grammar and strategies to promote English-medium reading comprehension. The English-centric nature of these classrooms might result in monolingual contexts that implicitly or explicitly prohibit other languages (Auerbach, 2016; Gebhard et al., 2019). Through professional development, teachers can explore the interconnection between students' languages to develop (a) understandings of how reading and writing develop across languages, (b) metalinguistic awareness as a scaffold for learning English, and (c) practices to foster authentic language use in classrooms (Beeman & Urow, 2012; García et al., 2017; Hornberger, 2003; Roehr-Brackin, 2018). In this way, ESL and ELA teachers can focus on developing students' English, while also emphasizing dynamic connections across languages to build multiliteracies (Valdés, 2020).

Content- and special-area teachers mediate disciplinary learning in math, science, social studies, fine arts, technology, and physical education. Although some may come with knowledge of language and literacy in the content areas, their preparation focuses primarily on content-area expertise and content-specific pedagogy. Language-focused capacity building can contribute to local efforts to deepen students' multiliteracies, as well as enhance learning by developing learners' disciplinary language and scaffolding access to rigorous content (Bailey, 2007; Lucas et al., 2008). Content teachers need opportunities to explore (a) how language develops simultaneously with content-area learning, (b) how to use strategies to scaffold content-area instruction to support language development, and (c) how students' bilingualism can enhance content instruction, for example by using cognates and connecting to previous learning in other languages (Cruz & Thornton, 2013; Kersaint et al., 2013; Latta & Chan, 2010; Nutta et al., 2010). By embracing students' developing biliteracy in content-area classrooms, educators can model and encourage real-world language use in the context of disciplinary practice.

Even though the SoBL separates languages for the purposes of assessment, teachers can make principled decisions about whether and how to strategically leverage translanguaging as a tool for promoting specific aspects of proficiency development in classroom instruction. For example, content-area teachers might encourage students to brainstorm what they know about disciplinary topics, using their rich linguistic repertoires to help them learn and think more deeply.

Facilitating Professional Learning To build requisite expertise, school and district stakeholders typically look to professional development. In Morton, Melody works with her team of biliteracy coaches and a statewide professional organization to facilitate the learning of world language, ESL, ELA, and content-area teachers across three high schools. Through differentiated professional learning opportunities, she encourages educators in various contexts to espouse the language lens in their practice, which also connects to the district's goal of encouraging biliteracy. Biliteracy coaches work directly with language teachers to enrich daily practice, while an external expert facilitates language-focused professional development with content teachers. Both facets build toward the district's defined purpose to nurture students' biliteracy, providing opportunities for teachers to hone their practice over time, rather than participating in one-off workshops without coherence or focus on larger goals. When deliberating professional development as a part of implementation efforts, consider a long-term trajectory of learning grounded in local goals.

Many schools have structures in place to house efforts to build capacity for language. Department and grade-level teams, as well as other iterations of professional learning communities (PLCs), provide locales for ongoing learning and application centered on language. We recommend selecting a core professional text to mediate discussions aligned to the local context (see Table 5.1). Educators might select texts to develop understandings about language (Adger et al., 2018), consider language implications from the New Standards (Heritage et al., 2015) and the World-Readiness Standards for Learning Languages (National Standards Collaborative Board, 2015), or develop pedagogies surrounding ***translanguaging*** that are appropriate for the intended program goals and instructional contexts (García et al., 2017). When possible, focal texts should connect with larger priorities spanning the school or district, such as Melody's choice to situate the language lens within the district's use of Understanding by Design (Heineke & McTighe, 2018). Teachers can collaboratively select and read chapters, consider and apply the ideas in classrooms, and then bring student re-

Table 5.1. Potential Texts for Professional Learning Communities

AUDIENCE	TEXT INFORMATION
World Language Teachers	Glisan, E. W., & Donato, R. (2017). *Enacting the work of language instruction: High-leverage teaching practices.* ACTFL.
	Glisan, E. W., & Donato, R. (2021). *Enacting the work of language instruction: High-leverage teaching practices. Volume 2.* ACTFL.
	Shrum, J., & Glisan, E. (2016). *Teacher's handbook: Contextualized language instruction* (5th ed.). Cengage Learning.
Bilingual and EL Teachers	Beeman, K., & Urow, C. (2012). *Teaching for biliteracy.* Caslon.
	España, C., & Herrera, L. Y. (2020). *En comunidad: Lessons for centering the voices and experiences of bilingual Latinx students.* Heinemann.
	García, O., Ibarra Johnson, S., & Seltzer, K. (2017). *The translanguaging classroom: Leveraging student bilingualism for learning.* Caslon.
General Education Teachers	Adger, C. T., Snow, C. E., & Christian, D. (2018). *What teachers need to know about language* (2nd ed.). Channel View.
	Heineke, A. J., & McTighe, J. (2018). *Using Understanding by Design in the culturally and linguistically diverse classroom.* ASCD.
	Heritage, M., Walqui, A., & Linquanti, R. (2015). *English language learners and the New Standards: Developing language, content knowledge, and analytical practices in the classroom.* Harvard Education Press.
	Snyder, S., & Staehr Fenner, D. (2021). *Culturally responsive teaching for multilingual learners: Tools for equity.* Corwin.

sponses and reflections to push discussion forward. While the PLC likely includes colleagues within grade-level and departmental teams, language-focused teachers or coaches may be strategically dispersed to facilitate and support conversations.

Before diving into professional development efforts, it is important to build colleagues' buy-in and awareness (Drago-Severson, 2009; Turnbull, 2002). We want administrators to assert that all practitioners facilitate language development and make biliteracy a priority across the school or district. We want teachers to recognize their roles in language development and see how the language lens can enhance their instructional practice and subsequent student outcomes. Both to initiate and maintain these capacity-building efforts, we need our colleagues to appreciate how the language lens enhances wider practices and goals. In the Morton School District, Melody continues to grapple with the buy-in of secondary content-area teachers. While language-focused teachers embrace their role in biliteracy development, some content-area teachers need support to see how the language lens enhances learning in disciplines such as geometry and chemistry. She finds that partnering with a state organization that provides professional development supports these efforts by having other expert voices to reiterate her messaging regarding language and biliteracy.

Beyond capacity-building efforts with existing teachers, stakeholders can consider how to strategically hire new faculty with requisite expertise to support language and biliteracy development. In Morton, Melody collaborates with the district's director of human resources to develop partnerships with universities that prepare strong language teachers, as well as those that prepare all teachers with ESL endorsements alongside content-area licensure. In addition to hiring for language-focused preparation, districts can target candidates based on language competencies, such as recruiting and prioritizing those who are bilingual and biliterate themselves to serve as models for students and weave home languages into their classrooms. This strategic recruitment is where we envision the SoBL as having rich potential in the future to develop a pipeline for future teachers. Districts and universities might partner to (a) recruit SoBL recipients into teacher preparation programs, (b) build from their rich language competencies to develop expert teachers, and (c) support their induction in local schools to support students' biliteracy in world language, bilingual, and EL programs.

Fostering Partnerships with Community Organizations

Situated in a culturally and linguistically diverse suburb of a large metropolis, Walsh School District (a pseudonym) sought to expand its language programming to match the linguistic backgrounds of its constituents and bolster progress toward the goal of students graduating bilingual and biliterate. In addition to long-standing Spanish dual and heritage language programs, leaders had partnered with educators to create similar programs for Vietnamese and Somali, the second and third most prevalent languages used by families. When approached by a community organization about offering formal instruction in Samoan, a top-ten language in the district, district stakeholders jumped at the opportunity. The organization, which centered on revitalizing the Samoan language and culture, knew of the district's work in language education, as well as the many students and families who spoke Samoan at home.

With significant collaboration between the community organization and the district's language learning department, they started an afterschool program that ran two days a week. They identified the high school with the highest population of Samoan students to house the program, which initially attracted 35 students from around the district. While the district provided space and recruited students, volunteers from the community organization provided all instruction, which utilized Samoan cultural traditions to facilitate authentic language learning. Despite its success, stakeholders realized that short and intermittent time after school was not advancing students' proficiency in Samoan. The community organization asked for time during the school day, and district leaders worked to run an elective class where a world language teacher of record partnered with the community organization teacher to provide daily Samoan instruction.

When seeking to implement the SoBL in schools, *community organizations* emerge as critical partners to promote equity and allow all students to achieve and demonstrate biliteracy. Schools often offer a limited number of languages for formal study, guided by available funding, curricula, and teachers with requisite language skills. But students like Aadalarasi enter educational spaces with rich linguistic competencies beyond Spanish, French, German, and other traditionally offered languages. To promote all students' budding multiliteracies, educators can seek out external partnerships beyond the walls of schools to enhance implementation for less commonly taught languages. The aspiration is to develop mutually beneficial partnerships, which endeavor to support school- and district-oriented goals for the SoBL and organizational goals related to the maintenance of heritage languages. By starting with students' linguistic resources, stakeholders can prioritize partnerships to extend the reach of the recognition, as happened in the Walsh school district with Samoan, Somali, and Vietnamese. These efforts begin by exploring potential opportunities and then working collaboratively to develop partnerships that aim to nurture heritage language maintenance and biliteracy.

Exploring Potential Opportunities Developing external partnerships starts with awareness of community resources, which connects to the exploration of the linguistic landscape that we discussed in Chapter 2. Because of the need to build partnerships for less commonly taught languages, *heritage language schools* emerge as key resources to probe. Communities often initiate heritage language schools due to the desire to preserve cultures, languages, and connections across generations (Kelleher, 2010). These efforts vary by context with different organizations (e.g., schools, churches, cultural centers), instructional methods (e.g., available resources, pedagogical approaches), staffing (e.g., trained teachers, parent volunteers, tribal leaders), and funding (e.g., tuition, grants, donations). Because of the grassroots nature of these varied efforts in local settings, no comprehensive list exists detailing all heritage language schools across the United States. To find organizations that exist within a community, begin with internet searches but center on word-of-mouth leads from students, families, and colleagues.

Community language schools are often easier to find due to their formal designation as schools. Schools focusing on the development and maintenance of heritage languages have been around for decades, seeking to develop language competencies to maintain connections between families and communities and facilitate potential return to home countries (Borowczyk, 2020; Kelleher, 2010). Linguist Joshua Fishman (2001) has documented community-based language schools across the country, identifying over 6,000 schools teaching 145 different languages, including 91 Indigenous languages. Most schools prioritize immigrant languages, primarily Chinese, French, Hebrew, Italian, Japanese, Korean, Polish, Portuguese, Spanish, Ukrainian, and Yiddish (Kelleher, 2010). These schools include those that meet every day like traditional K-12 schools, as well as afterschool programs, evening classes, weekend classes, and summer programs (Fishman, 2001; Liu, 2010). The Center for Applied Linguistics (www.cal.org) maintains a database of community language schools, as well as other resources related to heritage language learners. You can also explore the Coalition of Community-Based Heritage Language Schools (www.heritagelanguageschools.org), a nationwide organization that connects, supports, and advocates for community language schools, and reach out to those in your community or send information through students who attend their programs.

Not only do formal language schools facilitate language learning, other groups within communities, such as tribes, churches, and cultural centers, do so as well. Distinct from community language schools, these organizations often approach language development not through formal study but through participation in cultural traditions and practices (Kelleher, 2010). For example, volunteers from the Samoan organization engage Walsh students in chanting, singing, and dancing that incorporate the Samoan language as the primary medium. In the North School District, educators collaborate with tribal leaders to offer Paiute language classes, which involve three interwoven lenses on culture, language, and history. These are just two examples of valuable school and community partnerships that foster students' biliteracy and heritage language maintenance as a component of SoBL implementation. Discovering these stakeholders is the first step, but it may be hindered by lack of web presence or formal designation as heritage language programming. We recommend talking to students, families, colleagues, and community members to ascertain potential partners for focal languages.

Word-of-mouth discussions can also point you in the direction of individuals who might be valuable partners for working toward SoBL goals. While over

400 languages are used by U.S. residents, not all are represented by community organizations in a given region. For this reason, SoBL coordinators may come up empty in searches for language schools or cultural organizations offering formal opportunities for language learning. In these instances, school-based educators might collaborate with interested individuals with the requisite language background and experience to design and offer opportunities for instruction and assessment in the target language. Walsh district leaders have initiated Somali language study in collaboration with a multilingual teacher from Somalia who teaches French in the district. Illinois districts have enlisted biliterate parents with teaching backgrounds to collaboratively develop Polish assessments. In Hawai'i, stakeholders work with university faculty specializing in modern languages to craft assessments in needed languages. Whether with community-based schools, organizations, or individuals, partnerships outside of schools can enrich and extend SoBL efforts.

Too often, schools only recognize and support biliteracy development in the languages formally taught in the schools. Equity can be enhanced by building partnerships with community organizations and individuals to target both programming and assessment opportunities in students' home languages.

Developing Meaningful Partnerships After finding community organizations or individuals that might be a good match, it is important to initiate the work using a mutual-benefit partnership model where both schools and communities benefit from the collaboration (Kruger et al., 2009). In her research on community language schools, Borowczyk (2020) shares that community stakeholders recognize a multitude of benefits of the SoBL initiative and subsequent partnerships with schools. Her findings indicate that educators from Czech and Slovak, Polish, Lithuanian, French, and German language schools across the country envision the SoBL as a way to credential heritage languages in a way that matters in the United States, thus bolstering the recognition of students' language competencies, retention in community-based language study, and public awareness of the community and organization. In addition to embracing these opportunities, the formation of mutually beneficial partnerships might also respond to common challenges faced by heritage language schools, including program funding, meeting space, student recruitment, parental support, instructional materials, and staff development (Adger & Locke, 2000; Liu et al., 2011).

For school stakeholders reaching out to community organizations, or vice versa, we recommend starting with a brief overview of the SoBL initiative, as well as directly stating the local goals for promoting and recognizing students' biliteracy. Depending on the context, it may also be necessary to provide background on the district or school, including details on current language programming and the number of students from the focal language background. This is particularly important when reaching out to organizations outside of the school's immediate community, or where multiple school districts overlap in one general region. When reaching out for the first time, we recommend connecting with the mission of the organization to demonstrate knowledge of their work and immediately ground the potential partnership in mutual benefit. In other words, communication might emphasize how collaboration can support school-based educators' goals for equity in SoBL implementation and biliteracy development, as well as community-based organizers' aspirations to maintain heritage languages and cultures.

After forging the connection between school and community stakeholders, it is important to determine the logistics of the partnership. In their work on school-community partnerships in support of language minority students, Adger and Locke (2000) recommend starting small and building carefully with two key steps. The first step is to outline a shared vision, which should integrate the purposes of both school and community partners. For example, leaders in the Walsh district aim for all students to graduate biliterate, and their community partner aspires to maintain Samoan heritage through language and cultural traditions; together, they seek to support Samoan students in deepening their heritage language and culture as a means to develop biliteracy. The second step is to set responsibilities, which involve high to low levels of integration depending on the partner's needs and capacity. Modeling the notion of thoughtful growth over time, Walsh now exemplifies high-level integration with partners offering formal language study in schools. In Elmwood, Jason partners with organizations for supplementary services, such as collaborating to design and score assessments in Polish or Marathi. By defining vision and responsibilities in advance, partnerships can be built on foundations of clarity and transparency.

Even once the logistics have been determined, partnerships need to be nurtured over time. Unlike schools with firm institutional grounding and funding sources, community organizations and heritage language schools often grapple with fluctuating resources, personnel, and program offerings (Adger & Locke, 2000; Liu et al., 2011). Therefore, school-community partnerships must be dynamic to respond to changing contexts, challenges, and needs to ensure continued mutual benefit. Partners should maintain open lines of communication with routine points of collaboration, such as an annual meeting to review progress towards goals and to reflect iteratively on the ongoing partnership. Schools and district SoBL coordinators can also include community partners in regular updates and SoBL celebrations, specifically recognizing their contributions to students' heritage language maintenance and resulting biliteracy.

Connecting with Professional Organizations

Following legislation passed in 2014, the state of Minnesota offers Bilingual and Multilingual Seals and World Language Proficiency Certificates. As it is in most states, the SoBL is facilitated through the Department of Education, where state administrators and expert language educators offer a variety of supports to districts and schools implementing the SoBL. The state legislation allows for recognitions in all languages. The Minnesota Department of Education worked with stakeholders to design language proficiency assessments in various languages used by Minnesota students who wish to pursue recognition for their biliteracy. Responding to state demographics, they have developed proficiency-based assessments in languages such as Somali, Hmong, Karen, Dakota, and Ojibwe. These assessments are then available to local schools and districts seeking to expand their SoBL implementation (Minnesota Department of Education, 2021).

In addition to the Minnesota Department of Education, the state has a number of professional organizations with supports for SoBL implementation. The Minnesota Council on the Teaching of Languages and Cultures hosts an annual conference and regular workshops for language teachers. MinneTESOL provides supports for teachers of Minnesota's linguistically diverse EL population through conferences, interest-based groups, and a professional journal publication. Housed at the University of Minnesota, the Center for Advanced Research on Language Acquisition (CARLA) serves as a central hub for research, professional development, and resources to improve language teaching and learning. These organizations share in the goal of supporting language education in schools and communities, with specific efforts and resources for educators implementing the SoBL.

While much of our focus throughout this book has been on implementation in local settings, it is important to consider partnerships and collaboration more broadly via national, state, and regional networks. Professional organizations can serve as integral links among stakeholders across contexts, bringing together those working on the SoBL in separate contexts and fostering collaboration and expansion of these important efforts. In Minnesota, for example, local educators tap into various resources and collaborations among national, state, and regional organizations to support SoBL efforts in schools and districts. In this section, we describe different avenues for exploring networks that might benefit your work.

National Organizations Although states initiate and implement unique iterations of SoBL legislation, national organizations have come together to support and sustain efforts across the United States. SealofBiliteracy.org is an excellent place to begin exploration of national resources, because it provides links to individual state websites and the latest resources, frequently asked questions, and other information to guide implementation. Serving as a national platform for the SoBL, the website is maintained by Velázquez Press and Californians Together, the advocacy group that initiated the SoBL movement (Olsen, 2020). Stakeholders at these organizations commonly support state leaders seeking to enact SoBL legislation, but resources and updates can also benefit local educators as they think through implementation.

Various professional organizations partner with SealofBiliteracy.org and Californians Together to provide cohesive national supports for SoBL implementation. As described in Chapter 1, national organizations including ACTFL, NABE, NCSSFL, and

TESOL International collaborated to craft guidelines for implementation. These partners released revised recommendations in 2020 with additional organizations, including the MLA and NAELPA, joining the charge. Sharing a commitment to high-quality language education, these organizations offer publications, conferences, and professional development opportunities on all facets of language education, as well as language education specific to the SoBL. These offerings include the latest research and perspectives on the SoBL from researchers and practitioners across the country.

State Organizations Since SoBL policy is enacted by states, state-level organizations provide targeted support for local implementation. National language organizations have formal or informal relationships with state organizations that often lead efforts to adopt the SoBL in their state. In New Jersey, language educators from FLENJ, NJTESOL, and NJBE—linked to ACTFL, TESOL, and NABE respectively—have collaborated to initiate, pilot, and implement the initiative across the state. This in-depth, cross-context work with the SoBL situates state organizations as experts, advocates, and resource hubs for local districts and schools. Washington's state language organization WAFLT, facilitates the assessments for less commonly tested languages. In Massachusetts, TESOL affiliate MAT-SOL engages in advocacy work to ensure equity in the SoBL for ELs. State language organizations often partner and collaborate with language educators in the state department of education, which houses and administers the SoBL. Together, state-level organizations can provide procedural supports for SoBL implementation.

State language organizations also provide an array of professional development opportunities to enhance SoBL work in schools. While the offerings of these organizations vary by state, key trends emerge for resources: online materials, annual conferences, workshops, webinars, and networking opportunities. The first step is often the organization's website, where many have specific pages with resources dedicated to the SoBL. Some organizations also offer professional publications, such as journals for language practitioners with research-based recommendations to guide practice within the unique contexts of that state (e.g., *CABE Journal* in California, *INTESOL Journal* in Indiana). State language organizations typically host conferences, such as the fall and spring conferences of the Foreign Language Association of North Carolina, which serve as excellent locales for professional development

and networking with others implementing the SoBL across the state. Membership in these state organizations also yields various opportunities for ongoing professional learning and support through workshops, roundtables, panels, and webinars.

Regional Networks Regional networks can grow from state-level collaborations, connecting individuals engaged in SoBL implementation in the same communities and regions. In our work with various districts in Illinois, we have found these regional networks to be particularly valuable for those leading SoBL efforts in schools. In the suburbs north of Chicago, a group of world language department chairs has formed an informal network to support one another's work. Having connected through involvement in ICTFL, the state affiliate of ACTFL, they maintain communication across their high schools to support one another's work in language education. Justin at Stevenson High School, like department chairs in neighboring communities, uses the network of thought partners to brainstorm ways to boost enrollment and encourage best practices for authentic language instruction (see Fisk, 2020).

Regional networks are particularly valuable for SoBL implementation. With similar linguistic landscapes across their communities, the world language department chairs (who also serve as SoBL coordinators in their schools) have leaned on one another since the enactment of the policy in Illinois and adoption in their individual districts. Together, they seek to expand access to the SoBL for their students by, among other initiatives, securing assessments in less commonly tested languages for their highly multilingual populations. After partnering with an external organization to develop an assessment in Marathi, a language used by Indian residents in the north suburbs, Justin shared these resources with this network. Another potential line of collaboration lies in placing joint orders for assessments to take advantage of bulk-purchase discounts from test-making organizations. By pooling resources and sharing ideas across small school districts, these coordinators deepen SoBL efforts.

Aligning with Institutions of Higher Education

At Grand View University in Des Moines, Iowa, Dr. Amy Schumann wanted to ensure the impact of the SoBL beyond high school graduation. Grand View faculty sought to increase the university's bilingual student population, and Dr. Schumann saw the SoBL as supporting this goal. She approached her modern language department colleagues about the possibility of awarding college credit to SoBL recipients. Department faculty wanted to recognize students' achievement but did not want enrollment to drop in their department. A minor in a world language at Grand View University is 22 credits, eight of which are preliminary courses. Due to concerns that students who might otherwise have taken a modern language course might request SoBL credits but not enroll in additional language courses, department faculty decided on a retroactive credit policy.

As a result, SoBL recipients can request credit for these preliminary courses, giving them eight credits, following completion of one course in the department. SoBLs in languages not taught by the department yield elective credits upon completion of any course in the department. For example, students with the SoBL in Hmong, which is not taught at Grand View, can take Spanish I and receive eight elective credits for the Hmong SoBL. Students with a SoBL in Spanish, a language offered by the department, receive their credits as Spanish courses. Completion of one 3-credit course in the department, plus the eight credits for the SoBL, gives students half of the credits necessary for a language minor.

The department has used the new policy as an incentive to recruit bilingual students from area high schools, seeing an increase in modern language minors and majors. Further, the use of the SoBL for placement into courses has added another option, so that students with the SoBL do not have to pay the fee required to take the College Level Examination Program.

Whereas state SoBL policies center on K-12 schools, institutions of higher education (IHEs) emerge as integral partners to extend the reach and impact of the recognition. Language departments at IHEs, typically housed in the general arts and sciences, offer world language courses, minors, and majors, with the potential to use the SoBL for placement or credit. Schools and colleges of education prepare world language, bilingual, and EL teachers, employing faculty with expertise to support SoBL efforts. In a climate where world language and language teacher preparation programs have languishing enrollment, the SoBL offers a promising tool for recruitment. Given the shortage of language teachers and bilingual professionals, we see these collaborations as a win-win: students' knowledge of postsecondary opportunities increases interest in language study, and IHEs benefit from increased enrollment.

Modern Language Departments The SoBL is a powerful tool for encouraging students to continue language study and deepen proficiency at the postsecondary level. IHEs increasingly use the SoBL for placement and awarding college credit. In Illinois and Minnesota, legislation requires IHEs in state systems to award college credit for the SoBL when students request it. Maine's Department of Education and university system have a similar agreement. IHEs in other states, such as Grand View University in Iowa described in the vignette, voluntarily enact policies to recognize students' biliteracy. Depending on the institution, language departments may use the SoBL (a) for a placement in coursework, using the recognition to start students in the appropriate course based on their demonstrated proficiency; (b) for credit, providing course credits based on the recognition upon students' enrollment; or (c) for retroactive or back credits, where students complete one course in the department to then earn credit for their SoBL (see Table 5.2).

Offering credit to SoBL recipients has benefits for both students and IHEs. For students, such policies may increase motivation to enroll in higher education, can help to level the playing field for students who did not have access to AP courses, and can reduce tuition costs, making college more accessible. ELs are often underrepresented in high school courses tied to college credit (Callahan, 2005; Callahan et al., 2010; Harklau, 1994, 2013; Wang & Goldschmidt, 1999), so the SoBL provides a way for students to receive credit for the linguistic resources they possess. In our research, students have reported that the possibility of receiving college credit served as an important motivating factor in their decisions to pursue the SoBL (Davin, 2021a; Davin & Heineke, 2018). For IHEs, the SoBL offers a tool for recruitment and placement, with initial evidence suggesting increased enrollment in modern language departments (Davin, 2021b). Faculty also note enhancements to placement decisions. For example,

Table 5.2. Sample University Policies for SoBL Placement and Credit

UNIVERSITY	POLICY	DETAILS
Kansas State University	Placement and Back Credits	Gold SoBL (Intermediate Mid) leads to placement in Spanish 301, and Platinum SoBL (Advanced Low) leads to placement in Spanish 410; a student who completes the course receives retroactive credit for prerequisite courses
Pittsburg State University	Placement and Back Credits	SoBL recipients enroll in the 5th semester course and receive back credits for previous courses after passing with a grade of C or higher; only three additional courses are needed for a minor and six for a major
Southern Connecticut State University	Credits	SoBL recipients receive nine credits in the focal language, in place of three introductory level courses
University of Hawai'i at Manoa	Back Credits	SoBL recipients can request up to 12 back credits once they pass a modern language course with a grade of C or higher
University of Illinois Urbana-Champaign	Credits	SoBL in any language from any state yields eight credits
University of Maine system	Credits	SoBL at Intermediate Mid yields six credits SoBL at Advanced Low yields nine credits

whereas students might previously have enrolled in a course below their abilities, use of the SoBL ensures placement in levels appropriate for their proficiency levels.

 **The SoBL has the potential to reduce inequities for heritage language learners seeking college credit. When colleges only accept AP scores, students proficient in less commonly taught languages cannot earn credits. Equity emerges when states, universities, and colleges allow the SoBL to count for college credit, and when local districts and schools seek to provide multiple avenues to award the SoBL in all languages.**

Partnerships with language faculty at nearby colleges and universities can lead to opportunities for students to achieve credit for their biliteracy, as well as support implementation efforts in schools. In some states, stakeholders have collaborated with university faculty to design assessments in less commonly tested languages (Heineke & Davin, 2018). In Hawai'i, for example, state-level leaders in SoBL work sought the collaboration of faculty at the University of Hawai'i at Mānoa. In a department organized into East Asian, Indo-Pacific, and European and American languages, faculty had the requisite language expertise to support the design of assessments in languages used by Hawaiian students but not regularly offered by assessment companies.

This partnership also prompted additional actions, such as the university accepting the SoBL for college credit (see Table 5.2).

Colleges and Schools of Education Another potential line of IHE partnerships lies in education-focused programs, including those related to world language, bilingual, and EL education. In our work as university faculty in schools of education in Illinois and North Carolina, as well as our research on other contexts, we have seen various ways that schools and universities can partner to provide professional development for teachers, develop pipelines for language teachers, and advocate for SoBL policy changes (Heineke & Davin, 2018, 2021; Sherf et al., 2020). By reaching out to university faculty at nearby institutions, you might find additional sources of support and collaboration in line with your goals.

Education faculty support schools and districts in a variety of ways, such as consulting on program design and providing professional development. Some universities house centers and projects specifically focused on language education, such as CARLA at the University of Minnesota, described in the previous section. In these contexts, expert practitioners and researchers in language education have funds and multiple avenues to provide educators with high-quality, research-based professional development and resources to support teaching, learning, and biliteracy development. Even when designated centers do not exist, language education faculty might welcome opportunities to collaborate with schools on these important efforts. They might also tap into their connections across schools to connect stakeholders engaging in this work.

School–university partnerships can also be leveraged to recruit biliterate students into teacher education programs and respond to nationwide shortages of world language and bilingual teachers. In collaboration with partner districts, education faculty at Loyola University Chicago are working to develop bilingual teacher pipelines where (a) students develop biliteracy in partner districts, (b) biliterate high-school graduates enroll in teacher education programs, (c) teacher educators prepare candidates as expert pedagogues in language education, and (d) teachers return to classrooms to promote students' biliteracy. As a part of these efforts, faculty successfully lobbied the Illinois State Board of Education to accept the SoBL in place of the bilingual proficiency exam, streamlining the pathway to licensure. These potential pipelines benefit both IHEs and schools, seeking to leverage students' biliteracy, provide pathways to teaching, and strengthen language programming in schools.

Connecting with Businesses and Future Employers

In 2017, Missouri legislators passed the SoBL, which districts across the state can enact to recognize students' biliteracy. Rick (a pseudonym), an administrator in the Department of Elementary and Secondary Education, sought to bring businesses and industry to the fore to deepen the impact of the recognition for individual students and larger communities in Missouri. With state leaders focusing on workforce development, he aligned his message to emphasize the benefits of bilingualism in various careers by pointing out how bilingual nurses, emergency responders, and insurance agents could positively influence communities.

Once the SoBL passed, Rick asked non-profit and business leaders to endorse it, securing publicly posted letters of support from regional chambers of commerce and companies like Ameren, Mastercard, and Midwest Bank. He also partnered with a regional non-profit organization that works to recruit highly-skilled international workers, which facilitated his connections to various companies. Rick has collaborated with various universities across the state but recognizes that not all students pursue postsecondary education. For this reason, he situated industry support as integral to encouraging all students to achieve biliteracy.

In addition to individual connections with lawmakers and business leaders, Rick worked to establish the SoBL as an official credential with the Missouri Department of Labor. In this way, the SoBL would not only recognize students' biliteracy but also serve as a formal credential to demonstrate students' competencies to future employers. Overall, he found that external stakeholders wanted to support Missouri students in being successful in their careers through the attainment of biliteracy.

State SoBL legislation typically highlights the value of biliteracy in connection with readiness for both college and career. As described in Chapter 1, biliteracy involves integral skills and competencies that facilitate both domestic and international business, but many companies find shortages of biliterate individuals to hire for critical positions (Commission on Language Learning, 2017). Most businesses prefer bilingual employees over monolinguals, with many prioritizing bilingual candidates when hiring (Callahan & Gándara, 2014; Damari et al., 2017). As SoBL efforts roll out across the country, partnerships between stakeholders in education and industry are just beginning to emerge as potential ways to enhance implementation.

Awareness and buy-in are integral first steps when reaching out to external stakeholders with business interests. In Chapter 1, we discussed enlisting support from district administrators and school boards by aligning the SoBL with existing initiatives. This same approach works when asking legislators and business leaders to endorse the SoBL or extend its use for industry credentialing. Rick's efforts in Missouri demonstrate strategic alignment between the SoBL and the state's priority on workforce development, as he maintains a consistent message about the value that bilingual and biliterate workers bring to communities in industries like healthcare and public safety. He shares information about the SoBL to build awareness and highlights key points relevant to the target audience, whether those are (a) the priority on workforce development among lawmakers, (b) potential contributions to the community for regional and local chambers of commerce, or (c) the demand for biliterate workers in particular careers and companies. When companies buy in to the initiative, they submit formal letters that Rick posts on the department website. Districts can then use these to market the SoBL to students.

In addition to states seeking out formal endorsements and hiring commitments, local stakeholders can introduce the SoBL into everyday interactions with employers. Many companies and organizations do not know about the SoBL, so they may not realize its significance when recruiting or hiring. Educators and students can share information about the SoBL with external actors and advocate for its use in hiring decisions. Take for example the student vignette of Kaaha in Chapter 1, who landed a job at a call center after sharing her SoBL recognition with the interviewer. Another student in Iowa obtained a job as a bilingual paraeducator, using the SoBL as a credential to demonstrate the requisite language competencies. In both examples, those familiar with the SoBL shared their knowledge with employers, who eagerly embraced the opportunity to hire individuals with demonstrated biliteracy skills. Each time one door opens and stakeholders share information about the SoBL with employers, more open doors are likely to follow for future students.

Businesses can indeed encourage students to pursue the SoBL, but other facets of partnerships can also support learners on the path to developing biliteracy. We have seen examples of national companies partnering with districts to provide instructional resources and experiences that nurture biliteracy. For example, Istation is an educational technology company providing adaptive and personalized curriculum in Spanish. The company supports schools implementing the SoBL by demonstrating how its software can build students' Spanish competencies even in English-medium classrooms. In addition, local companies can provide students with authentic contexts for practicing their language skills. In suburban Milwaukee, one district partners with businesses and organizations where aspiring SoBL recipients use their bilingualism as a part of volunteer opportunities and service-learning projects. We encourage exploration of various partnerships and

innovative thinking around different avenues to bolster interest and application of the SoBL in multilingual communities and society as a whole.

Chapter Summary

In this chapter, we focused on the fourth facet of the framework, centered on collaboration with **Partners** to support SoBL implementation. Drawing from theory and research on the multiple layers of stakeholders involved in language educational policy, we explored ways to enlist the support of educators, community partners, professional organizations, universities, and businesses. Specific goals for SoBL implementation should drive collaboration, using various partnerships to achieve those goals with an all-hands-on-deck approach that extends the reach and responsibility for the SoBL beyond one person or department. Building buy-in and awareness is key, as other stakeholders may not have the language-specific expertise to visualize the pertinence and potential of this initiative. By carefully and thoughtfully planning out pathways to meaningful collaboration, you can achieve commitment and support from various sources to bolster SoBL implementation. Partnerships take time to initiate and nurture, so those individuals leading SoBL efforts might carefully consider which stakeholders to prioritize and which to defer as future avenues of support.

Questions for Discussion and Reflection

1. Reflect and engage in discussion with your team. How can you extend your efforts in SoBL implementation beyond yourself or your department? How can you utilize the initiative to promote biliteracy more broadly across the school, district, and community? Discuss both the opportunities and the challenges to forging new partnerships.

2. Consider the current expertise in your school or district. What do teachers across grade levels and content areas know about language and biliteracy? To support students in achieving biliteracy, how can they infuse a language lens into their classroom practice? Use Tool 5.1 to gather related data directly from teachers.

3. What components are integral to developing and maintaining mutually beneficial school–community partnerships? What do you see

each partner committing to and receiving from the work? How would you assess the partnerships that you have now? What partnerships can you forge in the future? Use Tool 5.2 to brainstorm potential partners to support your progress toward your goals for SoBL implementation.

4. Amassing available resources is integral when implementing the SoBL. Use Tool 5.3 to discover different organizations that might support your work. What resources are available to you from national, state, and regional professional organizations? Connect with these groups via social media and email lists.

5. Biliteracy is an incredible asset for both college and career, and your SoBL efforts can receive significant support from colleges, universities, and businesses that eagerly await biliterate individuals from your school. Continue to add to Tool 5.3 with information on potential partners that might encourage students to pursue the SoBL to achieve college credit or job attainment following high school graduation.

Further Reading

- Borowczyk, M. (2020). Credentialing heritage: The role of community heritage language schools in implementing the Seal of Biliteracy. *Foreign Language Annals, 53*, 28–47. https://doi.org/10.1111/flan.12439

- Cohan, A., Honigsfeld, A., & Dove, M. G. (2019). *Team up, speak up, fire up! Educators, students, and the community working together to support English learners.* ASCD.

- Epstein, J. L., Sanders, M. G., Sheldon, S. B., Simon, B. S., Salinas, K. C., Jansorn, N. R., Voorhis, F. L. V., Martin, C. S., Thomas, B. G., Greenfeld, M., Hutchins, D. J., & Williams, K. J. (2019). *School, family, and community partnerships: Your handbook for action.* Corwin.

- Garcia, O., & Wei, L. (2014). *Translanguaging: Language, bilingualism, and education.* Palgrave Macmillan.

Tool 5.1. Auditing Teachers' Related Expertise

Directions: Use this tool to gather data on your colleagues' expertise related to language and biliteracy. You can (a) print and have teachers respond on paper copies or (b) transfer the prompts to an electronic survey and modify as desired.

PROMPTS	RATING STRONG (5) TO WEAK (1)				
Rate your knowledge of the following concepts:					
Students' language usage in homes and communities	5	4	3	2	1
Students' language abilities in English	5	4	3	2	1
Students' language abilities in other languages	5	4	3	2	1
The school's world language programming	5	4	3	2	1
The school's bilingual education programming	5	4	3	2	1
The Seal of Biliteracy initiative and recognition	5	4	3	2	1
Rate your classroom usage of the following strategies:					
Consider the language demands in disciplinary learning	5	4	3	2	1
Tap into students' languages as resources for learning	5	4	3	2	1
Connect vocabulary with cognates in other languages	5	4	3	2	1
Encourage students to use other languages	5	4	3	2	1
Scaffold instruction with a lens on language	5	4	3	2	1
Provide bilingual or home-language resources	5	4	3	2	1
Commend students' bilingualism and biliteracy	5	4	3	2	1

Circle topics you would be interested in learning more about:

Language demands in content-area instruction

Pedagogy that utilizes students' home languages

Ways to bridge students' multiple languages

Classroom environments that support bilingualism

Instructional materials that support bilingualism

The Seal of Biliteracy initiative and recognition

Opportunities to learn another language

Tool 5.2: Researching Potential Partners

Directions: Return to your goals for SoBL implementation. First, brainstorm the languages where you need to grow your programming and assessments to meet your goals. Then, use Google or another online search engine to brainstorm potential partners in the community. Finally, use the ideas presented in this chapter to chart out ideas and next steps for connecting and initiating mutually beneficial partnerships to support students' biliteracy.

FOCAL LANGUAGE What languages need attention to reach goals?	POTENTIAL PARTNER Who might support these efforts? Who is the contact?	KEY DETAILS AND NEXT STEPS How might we initiate a beneficial partnership?

Tool 5.3: Exploring Organizations and Resources

Directions: Use Google or another online search engine to ascertain state and regional affiliates working on language education in your area, as well as colleges, universities, and businesses who might support progress toward your goals for SoBL implementation. Note the organization's name and website. List available supports for SoBL implementation, such as professional development, conferences, networking opportunities, and other resources.

ORGANIZATION	NAME AND WEBSITE	AVAILABLE RESOURCES
Department of Education		
State Organization of World Language Educators		
State Organization of TESOL Educators		
State Organization of Bilingual Educators		
Colleges and Universities		
Businesses		
Language Specific Organizations		
Other Organizations		

Chapter 6
Promotion: Increasing Awareness to Expand Reach

Neeb was born in Thailand to Hmong parents and moved to Minnesota as a child. We met him shortly after he had taken the SoBL assessment but before he had received his results. He was nervous. His parents complained that he spoke English too frequently, which caused tension at home, so he hadn't told them about the SoBL. One year later, Neeb excitedly shared that he had earned a Platinum SoBL, saying that he "felt proud of himself." When he had received the letter sharing the accomplishment, he initially hid it from his parents to surprise them at the award ceremony hosted by the school. He described how proud they were when they arrived at the ceremony and learned about the recognition of his biliteracy in Hmong and English. Neeb reflected that it was worth coming to school on a Saturday to take the SoBL assessment. He said that the SoBL motivated him to learn more about his own culture. He also felt that the recognition would be useful for his International Business major.

Guiding Questions

What do students and their families need to know about the SoBL?

What are the best ways to advertise the SoBL to students and their families?

In what ways should programs recognize SoBL recipients?

In this chapter, we examine the fifth facet of the framework: *Promotion*. The SoBL initiative is still relatively young in the United States. While some states have been implementing the policy for upwards of a decade, others are in the first years of implementation and still others continue to work toward adoption. Remember that many states had adopted the SoBL before publication of the implementation guidelines (ACTFL et al., 2015), and that policies vary in small but significant ways across states (see Chapter 1). As a result, what an individual might hear about the SoBL in one state or local setting might vary from their own context. Some states have detailed implementation guides (e.g., Massachusetts) and even online learning modules (e.g., New York), while others offer little guidance beyond the formal state legislation or code. Thus, a critical facet of SoBL implementation is promoting the policy so that everyone involved understands it and uses those understandings to nurture and honor biliteracy.

Research on the SoBL emphasizes the need for promotion with explicit lenses on equity and access (Davin & Heineke, 2018; Davin et al., 2018). As described in previous chapters, stakeholders initiated the SoBL to rectify unequal access to language programming and opportunities to develop biliteracy, particularly for ELs and heritage language learners (García & Otheguy, 2017; Olsen, 2020). Nonetheless, the policy has been criticized in recent years for more often recognizing students who learned world languages in school than those like Neeb who learned languages other than English at home (Schwedhelm & King, 2020; Subtirelu et al., 2019). One cause of this issue relates to uneven or narrow promotion. Students enrolled in world language classes are more likely to hear about the SoBL and understand its requirements than their peers who are not (Davin & Heineke, 2018).

Figure 6.1. Stakeholders to Consider When Promoting the SoBL

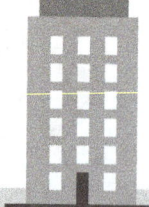

Administrators
Counselors
Teachers

Students
Families

Businesses
Community organizations
Postsecondary institutions

In this chapter, we describe how to promote the SoBL to ensure access, awareness, and opportunities for all students, including those like Neeb who are proficient in languages not taught in school. If you look back on the layers to consider when forging partnerships (Figure 5.1), you will see that SoBL promotion emerges in many of the same settings (Figure 6.1). In this chapter, we share examples and ideas from schools across the country for promoting the SoBL, including best practices for ensuring that all students and families know about the SoBL and its requirements. We explain the importance of promotion at the community level and discuss ways to reach these stakeholders. Finally, we conclude this chapter by describing ways in which districts and schools can recognize and celebrate SoBL recipients.

Considering Your Current Promotion

If you are new to SoBL implementation, this chapter offers ideas to think through and plan for SoBL promotion. Return to the interview that you conducted using Tool 1.2 with a neighboring district or school and re-examine how it promotes the SoBL and biliteracy. If you are working in a context that is already engaged in implementation, reflect on the ways that your district or school currently promotes the SoBL. Think about what information is shared, with whom it is shared, and who is involved in the sharing. What percentage of your faculty and staff know about the SoBL? What percentage of your students? What percentage of their parents? Think also about how you recognize students who receive the SoBL. Is their accomplishment lauded in the same ways as other honors in the school? Does your school recognize students at graduation? Do you inform their parents and the community of the accomplishment?

While there is no one best way to divide the promotional work of the SoBL, it must be collaborative. Administrators, counselors, and teachers must all comprehend the importance of the program to deliver a consistent message to students. Regardless of your role, as you read this chapter think about how you can contribute to expanding the word about the SoBL across the school and community, and how this work could be shared across the individuals in your context. With many voices and efforts promoting holistic SoBL efforts, including **_Purpose, Proficiency Assessments, Programs_**, and **_Partners_**, more students can be aware of the multifaceted efforts around biliteracy and determine whether and how they wish to pursue the recognition.

Developing Awareness Among School Colleagues

Justin embraced the opportunities and challenges that came with his role of leading SoBL implementation at Stevenson High School, a Midwest suburban high school with 4,000 students. With the state's legislation requiring public universities to give students credit for the SoBL, the initiative fit with the school's prioritization of college attainment. As department chair of ELs and world languages, Justin worked with all language teachers at the school, including ESL, French, German, Hebrew, Latin, Mandarin, and Spanish. He maintained regular communication with the principal and director of curriculum to maintain support for the SoBL, particularly funding for the various assessments needed for less commonly taught languages.

A second challenge came with building his colleagues' awareness of the SoBL, a critical step for recruiting students both inside and outside of language programming. Justin began with faculty in his department, facilitating professional development around best practices in teaching ELs and world languages and providing updates on expanding assessment offerings in meetings with teachers. He also connected with faculty overseeing various cultural clubs, including the Polish, Hebrew, and Indian student organizations. Recognizing the integral role of school counselors, he held lunch-and-learn sessions to share information about the SoBL, such as a session focused on the new Hindi and Polish portfolio assessments. Whereas language teachers could recruit in their classes, he saw counselors as critical to spreading the word more broadly to students (Fisk, 2020).

SoBL promotion begins at the school, where administrators and faculty must be knowledgeable about the program. In schools with the most successful outcomes in implementing the SoBL, efforts extend beyond one person or department to collaborative engagement of various educators (Heineke & Davin, 2021). Like Justin at Stevenson High School, those leading SoBL efforts must seek to engage administrators, counselors, and teachers—developing and maintaining awareness of the recognition to prevent siloes and enhance the initiative's reach across the school. In this section, we focus on promotion within the school, exploring who should be involved and how to build colleagues' awareness of the program.

Involving Pertinent Colleagues Administrators oversee the operations of a school, making them central to dissemination of communication across stakeholders, as well as prioritization of time, space, and resources. With appropriate buy-in and awareness, principals, assistant principals, deans, and directors use their roles to enhance the reach of the initiative, such as including important information in regular communications with students, parents, and educators. Using budgetary discretion, leaders can provide resources such as flyers and materials for learning sessions and award celebrations. They can also free up time for individuals to focus on SoBL implementation. As department chair, Justin connects regularly with administrators, who are keenly aware of the recognition and eager to enhance access as the SoBL connects to the high school's goals for college preparedness among its linguistically diverse student population. Admin-

istrators facilitate several logistics, such as parent communication and award ceremonies, as well as free up Justin's time to focus on SoBL logistics and departmental efforts.

Counselors often have a touchpoint with every student in a given school, which makes them integral to communicating recognition details across the student body. They are likely to know or have access to students' language backgrounds and to have knowledge of their future aspirations. Thus, counselors are a critical link in encouraging students to pursue the SoBL, especially for ELs or other students not in world language classes who might not hear about the SoBL otherwise. To fill this role, counselors need to be aware of (a) SoBL requirements, (b) testing dates, and (c) available funds to pay for proficiency assessments. They should also know (d) which colleges and universities award credit for the SoBL, and (e) how tiers of the SoBL, when applicable, correspond to credit. At his large suburban public high school, Justin recognizes counselors as integral to capturing the many students who use another language at home. By partnering with counselors, he extends the reach and equity of the initiative.

Districts should seek bilingual counselors whenever possible. If a school has a high population of students who speak the same language, a counselor who speaks that language can be a great asset in supporting students and families. Even without a shared heritage language, a multilingual counselor's knowledge of another language and culture is an asset to any school.

In our research, students consistently cite teachers as one of the biggest influences in their decision to pursue the SoBL (Davin & Heineke, 2018; Davin, 2021a). Language teachers, including those in world language, bilingual, and EL classrooms, connect directly to the initiative and have the most urgency to be aware of implementation details. Many of the students we have interviewed reported that they learned about the SoBL from teachers who knew they were bilingual and encouraged them to take the SoBL assessment. But beyond encouraging students to take the SoBL assessment, teachers across K-12 schools are instrumental in validating heritage languages. All teachers need to understand that first language literacy is critical to second language literacy and that language is inextricably tied to identity (Norton & Toohey, 2011). Small actions like allowing students to use home languages in the classroom or asking students about their cultural and linguistic identities go a long way in supporting students' bilingual identities, which ultimately bolsters the number of students demonstrating biliteracy.

Building and Maintaining Awareness Involving stakeholders within school buildings starts with building awareness. This needs to be done strategically to inform colleagues without overwhelming them or demanding extensive time and effort. Anyone who works in schools knows the heavy workload of every person in the building: administrators have a hand in every pot, and other educators do all that comes with their roles while also sponsoring clubs, coaching sports, tutoring students, and leading initiatives in their fields of expertise. Just as the bilingual or world language department might lead SoBL efforts, the special education team drives inclusion efforts, the history department spearheads civics efforts, social workers facilitate social-emotional learning efforts, and counselors steer college readiness efforts. But these efforts cut across schools, making it key to break down siloes between departments. The goal should be to make colleagues aware of important information in a streamlined manner that respects their unique roles, responsibilities, and workloads.

The first step is to build initial awareness. Tool 6.1 can support brainstorming of the various stakeholders in the school building who might contribute to SoBL efforts and goals in order to seek out their support and partnership. Like the trajectory of dialogue with district administrators, the conversation might begin with general information on the SoBL, research regarding the benefits of biliteracy, and local goals for implementation before moving into specific asks to support implementation. Because colleagues wear multiple hats and have other initiatives to maneuver, it is important to be specific on what they can do to support the initiative and provide resources to aid in their work. For example, Justin initiated in-school partnerships via individual meetings with administrators, followed by lunch-and-learn sessions with counselors where he provided an easily utilizable one-pager with key information like available languages and testing dates. Justin has discovered the value of targeting specific individuals or groups of colleagues when building awareness, so he holds smaller meetings to allow for more personal conversations focused on each person's unique role and potential contributions.

Deficit-based presumptions may exist in schools and directly influence how educators define their expectations for students, including students of color and those labeled as ELs. When working with educators, you may first need to deconstruct existing assumptions to ensure that colleagues embrace the linguistic assets of all students and the potential for all students to develop biliteracy.

Following initial touchpoints with internal stakeholders, efforts should shift to keeping everyone aware of the latest information so that they can then share with students and families. We recommend selecting a medium already being used to share information across the school site, such as the monthly faculty newsletter, weekly email blast, or blogs on the school website. Regular updates might include (a) upcoming testing dates, (b) any new languages being offered for testing, (c) the number of students taking tests and receiving recognition, (d) exciting innovations to programming and practices, and (e) featured SoBL recipients with stories on future plans for college and career. In addition to providing periodic updates, you might also invite colleagues to formal events and celebrations involving the SoBL, which can maintain their enthusiasm and recognize their contributions toward the initiative.

Conveying Information to Students and Their Families

Sycamore School District (a pseudonym) is a culturally and linguistically diverse school district in suburban Illinois. During focus group interviews with high school students who had taken the SoBL assessment, Sean (a pseudonym), the world language coordinator, was surprised to hear students consistently report not telling their parents about the SoBL. Some students described tension at home related to their primary use of English instead of the home language and explained that they didn't want to tell their parents about the program until they knew whether they had passed the SoBL assessment. Others who had already received their results described how excited their parents became after learning that their children had earned the SoBL.

Several years later, the language coordinator reached out to us to follow up. He now offers a Parent World Language Night once a semester to discuss language proficiency, the SoBL, and the district's world language programming. At the meeting, Sean discusses the concept of proficiency and shares information with parents about the (a) sequence of study available in the district, (b) levels of proficiency students are expected to reach, and (c) requirements for the recognition. He shares past data from the SoBL assessments and explains how they correspond to the available sequences of study. He also provides parents with information regarding the logistics of the SoBL assessments, including how students can sign up.

While we know that a common barrier to consistently graduating biliterate students relates to language programming and curriculum (see Chapter 4), another common barrier is a lack of information about how to receive the recognition (Davin & Heineke, 2018). In our research in Illinois, most students knew that they could earn college credit with the SoBL, but few could explain how to earn a SoBL. Students did not realize that they had to demonstrate English proficiency as well as world language proficiency. They knew that they had to take a test of the world language, but they did not know what types of tasks or questions were on the test. In this way, the SoBL existed as an enigmatic initiative within the school—students knew it existed, but the details for achieving it remained unclear.

In addition to students' lack of clarity, many parents are unaware of the SoBL, as demonstrated in the vignette with Sycamore. During a focus group in another context, a woman attending as a translator expressed shock that she had not heard of the SoBL. As the parent of a child at the same high school, she could not believe that her daughter had not told her about the recognition. We were less surprised; in our many focus groups over the years, students report not informing their parents, particularly those who speak heritage languages, due to tensions at home related to language use (Davin, 2021a). Some students, like Neeb described in the opening vignette, are afraid to tell their parents about the SoBL in case they do not score high enough on the SoBL assessment, which might exacerbate the situation. While parents may have access to information about the SoBL from other outlets, it can get lost in the sea of competing initiatives in schools. As educators, we must communicate frequently, early, and in various languages with parents about the SoBL so that they can encourage their children's biliteracy development.

What Students and Their Families Need to Know

To promote the SoBL, students and their families require as much information as possible about the SoBL program and process. Our research has shown that students often know much less about the SoBL than administrators and teachers realize, which can deter their participation (Davin, 2021a; Davin & Heineke, 2018). For students, especially ELs, the decision to take an additional high-stakes test to receive the SoBL is not an easy one (Davin, 2021a). In many contexts, students must pay for their own SoBL assessment, and families may be reluctant to do so unless they understand the potential benefits. Thus, it is important to provide all relevant information before asking students to voluntarily take and pay for a test, especially a test that assesses something as personal as a heritage language. We use the four previous framework facets to shape communication, including (a) *Purpose*, benefits, and requirements, (b) the logistics and caveats of *Proficiency Assessments*, (c) proficiency and *Programming* for biliteracy development, and (d) *Partners* and opportunities for collaboration.

Purpose Students and their families need to know the purpose of the SoBL, its potential benefits, and its requirements. In one district, educators implemented the SoBL to (a) convey multilingualism as an asset, (b) provide opportunities to earn college credit, and (c) promote racial equity (Hancock & Davin, 2020). They shared these purposes across the school, to homes, and throughout the community to promote the policy. When we asked students at this district about the benefits of the SoBL, almost everyone talked about college credit. As this example illustrates, the purpose of the SoBL and its benefits likely connect. Other benefits mentioned by students in other contexts include high school credit, college credit, employability, increased confidence in language skills, data for instructional decision making, and proof of language proficiency (Davin & Heineke, 2018; Davin et al., 2018; Hancock & Davin, 2020).

You have already defined your purpose for SoBL implementation (see Chapter 2). In addition to the larger purpose of the efforts as conceptualized by school and district stakeholders, you can seek the perspectives of students and families. Consider reaching out to former students who received the SoBL to ask them how the recognition has benefitted them, invite them to speak with current students, or encourage them to create a video in their world language sharing their perspective. You might also search YouTube for videos in which students and families discuss their perceptions of the SoBL. These motivational lenses on purpose and benefits can be shared with students and parents alongside information on the requirements of the SoBL in your state (see Chapter 1), such as required levels of language proficiency and evidence of world language and English proficiency.

 **Heritage language learners and ELs are less likely to know about the SoBL than world lanaguage learners (Davin & Heineke, 2018). To ensure equity, administrators, counselors, and teachers must promote the SoBL far and wide and in a variety of languages, rather than solely through world language programming.**

Proficiency Assessments Students and their families need logistical information about the assessment process, including the required steps and timeline to receive the SoBL. For example, some schools require students to submit applications early in the school year stating that they intend to pursue the SoBL. Although they represent an additional hurdle for students, applications can promote the opportunity and allow schools to better prepare for how many tests are needed and in what languages. Students and families also need to know (a) when and where the test is offered, (b) how long the test takes, (c) how to sign up, and (d) how much they need to pay. The topic of cost can be a sensitive one. As we have suggested in previous chapters, districts should make every effort to pay for these assessments, particularly for families with low incomes.

Additionally, all stakeholders need to understand the limitations of language proficiency assessments. Pertinent for approaching all tests in all content areas, *critical testing literacy* aims to help stakeholders and students understand the shortcomings of assessments. For example, the French spoken in Canada and the French Creole spoken in Louisiana are quite different from the French measured by most SoBL assessments. A student proficient in one of these other language varieties or dialects might struggle on a SoBL assessment. Educators should recognize that tests can have important implications for students' identity formation, especially for ELs whom such tests might label as not proficient

in their home languages (Davin, 2021a). Sharing assessment pitfalls with students and families can serve to alleviate these tensions and make visible the problematic nature of the SoBL relying solely upon formal assessments (Valdés, 2020).

Proficiency and Programming To understand SoBL requirements and assessments, students and families need to understand language proficiency, including the proficiency levels required for the SoBL across domains (listening, reading, speaking, writing). Whereas students enrolled in world language classes might be familiar with the construct of proficiency, others might not. Our research has shown that heritage language learners may choose not to take the SoBL assessment due to a fear of not scoring highly enough. For example, one student explained that he did not take the SoBL assessment because he struggled with spelling in Spanish—a struggle that likely would not have hindered his ability to receive the recognition (Davin, 2021a). Informational sessions should explain proficiency and provide texts at various proficiency levels so students can self-assess their proficiency. Another effective way to help students make an informed decision is to use a self-assessment checklist (see Appendix 2).

As students reflect on their proficiency in various languages, educators can also provide information on various language programs that support biliteracy development. As described in Chapter 4, this is where the SoBL holds untapped potential and can go beyond an insignia stamped on transcripts or diplomas (Schwedhelm & King, 2020). If students and families believe in the purpose (biliteracy development) and understand the means to achieve the recognition (proficiency assessment), then you also want to provide them with paths to achieve their goals. To do so, you can provide information about the SoBL itself with details on language programs to pursue in school and community settings, as well as different avenues for developing and maintaining languages in homes.

Partners and Collaboration In addition to passing information along to students, parents, and families, invite them to serve as partners in these efforts. Through our work across the country, we have seen parents and families play integral roles in SoBL implementation (Heineke & Davin, 2021). In many districts, parents and family members have emerged as instrumental in helping to find evaluators for alternative assessments of less commonly used or tested languages. In the Morton School District,

Melody invites parents to capture their pride and joy in their children's biliteracy in videos. As you share information on the multifaceted SoBL efforts in your context, be sure to frame them as flexible and collaborative so that parents and family members see themselves as part of the efforts. Encourage them to ask questions, share information, and contribute their perspectives to shape ongoing implementation.

How to Advertise the SoBL to Students To ensure that all students know about the SoBL, educators should consider using multiple outlets to convey information (Fisk, 2020). It is not enough to advertise the SoBL in world language courses or language clubs; promotion should extend across the school. You might also advertise in a variety of languages. Even though students pursuing the SoBL are likely proficient in English, posters or videos in other languages may draw more attention and interest. Table 6.1 lists ways that schools and districts often promote the SoBL.

Table 6.1. Ways to Promote the SoBL to Students

- Create a link from the school's webpage that provides information
- Advertise testing opportunities via social media
- Create an informational video
- Host student interest meetings
- Hang posters around the school in multiple languages
- Advertise in the school's news show or daily announcements
- Invite previous SoBL recipients to talk about their experiences
- Invite previous SoBL recipients to record videos about earning the SoBL
- Advertise in world language, bilingual, and EL classes
- Advertise in advisory or homeroom periods
- Include item in student advising surveys asking about intentions to pursue the SoBL

Beyond advertisements intended for all students, targeted invitations can also increase participation. An informal "You should really pursue this!" from a student's counselor or teacher can be impactful, especially for students who have been disenfranchised by U.S. schooling and may not be accustomed to participating in school programs. Formal individualized efforts are also important. One SoBL coordinator noticed that a school in her district yielded few recognitions despite the linguistically diverse student population. After reviewing Home Language Survey data, she decided to send personalized invitations to all students who had indicated other languages spoken in homes. She printed and sent invitations to families and students, along with the application to take the SoBL assessment. Another SoBL coordinator sends letters throughout the school year telling students which criteria they have met and which they still need to meet. For example, a student who has already passed the SAT is told that they are halfway there and only need to pass the world language assessment.

The timing of advertising is also critical. Promotion needs to begin early so that students have time to plan and prepare. In our research, most students indicated that they did not learn about the SoBL until their senior year of high school, at which point it was too late for them to develop biliteracy and receive the SoBL prior to graduation (Davin & Heineke, 2018). Some students lamented that had they known about the opportunity, they would have practiced particular domains of language more (Davin, 2021a). Minimally, educators should inform students and families about the SoBL when they arrive in high school, but ideally, students need information even earlier. Knowledge that the SoBL exists can send the early and critical message that educators recognize and care about students' home languages and cultures. This message can encourage students and their families to seek out programs and pathways to develop biliteracy.

How to Advertise the SoBL to Families Many of the ways that we recommend advertising the SoBL to students also apply to advertising to families, although it becomes even more important to communicate information in a variety of languages. Table 6.2 displays ideas for informing families about the recognition. We recommend reaching out to partners in the community for help with communication. Community language schools or local universities may be able to recommend individuals who can serve as translators at parent meetings or who can dub informational videos. These same individuals, or perhaps even your students, can also be invaluable resources for translating items like informational flyers or posters. Some districts and schools, like Stevenson High School described in a previous vignette, have a ***Bilingual Parent Advisory Committee (BPAC)***, a committee composed of parents of ELs at the school that works with educators to make programmatic decisions. These types of organizations can help promote the SoBL to families in the community.

In addition to logistical considerations, you also want to reflect upon parents' and families' perspectives on biliteracy development, particularly for those who use languages other than English at home. As reflected in the vignettes above, families often have strong viewpoints on language use, ranging from those who wish for their children to maintain their home language to those who prefer that their children learn and use English to avoid societal stigmas that they may have faced (e.g., Surrain, 2018). Educators seeking to advertise the SoBL to families need to be aware of these complexities and frame the initiative to demonstrate its value and benefits. For parents who want their children to maintain their home language, the SoBL can serve to realize those aspirations by giving additional, school-based encouragement to students. For families who want kids to learn primarily English at school, the SoBL can reinforce the value of their home language and demonstrate how both languages can serve their children's learning, development, and achievements inside and outside of school. Involving parents and families as active and collaborative partners is an integral step to welcoming these diverse perspectives and allowing them to shape SoBL implementation.

We recommend that stakeholders use Tool 6.2 to create a promotion plan for rolling out information about the SoBL to students and their families, including methods, point persons, and types of information. Some methods might provide an overview of the SoBL (e.g., informational videos, school webpage) and others should include logistical information about testing (e.g., posters, daily announcements). As you draft your plan, remember the importance of building awareness early. Parents can support language development in a variety of ways. Learning about the SoBL long before their child's graduation can encourage more use of the heritage language at home, the procurement of additional texts in the heritage language, or supplemental language classes at community language organizations. Additionally, by gleaning parents' perspectives and insights in early grade levels, you can shape your subsequent implementation efforts to respond to their unique desires and goals. The **Purpose** of SoBL implementation, as well as the **Proficiency Assessments, Programs, Partners**, and **Promotion** enacted to achieve that purpose, should dynamically change to maintain the best interests of students, families, and communities.

Enhancing Communication with Communities

Susy, the world language coordinator of Forest School District (pseudonyms), has made it her mission to ensure that all teachers, students, and families know about the SoBL and how to achieve it. At the beginning of each school year, she sends a PowerPoint describing the SoBL for department leads, to present to their teachers, including (a) what it is, (b) how to earn it, (c) how it came about, (d) recent data, and (e) how many recipients each school had the previous year. The teachers at every school in the district then give the same presentation to students during the advisory period. Susy keeps a district webpage about the program updated, sends multiple emails about the program to families each year, and sends text messages that remind students and their parents/guardians to sign up for language assessments.

Susy also engages in community outreach. She provides posters in various languages to hang throughout schools in her district and encourages administration to advertise the opportunity in morning announcements. She also hosts booths at local events, such as parent/teacher nights. She works with colleagues in the dual credit office to advertise the SoBL to local colleges in the area,

Table 6.2. Ways to Promote the SoBL to Families

- Send an informational flyer to each student's home in the home language
- Create a link from the school's webpage that provides information in a variety of languages
- Advertise testing opportunities via social media in a variety of languages
- Host a webinar about the program that includes time for questions
- Post an informational video with captions in a variety of languages
- Host parent interest meetings with translators available
- Hang posters around the school in multiple languages

some of whom offer students credit for SoBL attainment. She tells students that spending $20 on a SoBL test could save them as much as $1,000 in college tuition. Annually, she participates in a program at a local university where the parents of eighth graders are invited to attend and learn about high school. Susy offers a session on the SoBL where parents can learn all about the program and receive handouts and literature.

Moving beyond the school and the home, stakeholders can strengthen SoBL implementation and the impact of the recognition through promotion efforts across the community. Promotion should include local community language organizations, businesses, and institutions of higher education (IHEs). As described in Chapter 5, these partners can support implementation by providing resources to facilitate testing but are also important in ensuring that the SoBL is impactful beyond high school graduation. In this section, we discuss ways to spread the word in the community.

Spreading the Word Around the Community
Community language schools are integral partners due to their interest in language and culture preservation; however, because the SoBL is relatively new, organizations may be unaware of the initiative. When the MNTS Tamil School, presented in a vignette in Chapter 5, learned about the SoBL, the director began working to make it available for students in the Saturday school. He and his teachers collaborated with the Minnesota Department of Education (MDE) to create a Tamil test and with both MDE and ACTFL to train raters. The school now offers the assessment to its students, reports the results to students' school districts, and awards college scholarships to SoBL recipients. Participation in the SoBL has improved the school's enrollment, motivating many students to continue the study of Tamil into high school (Davin et al., 2019). We are often contacted by other community language schools who are interested in offering the SoBL but require additional information.

You can also reach out to nearby colleges and universities, including modern language departments and schools of education (see Chapter 5). If your students consistently attend a few institutions in your region or state, then reach out to ensure those IHEs' awareness about the SoBL. Although many colleges and universities are leveraging the SoBL for placement and credit in world language coursework, more are not (Davin, 2021b). Nonetheless, we have found that most IHEs eagerly embrace the SoBL, which promotes world language study and helps appropriately place students in coursework. By looping in these stakeholders and providing information about the SoBL, as well as inviting them to SoBL events, you might initiate their work to use the SoBL for placement or credit, while you encourage more students to consider the SoBL in pursuit of postsecondary goals.

Finally, you can connect with businesses and future employers, bringing them into the communication loop about SoBL recipients in your school or district. One of the original goals of the SoBL initiative was to provide potential employers with a clear sign of students' biliteracy. Nonetheless, many companies remain unaware of the recognition, which results in them not taking advantage of this indicator in recruitment and hiring decisions. While information is beginning to spread to IHEs, less is being done with potential employers. An exemplary model is the work being done in Missouri, where stakeholders are explaining the SoBL to major employers in the state and seeking letters of endorsement (see Chapter 5). We encourage others to follow a similar model to connect with businesses and enlist their support. You might prioritize companies in your community that hire students following graduation, such as the call center where Kaaha secured a job, as described in the vignette that starts this book.

Extending Beyond Your Context Through Social Media Many states, districts, and schools leverage social media to promote the SoBL to a wide audience. Social media offers an easy way to get messages, pictures, or videos out to faculty, students, families, and the larger community. By tagging community language organizations, state language organizations, or even the broader SealofBiliteracy.org, educators expand promotional efforts to wider audiences. Social media also allows for the promotion of the SoBL in many languages. Platforms such as Facebook can automatically translate posts into the viewer's language.

One of the most popular social media outlets for this type of promotion is Twitter. Table 6.3 shows a selection of various Tweets that promote the SoBL. Programs and individuals post tweets to (a) promote the program and celebrate SoBL recipients (e.g., gadoeworldlanguages, 2021), (b) explain implementation (e.g., Budke, 2020), and (c) advocate for more equitable implementation (e.g., Swartzloff, 2019).

Tweets like that of Cisneros (2019), whose audience is the parents of elementary school students, are an excellent way to promote the SoBL early. Perhaps our favorite is the final Tweet in Table 6.3, one from a student tweeting out her accomplishment and stat-

Table 6.3. Tweets That Promote the SoBL

- Congratulations to Daisy for qualifying to receive the first Spanish Seal of Biliteracy in the history of Seminole County! The Seal is available to Ga students in over 100 languages. Yearly, 2,000+ graduating seniors in Ga earn the Seal of Biliteracy in over 20 languages. [Picture of student included] (gadoeworldlanguages, 2021)

- It's #BilingualSeal testing season. Testing looks a bit different this yr w/ #covid19wl, but sharing my #2bilit2quit presentation about how we implement in my district #langchat #leadwithlanguages @mctlc ...[attached presentation] (Budke, 2020)

- Illinois, it's time to take a stand and provide equity for English learners and their WL learner peers. Let's start by making the English requirement more attainable on the IL State Seal of Biliteracy. @ISBEnews [linked to Education Week post] (Swartzloff, 2019)

- First day of school on the path to greatness! #Kindergarten #DualLanguage #bilingualism #DualLanguageRocks #LetsDoThis #BilingualSeal [Picture of kindergartener attached along with picture of SoBL emblem] (Cisneros, 2019)

- My pampo would be proud! #bilingualseal #graduation #happy #30days #18schooldays #may18 #fluent [linked to Instagram post] (Khiana, 2013)

ing that her *pampo*, an affectionate name in Spanish for a grandfather, would be proud (Khiana, 2013).

Another media platform through which districts and schools promote the SoBL is YouTube. Table 6.4 shows a selection of YouTube videos that promote the SoBL. Organizations like Californians Together (2018) have posted videos on YouTube to advocate the importance of bilingualism. Departments of education in states like Ohio and New York posted videos to explain the SoBL in those states. High schools like Farrington, featured in the Baliang America (2019) video, share videos of award ceremonies and discuss the importance of expanding access to less commonly tested languages. And finally, students often post videos about their accomplishment and what it means to them (e.g., Swartzloff, 2020).

Recognizing and Celebrating Students' Accomplishments

Abdi (a pseudonym) arrived to the United States when he was eight, proficient in Somali and just beginning to learn English. He explained that school was challenging, especially at first, because all of his classes were in English. When he heard about the SoBL, he was surprised to learn of the opportunity to take a test in Somali. Abdi decided to sign up to take the test but didn't mention it to his parents, who he explained were giving him a hard time for not speaking Somali at home with his siblings. He did not have a lot of experience reading or writing in Somali and was worried that

Table 6.4. YouTube Videos That Promote the SoBL

VIDEO TITLE	DESCRIPTION
The Seal of Biliteracy—Celebrating Students for the 21st Century (Californians Together, 2018)	Individuals from Californians Together, the advocacy group that began the SoBL, explain the SoBL and the importance of biliteracy.
ODE: Introducing Ohio's Seal of Biliteracy Program (Ohio Department of Education, 2017)	Administrator from Ohio's Department of Education explains the SoBL and its requirements.
Filipino students in Hawaii honored with Seal of Biliteracy (Baliang America, 2019)	Individuals from W. R. Farrington High School in Hawaii talk about how the program began and how they recognized students who spoke Tagalog and Ilocano.
Why earn your Seal of Biliteracy? (Swartzloff, 2020)	Two graduating SoBL recipients discuss why other students should pursue the SoBL.

he might not pass. Therefore, he didn't want to get his parents' hopes up. Abdi was thrilled to learn he had passed the test and earned a SoBL.

Abdi and his family were invited to a celebration at the end of the school year to recognize his accomplishment. The auditorium was packed with families speaking many different languages. Abdi's parents, grandmother, and four siblings came. They watched from the school auditorium as Abdi's name was called and he received a sash noting his accomplishment to wear at graduation. Local reporters were in attendance; the newspaper wrote a story about the event, and the nightly news aired a segment highlighting the ceremony.

A key aspect of SoBL promotion lies in celebrating students who receive the recognition. Such recognition is important to fulfilling the original purpose of the SoBL—to change deficit-based views of biliteracy. Each time stakeholders make biliteracy visible and elevate its status across the school, they chip away at the monolingualism that typically dominates the U.S. educational system (Crawford, 2000; Valdés, 2018; Valdez et al., 2016). Table 6.5 shows common ways that schools recognize SoBL recipients.

Table 6.5. Ways to Recognize SoBL Recipients

- Awards ceremony
- Notation on transcript
- Emblem on diploma
- Letter sent to parents and guardians
- Cord, sash, or medallion worn at graduation
- Announcement in local newspaper
- Announcement via social media
- Announcement on website or electronic billboard
- Notification to board of education
- Invitation to awardees to speak to younger students about the program
- Recorded video recognizing attainees

The most common way of recognizing SoBL recipients is with a notation on the transcript. This notation is often accompanied by a special emblem adhered to the diploma. These gestures are import-ant, but they are not enough to send the message that biliteracy is lauded or to build hype around the program. A ceremony like the one that Abdi attended can reinforce the message that schools recognize and honor multilingualism and ensure that students, their siblings, their families, and others in the community know about the program.

For some students, earning the SoBL may be one of the first times they receive recognition in school, so the recognition needs to be accompanied with the accolades and attention deserving of achieving biliteracy. In one heart-breaking anecdote, a colleague relayed that a student's parent called to make sure that the recognition was not an error, stating that her son "did not usually win awards." Additionally, in states where a student can earn the SoBL via seat time in lieu of a language assessment, we have met students who did not realize that they had earned the SoBL. Holding an awards ceremony is a wonderful way to build hype around the program and increase awareness, hopefully leading to increased participation.

One simple way to recognize students is to give all SoBL recipients a special cord or sash to wear around their neck with their robe at graduation, similar to honors cords. This practice sends the message that biliteracy is synonymous with doing well in school and maintaining high grades. Rather than cords or sashes, some districts instead give students medallions that are worn at graduation to recognize their SoBL attainment. In high school settings, these celebrations and recognitions tied to graduation (e.g., diplomas, transcripts, senior award ceremonies) provide students and families with deserving sources of pride and accomplishment.

Promoting the SoBL Through Pathway Recognitions If you are implementing the SoBL in K-12 settings, you do not want to wait until senior year to celebrate students' biliteracy. To enhance implementation and participation in language programming, you can incorporate opportunities to commend students' developing language skills across their schooling trajectory. As described in previous chapters, pathway recognitions are an excellent way to build hype around the SoBL and ensure that students learn about it early in their schooling.

Framingham Public Schools in Massachusetts have embraced the pathways initiative due to its alignment with the district's vision to prepare "each student to learn and live productively as a critically-thinking, responsible citizen in a multicultural, democratic society" (Santos, 2019, n.p.). Serving families from 72 language backgrounds, educators offer dual-language programs in Spanish and Portuguese starting in preschool, as well as world language programs in Spanish, French, Italian, Latin, and Mandarin in middle and high school. Pathway recognitions provide an opportunity to recognize the developing biliteracy of all students, including those who speak heritage languages other than those formally offered in schools. Using the Language Opportunity Coalition's (2021) designations for participation, attainment, and achievement, they recognize students' biliteracy at the end of elementary school in 5th grade, at the end of middle school in 8th grade, and at the end of high school in 12th grade. In addition to students who receive LOC pathway recognition, the district bestows its own investment award on individuals who do not meet state requirements but still commit to biliteracy development.

As you seek to promote the SoBL, consider how pathway recognitions might be incorporated as part of these efforts. You might start by revisiting your state's SoBL policy to determine whether pathways have been fleshed out in your context. If so, those details can support determination of the pathway options (participation, attainment, achievement), grade levels (preschool, elementary, middle school), and related assessments. The national SoBL organization (www.sealofbiliteracy.org) also has valuable information for all schools and districts seeking to initiate pathway recognitions, including ideas for varied assessments (e.g., oral presentation, reading log, written essay) and sample documents from exemplar districts (e.g., pathway application). As you consider the various facets of this work throughout this book, maintain a longitudinal lens on biliteracy development and consider these pathways as a potential and central component of SoBL implementation. By extending trajectories and increasing recognition for students' ongoing language development, districts and schools can effectively promote and nurture students' biliteracy over time.

Districts and schools with pathway programs might consider recognitions and celebrations as students advance along the pathway toward earning the SoBL. Smaller forms of recognition along the way, such as a special luncheon, can increase other students' and parents' awareness. Such recognition might also encourage additional students to begin studying another language early enough in their schooling to enroll in language courses and work toward biliteracy.

Chapter Summary

In this chapter, we shared the final facet of the framework, centered on **Promoting** the SoBL within schools, homes, and communities. Drawing upon our research and experiences related to what students and teachers report as barriers to SoBL access, such as advertising, we provided recommendations on how to overcome these barriers. We also described the importance in building hype around the SoBL to encourage students to enroll in language programming and sign up for the required assessments. Schools across the country have found success in advertising through regular school communications and websites, as well as through social media that expands SoBL promotion beyond the walls of the school building to a wider audience. We concluded with ideas for how educators might celebrate the accomplishments of SoBL recipients to encourage biliteracy development and maintenance across the school and community.

Questions for Discussion and Reflection

1. As a team, discuss who can support promotional efforts for this work in your context. Use Tool 6.1 to reflect on relevant stakeholders who might assist in promotion of the SoBL. Consider the current responsibilities of this individual within the system as well as how they might potentially contribute to SoBL promotion.

2. Brainstorm ways that you and your colleagues can promote the SoBL. Using Tool 6.2, create an action plan for who oversees each communication outlet and when it should occur. List the languages in which you need to create advertisements.

3. Create a list of the contact information for the chairs of modern language departments at the colleges and universities where many of your students attend. Reach out to these individuals to inquire about whether they are aware of the SoBL and whether it is used for placement decisions or credit determinations.

Further Reading

- Davin, K. J., Heineke, A. J., & Egnatz, L. (2018). The Seal of Biliteracy: Successes and challenges to implementation. *Foreign Language Annals, 51*(2),1–15. https://doi.org/10.1111/flan.12336

- Deal, T. E., & Peterson, K. D. (2016). *Shaping school culture* (3rd ed.). Jossey-Bass.

- Marichal, N., Roldán, A. R., & Coady, M. (2021). "My language learners seemed like ghosts": A rural teacher's transformational journey implementing the Seal of Biliteracy. *The Rural Educator, 42*(1), 52-56. https://doi.org/10.35608/ruraled. v42i1.1180

Tool 6.1. Reflecting on Relevant Stakeholders

Directions: Reflect upon relevant stakeholders in your context. Examples include administrators, counselors, classroom teachers, resource teachers, instructional coaches, school psychologists, clerks, paraprofessionals, and parent and family liaisons. List important stakeholders in your context and brainstorm how each might contribute to SoBL implementation.

ROLE List the various colleagues in the school building.	RESPONSIBILITIES What does this person do for our school community?	POTENTIAL CONTRIBUTIONS How might this role contribute to SoBL efforts?

Tool 6.2. Promotion Plan

Directions: Brainstorm ways that you can promote the SoBL to students and families. Using the information you included in Table 6.1, create an action plan for who is in charge of each communication outlet and when it should occur. List the languages in which you need to advertise.

MONTH	ACTIVITY	LEADER
August	Ex. Send video to all language teachers, including English, that explains the SoBL	Ex. Susy Brinkworth (District language coordinator)
September		
October		
November		
December		
January		
February		
March		
April		
May		
June		
July		

Chapter 7
Moving Forward: Implementing and Evaluating Efforts

During a focus group, we asked students what schools could do to better support their language development. Faduma, a Somali student, explained that the school needed to improve language programming. She said that they needed to add more language classes, "because they don't have an Arabic class, they don't have a Somali class, they don't have a Thai class, and I feel like you should give the students more options on which language they want to take, instead of the basics of Spanish, Chinese, French." For those language classes that did exist, she wished for improvement. She said that the school should "offer a more rigorous language program, because what they have right now, it doesn't help you learn the language at all." She explained that she "took two years of Spanish and [couldn't] remember anything besides, 'Can I go to the bathroom?'" She expressed her desire that the school "have the requirement higher on how many language classes [one must take], how many years, and also have a language program that's just as rigorous as a college language class."

Guiding Questions

How can stakeholders initiate and refine SoBL implementation in schools?

What key features and planning stages encompass the action planning process?

In what ways can individuals advocate for equity in SoBL implementation?

To begin this final chapter, we return to the premise that undergirds this entire book: that all students should have the opportunity to develop home and additional languages in school. Historically, this has not been the norm in U.S. schools, but the rapid and voluntary adoption of SoBL policies across the states over the last 10 years suggests readiness for change. Previous research has indicated the potential of the SoBL to combat subtractive schooling practices, validate students' home languages and cultures, and promote the development of world and heritage language programs (Castro, 2020; Davin et al., 2018; DeLeon & Lavandez, 2020; Heineke & Davin, 2021; Marichal et al., 2021). While the accomplishments of policymakers, advocates, educators, and community members in policy adoption are profound, variations in the SoBL from one state to another present challenges. States and districts are left to grapple with the implementational details, such as how to support and assess languages not commonly taught in schools. The challenge of doing so often creates inequities in which only students proficient in commonly taught languages can receive the SoBL. Such inequitable implementation threatens the potential of the SoBL overall.

With this context in mind, this text aims to support educators in implementing the SoBL with a lens on equity. Because the SoBL emerged as a grassroots and unfunded initiative, local educators often find themselves working to implement the recognition with relatively little guidance. With this book, we seek to detail the work of various students, educators, scholars, and other stakeholders involved in implementing the SoBL in contexts across the United States. Whether you are initiating or revising your efforts, we hope that this book has invigorated your excitement and desire to engage in this work in your school or district. In this final chapter, we begin by reviewing key facets of the 5Ps framework for SoBL implementation. We then delve into action planning with four integral steps to support your team in either initiating or revising implementational efforts. We close by identifying how readers can use their roles to advocate for heritage language learners and ELs to promote equitable implementation. Ultimately, the goal of this chapter is to apply what you have learned and explored in your context.

Framing This Work in Schools

In planning for SoBL implementation, a critical starting point is defining your **Purpose**, the first facet of the framework as presented in Chapter 2. To be impactful and sustainable, SoBL efforts should be grounded in the focal school or district, specifically focused on how the work can enhance students' biliteracy in languages used in homes, communities, and schools (Heineke & Davin, 2021; Herrera, 2016). By centering the work around the backgrounds and best interests of the constituents, including students, families, and community members, stakeholders can initiate implementational efforts with a lens on equity. From there, the purpose of SoBL work should be strategically connected to the school's or district's larger vision, mission, and strategic plan as a means to bolster its visibility, encourage collaboration among stakeholders, and garner necessary funds for implementation. Everyone involved, including administrators, school board members, teachers, counselors, parents, and students, should recognize the purpose of the SoBL in the school or district, which promotes widespread awareness and extends these efforts beyond the silo of world language or bilingual departments that typically take the lead on these efforts.

The second facet of the framework, **Proficiency Assessments**, explained in Chapter 3, is perhaps the most complex facet of the framework. World language is not a content area that is historically accustomed to large-scale standardized testing and thus lacks the requisite resources and funding. Unlike other content areas in which all students in a particular grade can take the same assessment, world language is unique in that students in U.S. schools speak hundreds of different languages. Many of these languages do not have readily available and affordable assessments. Thus, it is challenging to ensure that all students have equitable pathways to the SoBL. Coordinators and teams must carefully manage assessment logistics such as where and when

to offer assessments, what technology is necessary, and who participates. Within language classrooms, teachers must consider how to design and evaluate classroom-based assessments to prepare students for the SoBL assessments.

The third facet of the framework, **Programs**, is also inextricably tied to the success of SoBL implementation. As explained in Chapter 4, the number of SoBL recognitions in a given district relates to the language programs offered, including types, languages, curricula, and instruction. Dual-language, heritage language, and world language programs with extended sequences of study nurture biliteracy and subsequently expand the pool of students eligible for the SoBL. Even students who use other languages at home likely require formal instruction to develop proficiency in all four domains (listening, reading, speaking, writing) to achieve the SoBL. But, as explored in Chapter 3, not all language programming is created equal in its design or implementation. Readers should critically evaluate and probe areas to improve programs, curricula, and instruction as a means to reach goals for biliteracy development.

The fourth facet corresponds to **Partners**, underscoring the importance of collaboration, cooperation, and communication across stakeholders. SoBL implementation can be labor intensive for individuals to tackle themselves, especially in contexts that do not have established procedures. In Chapter 5, we described the importance of the all-hands-on-deck approach for equitable implementation. Teachers, leaders, and counselors should be aware of SoBL efforts and understand their roles in promoting biliteracy with students. Individuals at community organizations, businesses, and universities emerge as critical partners in supporting implementation, particularly when prioritizing equity for heritage language learners and ELs. These internal and external partners not only support SoBL implementation but also have the potential to build awareness regarding the importance of multilingualism and biliteracy development. In other words, extending the SoBL work to a broader array of stakeholders not only distributes the work but but can disrupt stubborn and prevalent monolingual ideologies in schools and society.

The fifth and final facet of the framework is **Promotion**, which seeks to extend awareness of the recognition to students, parents, educators, and community members. In Chapter 6, we considered strategic and purposeful steps to promote awareness and recognition for all SoBL recipients. Many students may experience information overload from social media posts, the influx of emails, and competing news outlets in the digital age, compounding the challenge of raising awareness of the SoBL. This context may have been further intensified by the complexities around the COVID pandemic and the shift to distance and hybrid learning formats. Unlike the movie *Field of Dreams*, you cannot simply build the SoBL program in your school or district and expect students to participate. The goal is to leverage your programs and partners to promote the SoBL, advance its purpose, and improve language education in schools to expand equity and access.

Each facet of the framework represents a critical component of effective, equitable, and purposeful SoBL implementation. A weakness in any facet of the framework may diminish the power of the SoBL initiative and the recognition that students receive for their remarkable achievement of biliteracy. For example, a strong purpose, invested partners, and broad promotion does not yield SoBL recipients without high-quality and accessible language programming. Similarly, strong language programming and a well-articulated and context-sensitive purpose do not advance the policy without partners on board to carry out the logistics and spread awareness of the program. In our years of research and work in multiple settings across the country, we have yet to encounter stakeholders who did not recognize the need to refine and improve at least one of these facets of implementation. We encourage you to use the framework, as well as the action plan template and tools detailed in this chapter, to evaluate your potential areas of growth, as well as to applaud yourself on areas of strength.

Enacting the Framework: Action Plans for Implementation

Throughout this book, we have shared numerous ideas of how to approach SoBL implementation, delving into five facets for you to consider within the scope of your unique context. Research-based vignettes across the text have depicted stakeholders just like you working alongside their colleagues, students, and families to make this initiative thrive and bolster their overall goals and programs in language education. As you can likely tell from the many examples, there is no one-size-fits-all approach, as the policy offers the flexibility to allow educators to shape implementation in response to the linguistic landscapes in homes, communities, and schools. Flexibility is wonderful in allowing you to chart your own work on the ground, but also challenging given

that you may have grown accustomed to policy mandates with much stricter and more detailed guidelines for implementation and evaluation.

For us, the answer lies in a good action plan, which gives you and your collaborators the opportunity to lay out your roadmap for implementation. With your school, district, and community in mind, action planning prompts defining purpose and determining next steps to evaluate and enhance proficiency assessments, programs, partners, and promotional efforts. You can use any action planning tool of your preference, though we share a template previously used in our work in schools (Heineke et al., 2018). Drawing from the premise of backward design for school change (Wiggins & McTighe, 2007), we first set goals, then determine evidence of progress toward goals, and finally sketch out the trajectory of action steps to reach goals. These three stages of action planning are not linear, with the need for continuous reflection, review, and refinement of the action plan to match the changing contexts of schools (see Figure 7.1).

This is where the rubber meets the road, as the say-

Figure 7.1. Action Planning for SoBL Implementation

ing goes. In other words, now is the time to take all the reading and learning from across this book and put it into practice in your own setting. We hope that readers convene action planning sessions collaboratively with stakeholders from the school, district, and community. Whether you are just getting started with the SoBL or seeking to refine your current work, the action planning process will support your team in defining your purpose clearly, discerning how to collect aligned data to inform your efforts, and setting next steps to enhance pathways for students to develop and demonstrate biliteracy. We provide our template in Tool 7.1, as well as action plan examples in the appendices. You can see how the framework weaves into the template to support strategic connections between ideas and examples presented in the book and your unique context.

Defining Goals for Biliteracy Development The first stage of action planning involves defining the goals that you seek to accomplish through SoBL implementation. Like any good backward-designed plan, these goals then drive the rest of your work moving forward. In Chapter 2, we explored **Purpose** as the first framework facet that should drive SoBL efforts. As outlined in that chapter, begin by reflecting on language use in homes, communities, and schools as a means to ground your action plan in your unique context. Consider larger initiatives in your school and district, as well as existing and potential language programming. With that context in mind, define your goals in response to the question, What do we seek to achieve with the SoBL? Then collaboratively refine goals to be specific, measurable, attainable, relevant, and timebound (see Table 2.1 in Chapter 2; Doran et al., 1981). Above all, prioritize goals that benefit students, including heritage language learners and ELs.

Stakeholders might consider drafting both long- and short-term goals as a part of their action plan (see Tool 7.1). Long-term goals embrace the longitudinal trajectory of both biliteracy development and school change. We know that language takes years to develop (Collier, 1989; Hakuta et al., 2000) and that meaningful change in schools is complex and takes time (Fullan, 2007). Short-term goals scaffold work toward larger goals, providing tangible objectives to guide next steps on the ground. In the Walsh School District, which has been used as an example throughout the book, stakeholders set a long-term goal of all students graduating biliterate by a set year and short-term goals to expand language programs in community languages like Somali and Samoan. In this way, the long-term goal drives the overall work while the short-term goals scaffold progress toward the larger purpose of students' biliteracy.

Determining Data Points to Evaluate Progress
When approached through backward design, action planning then shifts to the second stage: the evaluation plan. This stage immediately follows the goal-setting stage to enhance alignment, in that what you evaluate should connect to what you are seeking to accomplish. In this stage, stakeholders predetermine the data points that will serve to inform both the long-term success of the efforts and ongoing progress toward goals over time. After drafting goals for the SoBL in your setting, your team should then brainstorm related data points, which should include both formal and anecdotal sources (see Tool 7.1). To borrow an analogy from Wiggins and McTighe (2005), the idea is to craft a scrapbook, not take a single snapshot. With multiple sources of data, you can evaluate SoBL implementation efforts and enhance future practice in pursuit of your goals.

Formal data points to assess SoBL implementation typically include proficiency assessment data and program enrollment numbers. For example, if the action plan targets a certain number or percentage of students becoming biliterate, then formal results of SoBL assessments provide aligned data on SoBL recipients and proficiency levels. If stakeholders seek to enhance heritage language programs and equity in SoBL distribution among heritage language learners, then data would be needed on the number of languages assessed, as well as the number of recognitions in each language. Teams pinpointing goals for ELs would want disaggregated data to understand how many current and former ELs receive the SoBL. As shown by these examples, it is critical to delineate sources that will provide aligned data to inform progress toward goals. For additional ideas on formal data sources, return to Chapter 3 (SoBL assessment data analysis) and Chapter 4 (program access and enrollment analysis).

Whereas formal data sources often provide hard-and-fast numbers to measure progress quantitatively, **anecdotal data** enrich the evaluation with qualitative stories, observations, and results. SoBL implementation can be captured and informed by listening to the voices and experiences of students, families, teachers, and community members. Take the example of Faduma in the vignette that begins this chapter, who had important perspectives to inform the implementational work of educators in her school. In other vignettes throughout the book, you have read about students' and educators' experiences with the SoBL. If you seek to measure the impact of the SoBL or understand the nuances of implementation on the ground, then hearing directly from stakeholders is an important component of the evaluation plan. Consider how to meaningfully and methodically capture the voices of students and stakeholders, such as through annual focus groups or reflections. In the Morton School District, for example, students and families create videos about biliteracy, which are shared at the annual SoBL celebration. Not only do the videos hold value for the students and families who create them, they provide artifacts for stakeholders to use when evaluating the impact and experiences tied to SoBL implementation.

Planning Action Steps for Implementation After defining goals and determining data to evaluate progress, the third stage of action planning involves charting the roadmap to reach the goals (Wiggins & McTighe, 2007). This implementational plan outlines the action steps needed to accomplish the goals, with clearly defined tasks, roles, resources, and timelines to enhance efficacious application in practice. When you reach this stage, consider using the 5Ps framework to brainstorm what needs to be done to achieve the predefined goals for SoBL implementation. Whereas the first facet *(Purpose)* aligns with setting goals in the first stage of action planning and the second facet *(Proficiency Assessments)* connects to pinpointing evaluation tools in the second stage of action planning, the remaining three facets—*Programs, Partnerships,* and *Promotion*—are integral to this third stage that seeks to pinpoint tasks and responsibilities.

For example, many stakeholders aim for SoBL work to expand access to biliteracy development, requiring action steps that involve refining existing or adding new language programs. As described in Chapter 4, you might determine the need to streamline world language curriculum by proficiency level or revisit how bilingual teachers use language allocations and bridging. Programmatic discussions often give rise to consideration of new partnerships, such as those described in Chapter 5 with community organizations, universities, and other educators. Ideas around promotion in Chapter 6 aim to expand access to the SoBL with additional approaches to assessment and recruitment. We suggest returning to these chapters as needed to glean ideas for inspiration in fleshing out the detailed steps of your implementation plan.

Logistical details become key in this stage of action planning. There is likely ample excitement around directions for SoBL implementation, whether that be expanding heritage language programming, developing new community partnerships, or gathering students' stories and voices for promotional efforts. But efforts may quickly stall without considering the necessary logistics to accomplish the task: (a) pertinent sub-steps, (b) assigned roles, (c) needed resources, and (d) a reasonable timeline. We like to pose four questions to provoke productive planning

for each task listed in the implementation plan: *What needs to be done? Who can support this work? What resources do we need? When should this be accomplished?* This collaborative discussion helps shift the action plan from theory into practice. Teams can also prioritize and organize timing of tasks to reach goals for SoBL implementation.

Ongoing Reflection and Refinement of Efforts The SoBL action planning template taps into the three stages of backward design for stakeholders to set goals, determine evidence, and plan action steps (Wiggins & McTighe, 2007). But action planning for SoBL implementation does not stop after these three seemingly linear and static stages. This initial plan gives you a place to get started but should be conceptualized as a dynamic and flexible roadmap that changes as needed as the work plays out in practice. For example, in the Walsh School District, stakeholders circled back to tweak the long-term goal for all students to graduate biliterate after realizing the on-the-ground challenges of achieving this goal, such as with students with severe and profound learning disabilities. Other districts have realized the need to collect additional data or revise action steps to reach goals. We recommend determining regular intervals for the SoBL team to reconvene to reflect, discuss, and revise the action plan to inform future implementation efforts.

In addition to maintaining this dynamic cycle where implementation and evaluation inform future efforts, consider how to amplify beyond your SoBL-focused action plan. As discussed in Chapter 2, stakeholders across the country have had success in promoting students' biliteracy and funding language programming when the SoBL ties to broader school and district goals (Heineke & Davin, 2021). Rather than maintaining the SoBL in the silo of bilingual and world language departments, work to merge and situate SoBL action plans into larger school improvement plans and district strategic plans. This allows for greater exposure and attention to these important efforts, potentially yielding enhanced funding and resources to support the work as it evolves over time. We urge administrators to participate in SoBL action planning teams to facilitate the amplification of the SoBL into the larger fabric of the school and district.

Reflecting on Biliteracy Efforts: Exploring Avenues for Advocacy and Change

If you purchased this book to support your work with the SoBL, you likely already recognize the great promise of the initiative to promote biliteracy and enhance language education in your community. We echo the advice of Fisk that "[the] perfect need not get in the way of [the] possible" (2020, p. 149), acknowledging that you must start somewhere with SoBL implementation. However, as he cautions, it is imperative to recognize the potential of the SoBL to exacerbate inequities in schools if it is not thoughtfully implemented with a lens on equity. Throughout this book, we have called attention to equity issues that commonly emerge during enactment of SoBL policies. These inequities coalesce around heritage language learners and ELs, particularly when the recognition is conceptualized and used to promote the elite bilingualism of White, English-dominant world language learners (Colomer & Chang-Bacon, 2020; Heineke et al., 2018; Subtirelu, 2020; Subtirelu et al., 2019; Valdés, 2020). Our intent was to place potential issues in the forefront of your mind as you navigate SoBL implementation in your setting. In this closing section, we emphasize collaborative and individual steps to take to advocate for equity and access as a part of SoBL implementation (Figure 7.2).

Promoting Change in States, Districts, and Schools
Various issues of equity emerge from nuances of states' SoBL policies, which can be changed through collaborative advocacy efforts in partnership with

Figure 7.2. Advocating Across Policy Layers

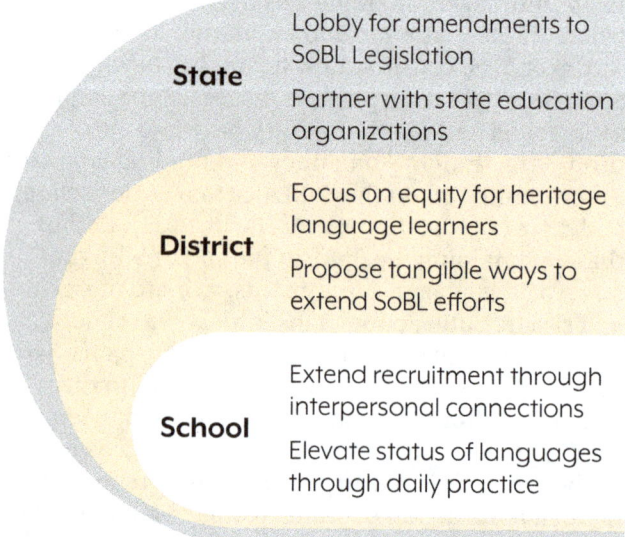

state organizations and legislators. In Massachusetts, for example, leaders of the state organizations for EL, bilingual, and world language education came together to lobby for an amendment to initial SoBL legislation with provisions to promote equity for ELs (Sherf et al., 2020). After getting to know

the intricacies of your state's policy and understanding the implications for your implementation in schools, brainstorm potential revisions to the legislation that would enhance equity. You might consider advocating for (a) removal of seat time as an indicator of world language proficiency, (b) alignment of minimum proficiency levels with those of other states, (c) alternative assessment options, and (d) acceptance of the SoBL for credit by colleges and universities. Use Tool 7.2 to identify equity issues in your state's policy, and reach out to contacts in state chapters of language education organizations (e.g., ACTFL, NABE, TESOL) to explore options and pathways for proposing amendments to current policies.

Even the most equitable policy can result in inequitable implementation, requiring a critical lens on local implementation. One common equity issue in district-level implementation emerges from the low-hanging fruit approach, where educators offer the SoBL only in languages formally taught at the school (e.g., Spanish, French). This approach results in the prioritization of elite bilingualism, where world language learners garner recognition for their biliteracy but heritage language learners do not. Educators can take specific steps to advocate for the equitable inclusion of heritage languages in implementation, including (a) involving students, families, and community members in SoBL discussions, (b) expanding assessment options to include home and community languages, (c) designing programs that develop and maintain heritage languages, (d) seeking funding from school boards to extend language assessments and programs, and (e) partnering with tribes and community language schools to support these expansion efforts. Whether you are working individually or collaboratively on the SoBL in your context, consider drafting a proposal with tangible next steps for administrators to expand the reach of the SoBL.

In addition to lobbying for larger changes to SoBL policy, whether in state legislation or local implementation, educators promote equity through their daily actions and decisions in classrooms and schools. Teams of teachers, leaders, and counselors can work together in explicit ways to expand the reach of the initiative in the school, such as (a) individually reaching out to students to advertise and share information on the SoBL, (b) connecting strategically with student groups and clubs to expand recruitment beyond formal language classes, and (c) providing flexible testing options and dates to maximize students' ability to take SoBL assessments. Educators can also implicitly support SoBL efforts by elevating the status of other languages in the classroom; this might include (a) talking in asset-based ways about students' language competencies, (b) encouraging students to use and develop multiple languages and literacies, and (c) incorporating culturally sustaining curriculum and instruction (Alim & Paris, 2018; Herrera, 2016; García & Wei, 2014). When teachers and other educators communicate their shared valuing of languages and biliteracy, schools become sites where all students develop and maintain rich language competencies.

Embracing Individual Agency to Promote Biliteracy Throughout this book, we have emphasized the importance of collaboration in implementing the SoBL. But individual actions also contribute to larger efforts, including those that promote equity. In other words, you do not have to be working in concert with a team to advocate for biliteracy and extend the scope of SoBL implementation in your context. We recommend first considering ways to tap into your particular role, expertise, and experience, followed by evaluating what lies within your locus of control to bring about change.

All educators and stakeholders bring unique sets of knowledge and experience to their roles. As you consider ways to advocate for equitable access to the SoBL, begin by reflecting upon the expertise that you bring to the table. For example, world language teachers might offer important insight into how schools set up heritage learner sections of world language courses to tap into these learners' unique assets and needs. Bilingual teachers may know of publishers and websites where they can find high-quality texts and resources in students' home languages to facilitate biliteracy. Community language teachers might use their expertise to develop alternative assessments in languages not taught in schools. Counselors could develop ways to connect individually and share information about the SoBL with ELs. Administrators may utilize their financial know-how to scrutinize budgets for additional funds for SoBL assessments. Whatever your role and expertise, you can find creative ways to promote equitable implementation of the SoBL.

In addition to your expertise, consider the scope of your advocacy to prioritize potential tasks. Regardless of your role, you have agency to influence SoBL policy in a multitude of ways. It may be helpful to reflect upon your role and recognize the varying types and intensities of your advocacy efforts (see Figure 7.3). To be sure, you can reach out to legislators and other stakeholders to lobby for changes to SoBL legislation to promote equity for heritage language learners and ELs. But you can also promote equity for the same students through smaller acts embedded in daily practice. For example, you might research and pass along various assessment options in the home languages used by students in your school. You also might ensure that your world language department purchases headsets for the speaking portions of SoBL assessments, as well as multilingual keyboard overlays to allow students to complete written assessments in writing systems such as those used in Arabic and Russian. In the grand scheme of SoBL implementation, reflect upon and prioritize the various ways you can ensure equitable access to the recognition.

Chapter Summary

In this chapter, we merged the five facets of the 5Ps framework—***Purpose, Proficiency Assessments, Programs, Partnerships***, and ***Promotion***—to support readers in developing actionable next steps to implement the SoBL in their settings. Using a backward-design approach to action planning, we detailed how to define goals for biliteracy, determine data sources to use to evaluate progress, and plan for the implementation of the SoBL in practice. We then called attention to the specific lens on equity woven throughout this text, encouraging readers to recognize and act upon equity issues emergent in their SoBL work. Through our work in contexts across the United States, we have seen the incredible promise of the SoBL when stakeholders attend specifically to equity and ensure that all students have pathways to develop and demonstrate their biliteracy.

Figure 7.3. Varying Intensities of Advocacy Efforts

| Research language assessments | Procure multilingual keyboards | Request funding from school board | Initiate community partnerships | Develop new language programs | Draft amendments to legislation |

Less intensive ← → More intensive

Questions for Discussion and Application

1. With your SoBL implementation team, discuss the 5Ps framework. First, discuss key points from each facet that stood out to you and align with your setting. Then, use the framework facets to center on the key components of the work in your setting. What is our **Purpose** for implementing the SoBL? How can we approach **Proficiency Assessments** to evaluate progress toward goals? How might we enhance language **Programs** to support students' biliteracy? What **Partners** can we engage to deepen this work? How can we **Promote** the SoBL to reach a wide array of students?

2. Use your previous discussions to draft an action plan for SoBL implementation. Use the action plan template provided in Tool 7.1 or another template of your choice to flesh out your goals and next steps for implementing the SoBL and evaluating your efforts over time. In addition to using the framework facets to brainstorm, be sure to organize and sequence the action steps and consider the important logistics (e.g., sub-steps, roles, resources, timeline). If they are not already on your SoBL team, be sure to share the action plan with school and district leaders for feedback and support.

3. Critically consider how the SoBL in your state and local context might deter heritage language learners and ELs from achieving the SoBL. Use Tool 7.2 to first brainstorm equity issues, including those with state policy and local implementation. Then leverage your expertise, as well as the ideas and examples throughout this text, to propose changes that would alleviate these issues. Pinpoint next steps to follow up with relevant stakeholders to seek actionable change and promote equity in your future SoBL efforts.

Further Reading

- Staehr Fenner, D. (2014). *Advocating for English learners: A guide for educators.* Corwin.

- Valdés, G. (2020). The future of the Seal of Biliteracy: Issues of equity and inclusion. In A. J. Heineke & K. J. Davin (Eds.), *The Seal of Biliteracy: Case studies and considerations for policy implementation* (pp. 177–204). Information Age.

- Wiggins, G., & McTighe, J. (2007). *Schooling by design: Mission, action, and achievement.* ASCD.

Tool 7.1. Action Plan Template for SoBL Goals, Evaluation, and Implementation

Directions: Use this template to draft an action plan for SoBL implementation. Use prompts to facilitate discussion and stimulate ideas for each stage of action planning: biliteracy goals, evaluation plan, and implementation plan. Also remember to determine logistics to continually review and revise your action plan in response to what you learn and experience during implementation.

PLANNING STEPS	ACTION PLAN	THINGS TO CONSIDER
Biliteracy Goals What do we seek to achieve with the SoBL?	Long-term goals: Short-term goals:	What are our aspirations for students' language and biliteracy development? Who should develop biliteracy? How do we aim to expand our language programming?
Evaluation Plan How will we know we achieved these goals?	Formal data: Anecdotal data:	What indicates success in reaching goals in five years? What indicates progress toward goals in one year? How can evaluation balance testing data with students' voices?
Implementation Plan What will enhance progress toward goals?	Proficiency Assessments: Programs: Partnerships: Promotion:	How can we refine and enhance access to existing programs to meet goals? What new programs and curricula could target additional students' biliteracy? Who can support this work, both inside and outside of our schools? How can we refine the logistics to promote the SoBL more broadly? For each task, note sub-steps, roles, resources, and timeline for completion.

Tool 7.2. Advocacy Considerations to Enhance Access and Equity

Directions: Take a critical lens on SoBL policy legislation and implementation in your state and local context. Use the tool below to (a) pinpoint the equity issue, (b) propose changes to rectify this issue, and (c) brainstorm the next steps to advocate for these changes. Examples are provided using common equity issues discussed in the chapter.

EQUITY ISSUE	PROPOSED CHANGE	NEXT STEPS
Ex: My state does not attach college credit to the SoBL, so recognitions in less common languages do not yield credit.	Allow SoBL (Intermediate Mid proficiency) to be accepted for college credit to recognize heritage language learners' biliteracy.	Email (a) state language organizations to see about advocacy and (b) former professors to see what universities might contribute.
Ex: My district situates the SoBL in world language classes so many heritage speakers do not have access to the recognition.	Extend SoBL assessment options in other languages and support individualized recruitment via counselors and ESL teachers.	Meet with (a) bilingual director to seek out home language assessments and (b) counselors and ESL teachers to build awareness.

References

A national security crisis: Foreign language capabilities in the federal government (S. Hrg. 112-663), U.S. Senate 112th Cong. (2012).

Abedi, J. (2010). *Performance assessments for English language learners.* Stanford Center for Opportunity Policy in Education. https://scale.stanford.edu/sites/g/files/sbiybj14851/f/performance-assessments-english-language-learners.pdf

ACTFL. (2010). *Use of the target language in the classroom.* Author. https://www.actfl.org/advocacy/actfl-position-statements/use-the-target-language-the-classroom

ACTFL. (2012a). *ACTFL performance descriptors for language learners 2012 edition.* Author. https://www.actfl.org/sites/default/files/pdfs/ACTFLPerformance-Descriptors.pdf

ACTFL. (2012b). *ACTFL proficiency guidelines 2012.* Author. https://www.actfl.org/publications/guidelines-and-manuals/actfl- proficiency-guidelines-2012

ACTFL. (2015). *Oral proficiency levels in the workplace.* Author. https://www.actfl.org/sites/default/files/guidelines/OralProficiencyWorkplacePoster.pdf

ACTFL. (2020). *What are the NCSSFL-ACTFL Can-Do Statements?* https://www.actfl.org/sites/default/files/can-dos/Can-Do%20Introduction%202020.pdf

ACTFL, National Association for Bilingual Education, National Council of State Supervisors for Languages, & TESOL International Association. (2015). *Guidelines for implementing the Seal of Biliteracy* (Joint report). http://www.actfl.org/sites/default/files/pdfs/SealofBiliteracyGuidelines_0.pdf

Adair-Hauck, B., & Donato, R. (2016). PACE: A story-based approach for dialogic inquiry about form and meaning. In J. Shrum & E. Glisan (Eds.), *Teacher's handbook: Contextualized foreign language instruction* (5th ed.). Cengage Learning.

Adair-Hauck, B., Glisan, E. W., Koda, K., Swender, E. B., & Sandrock, P. (2006). The integrated performance assessment (IPA): Connecting assessment to instruction and learning. *Foreign Language Annals, 39*(3), 359–382. https://doi.org/10.1111/j.1944-9720.2006.tb02894.x

Adair-Hauck, B., Glisan, E. W., & Troyan, F. J. (2013). *Implementing integrated performance assessment.* ACTFL.

Adger, C. T., & Locke, J. (2000). *Broadening the base: School/community partnerships serving language minority students at risk* (Educational Practice Report #6). The Center for Research on Education, Diversity and Excellence. https://escholarship.org/uc/item/8s47008n

Adger, C. T., Snow, C. E., & Christian, D. (2018). *What teachers need to know about language* (2nd ed.). Channel View.

Al-Hazza, T., & Bucher, K. T. (2008). Building Arab Americans' cultural identity and acceptance with children's literature. *The Reading Teacher, 62*(3), 210–219. https://doi.org/10.1598/RT.62.3.3

Alim, H. S., & Paris, D. (2018). What is culturally sustaining pedagogy and why does it matter? In D. Paris & H. S. Alim (Eds.), *Culturally sustaining pedagogies: Teaching and learning for justice in a changing world* (pp. 1-23). Teachers College Press.

American Academy of Arts & Sciences. (2017). *America's languages: Investing in language education for the 21st century.* Author.

American Councils for International Education (2017). *The national K-12 foreign language enrollment survey report.* www.americancouncils.org/

Anya, U. (2020). African Americans in world language study: The forged path and future directions. *Annual Review of Applied Linguistics, 40*(1), 97–112. https://doi.org/10.1017/S0267190520000070

Auerbach, E. R. (2016). Reflections on Auerbach (1993), Reexamining English only in the ESL classroom. *TESOL Quarterly, 50*(4), 936-939. https://doi.org/10.2307/3586949

Avant Assessment. (2017). *Avant STAMP results–national averages 2016–2017.* https:// d3itqxtdxl1nz0.cloudfront.net/pdfs/STAMP-National-Averages-Update-2017.pdf

Avant Assessment. (2021). *Language proficiency self-assessment.* https://theglobalseal.com/self-assessment

Baggett, H. C. (2016). Student enrollment in world languages: L'égalité des chances? *Foreign Language Annals, 49*(1), 162–179. https://doi.org/10.1111/flan.12173

Bailey, A. L. (2007). *The language demands of school.* Yale University Press.

Baliang America. (2019). *Filipino students in Hawaii honored with Seal of Biliteracy* [Video file]. YouTube. https://www.youtube.com/watch?v=UoUzZTTgyQs

Ball, D. L., & Forzani, F. M. (2009). The work of teaching and the challenge for teacher education. *Journal of Teacher Education, 60*(5), 497–511. https://doi.org/10.1177%2F0022487109348479

Ballinger, S. (2013). Towards a cross-linguistic pedagogy: Biliteracy and reciprocal learning strategies in French immersion. *Journal of Immersion and Content-Based Language Education, 1*(1), 131–148. https://doi.org/10.1075/jicb.1.1.06bal

Beeman, K., & Urow, C. (2012). *Teaching for biliteracy: Strengthening bridges between languages.* Caslon.

Bhatia, T. K., & Ritchie, W. C. (2013). Bilingualism and multilingualism in South Asia. In T. K. Bhatia & W. C. Ritchie (Eds.), *The handbook of bilingualism and multilingualism* (pp. 843–870). Blackwell. https://doi.org/10.1002/9781118332382.ch34

Bialystok, E. (1986). Factors in the growth of linguistic awareness. *Child Development, 57,* 498–510. https://doi.org/10.2307/1130604

Bialystok, E. (2007). Cognitive effects of bilingualism: How linguistic experience leads to cognitive change. *International Journal of Bilingual Education and Bilingualism, 10*(3), 210–223. https://doi.org/10.2167/beb441.0

Bialystok, E., Craik, F. I. M., & Freedman, M. (2007). Bilingualism as a protection against the onset of symptoms of dementia. *Neuropsychologia, 45*(2), 459–464. https://doi.org/10.1016/j.neuropsychologia.2006.10.009

Black, C., Chou, A., & Hancock, C. (2020). *The 2018-19 national Seal of Biliteracy report.* https://sealofbiliteracy.org/doc/2020-National-Seal-of-Biliteracy-Report-Final.pdf

Borowczyk, M. (2020). Credentialing heritage: The role of community language schools in implementing the Seal of Biliteracy. *Foreign Language Annals, 53*(1), 28–47. https://doi.org/10.1111/flan.12439

Budke, M. [@MeganBudke]. (2020, May 18). *It's #BilingualSeal testing season. Testing looks a bit different this yr.* [Tweet; link to presentation]. Twitter. https://twitter.com/MeganBudke/status/1262421454869708805

Burgo, C. (2017). Meeting student needs: Integrating Spanish heritage language learners into the second language classroom. *Hispania, 100*(5), 45-50.

Burkhauser, S., Steele, J. L., Li, J., Slater, R. O., Bacon, M., & Miller, T. (2016). Partner- language learning trajectories in dual-language immersion: Evidence from an urban district. *Foreign Language Annals, 49*(3), 415–433. https://doi.org/10.1111/flan.12218

Burnet, M. M. (2020). Signed, sealed, delivered: District-level adoption of the Washington state Seal of Biliteracy. In A. J. Heineke & K. J. Davin (Eds.), *The Seal of Biliteracy: Case studies and considerations for policy implementation* (pp. 105–122). Information Age.

Byram, M. (1997). *Teaching and assessing intercultural communicative competence.* Multilingual Matters.

Cai, M. (2003). Can we fly across cultural gaps on the wings of imagination? Ethnicity, experience, and cultural authenticity. In D. L. Fox & K. G. Short (Eds.), *Stories matter: The complexity of cultural authenticity in children's literature.* NCTE.

Calderón, M. E., Dove, M. G., Staehr Fenner, D., Gottlieb, M., Honigsfeld, A., Singer, T. W., Sinclair-Slaakk, S. M., Soto, I., & Zacarian, D. (2019). *Breaking down the wall: Essential shifts for English learners' success.* Corwin.

California State Board of Education. (2014). *California English language development standards.* Author. https://www.cde.ca.gov/sp/el/er/documents/eldstndspublication14.pdf

Californians Together. (2018, May 17). *The Seal of Biliteracy – Celebrating students for the 21st century* [Video File]. YouTube. https://www.youtube.com/watch?v=-RimfosMB5I

Californians Together, American Council on the Teaching of Foreign Languages, Modern Language Association, National Association for Bilingual Education, National Association of English Language Program Administrators, National Council of State Supervisors for Languages, & TESOL International Association. (2020). *Guidelines for implementing the Seal of Biliteracy* (Joint report). https://www.actfl.org/sites/default/files/resources/SOBL_Updated_Guidelines%20_October_2020.pdf

Callahan, R. M. (2005). Tracking and high school English learners: Limiting opportunity to learn. *American Educational Research Journal, 42*(2), 305–328. https://doi.org/10.3102/00028312042002305

Callahan, R., & Gándara, P. (2014). *The bilingual advantage: Language, literacy, and the US labor market.* Multilingual Matters.

Callahan, R., Wilkinson, L., & Muller, C. (2010). Academic achievement and course taking among language minority youth in U.S. schools: Effects of ESL placement. *Educational Evaluation and Policy Analysis, 32*(1), 84–117. https://doi.org/10.3102/00028312042002305

Carreira, M., & Kagan, O. (2018). Heritage language education: A proposal for the next 50 years. *Foreign Language Annals, 51*(1), 152–168. https://doi.org/10.1111/flan.12331

Castro, A. (2020). Validating the linguistic strengths of English learners: Los Angeles Unified School District's implementation of the Seal of Biliteracy. In A. J. Heineke & K. J. Davin (Eds.), *The Seal of Biliteracy: Case studies and considerations for policy implementation* (pp. 123–140). Information Age.

Cervantes-Soon, C. G., Dorner, L., Palmer, D., Heiman, D., & Choi, R. S. J. (2017). Combating inequalities in two-way language immersion programs: Towards critical consciousness in bilingual education spaces. *Review of Research in Education, 41*(1), 403–427. https://doi.org/10.3102/0091732X17690120

Chou, A. (2019). *2019 national Seal of Biliteracy report for 2017-2018 academic year.* https://sealofbiliteracy.org/doc/2019-National-Seal-of-Biliteracy-Report-Final.pdf

Cisneros, R. [@bubbasax]. (2019, July 25). *First day of school on the path to greatness!* [Tweet; thumbnail pictures included]. Twitter. https://twitter.com/bubbasax/status/1154517132798857216

Cohan, A., Honigsfeld, A., & Dove, M. G. (2019). *Team up, speak up, fire up! Educators, students, and the community working together to support English learners.* ASCD.

Collier, V. P. (1989). How long? A synthesis of research on academic achievement in a second language. *TESOL Quarterly, 23*(3), 509–531. https://doi.org/10.2307/3586923

Collier, V. P., & Thomas, W. P. (2017). Validating the power of bilingual schooling: Thirty-two years of large-scale, longitudinal research. *Annual Review of Applied Linguistics, 37*, 1–15. https://doi.org/10.1017/S0267190517000034P

Collins, L., & White, J. (2011). An intensive look at intensity and language learning. *TESOL Quarterly, 45*(1), 106–133. https://doi.org/10.5054/tq.2011.240858

Colomer, S. E., & Chang-Bacon, C. K. (2020). Seal of Biliteracy graduates get critical: Incorporating critical biliteracies in dual-language programs and beyond. *Journal of Adolescent & Adult Literacy, 63*(4), 379–389. https://doi.org/10.1002/jaal.1017

Commins, N. L., & Miramontes, O. B. (2006). Addressing linguistic diversity from the outset. *Journal of Teacher Education, 57*(3), 240–246. https://doi.org/10.1177%2F0022487105285591

Commission of European Communities. (2003). *Promoting language learning and linguistic diversity: An action plan 2004-2006.* Author.

Commission on Language Learning. (2017). *America's languages: Investing in language education for the 21st century.* Author. https://www.amacad.org/multimedia/pdfs/publications/researchpapersmonographs/language/Commission-on-Language-Learning_Americas-Languages.pdf

Cook, V. J. (1992). Evidence for multi-competence. *Language Learning, 42*(4), 557–591. https://doi.org/10.1111/j.1467-1770.1992.tb01044.x

Cook, V. J. (1999). Going beyond the native speaker in language teaching. *TESOL Quarterly, 33*(2), 185–209. https://doi.org/10.2307/3587717

Crawford, J. (2000). *At war with diversity: US language policy in an age of anxiety.* Multilingual Matters.

Creese, A., & Blackledge, A. (2015). Translanguaging and identity in educational settings. *Annual Review of Applied Linguistics, 35*, 20–35. https://doi.org/10.1017/S0267190514000233

Cruz, B. C., & Thornton, S. J. (2013). *Teaching social studies to English language learners.* Routledge.

Damari, R. R., Rivers, W. P., Brecht, R. D., Gardner, P., Pulupa, C., & Robinson, J. (2017). The demand for multilingual human capital in the U.S. labor market. *Foreign Language Annals, 50*(1), 13–37. https://doi.org/10.1111/flan.12241

Datnow, A. (2006). Connection in the policy chain: The "co-construction" of implementation in the comprehensive school reform. In M. I. Honig (Ed.), *New directions in education policy implementation: Confronting complexity* (pp. 105–124). State of New York Press.

Davin, K. J. (2021a). Critical language testing: Factors influencing students' decisions to (not) pursue the Seal of Biliteracy. *Harvard Educational Review, 91*(2), 179-203. https://doi.org/10.17763/1943-5045-91.2.179

Davin, K. J. (2021b). The Seal of Biliteracy: College credit and placement. *The Language Educator, 16*(2), 24–26.

Davin, K. J., Chavoshan, I., & Donato, R. (2018). Images of past teachers: Present when you teach. *System, 72*(1), 139–150. https://doi.org/10.1016/j.system.2017.12.001

Davin, K. J., & Heineke, A. J. (2017). The Seal of Biliteracy: Variations in policy and outcomes. *Foreign Language Annals, 50*(3), 486–499. https://doi.org/10.1111/flan.12279

Davin, K. J., & Heineke, A. J. (2018). The Seal of Biliteracy: Adding students' voices to the conversation. *Bilingual Research Journal, 41*(3), 312–328. https://doi.org/10.1080/15235882.2018.1481896

Davin, K. J., Heineke, A. J., & Egnatz, L. (2018). The Seal of Biliteracy: Successes and challenges to implementation. *Foreign Language Annals, 51*(2), 275–289. https://doi.org/10.1111/flan.12336

Davin, K. J., Rempert, T., & Hammerand, A. (2014). Converting data to knowledge: One district's experience using large-scale proficiency assessment. *Foreign Language Annals, 47*(2), 241–260. https://doi.org/10.1111/flan.12081

Davin, K. J., Troyan, F., Donato, R., & Hellmann, A. (2011). Research on the implementation of the IPA in an elementary Spanish program. *Foreign Language Annals, 44*(4), 605–625. https://doi.org/10.1111/j.1944-9720.2011.01153.x

Deal, T. E., & Peterson, K. D. (2016). *Shaping school culture* (3rd ed.). Jossey-Bass.

de Bot, K., Lowie, V., & Verspoor, M. (2007). A dynamic systems approach to second language acquisition. *Bilingualism: Language and Cognition, 10*(1), 7–21. https://doi.org/10.1017/S1366728906002732

DeLeon, T. M., & Lavandez, M. (2020). The new ecology of biliteracy in California: A study of the early implementation of the Seal of Biliteracy. In A. J. Heineke & K. J. Davin (Eds.), *The Seal of Biliteracy: Case studies and considerations for policy implementation* (pp. 49–66). Information Age.

Donato, R., & Davin, K. J. (2018). The genesis of classroom discursive practices as history-in-person processes. *Language Teaching Research, 22*(6), 739–760. https://doi.org/10.1177/1362168817702672

Donato, R., & Tucker, G. R. (2010). A tale of two schools: *Developing sustainable early foreign* language programs. Multilingual Matters. https://doi.org/10.1017/S0272263112000241

Doran, G., Miller, A., & Cunningham, J. (1981). There's a S.M.A.R.T. way to write management's goals and objectives. *Management Review, 70*, 35–36.

Drago-Severson, E. (2009). *Leading adult learning: Supporting adult development in our schools.* Corwin/Sage Press.

Echevarría, J. J., Vogt, M. J., & Short, D. J. (2013). *Making content comprehensible for elementary English learners: The SIOP model.* Pearson.

Egnatz, L. & Santos, V. D. O. (in press). *Seal of Biliteracy for all: Expanding assessment options toward access and equity for learners of less commonly tested languages.* Avant Assessment.

ELPA21. (2013). *English language proficiency standards.* Author. https://elpa21.org/wp-content/uploads/2019/03/Final-4_30-ELPA21-Standards_1.pdf

Epstein, J. L., Sanders, M. G., Sheldon, S. B., Simon, B. S., Salinas, K. C., Jansorn, N. R., Voorhis, F. L. V., Martin, C. S., Thomas, B. G., Greenfeld, M., Hutchins, D. J., & Williams, K. J. (2019). *School, family, and community partnerships: Your handbook for action.* Corwin.

Escamilla, K. (2010). Bilingual education programs: Maintenance, transitional, and dual language. In C. S. Clauss-Ehlers (Ed.), *Encyclopedia of cross-cultural school psychology.* Springer. https://doi.org/10.1007/978-0-387-71799-9_40

España, C., & Herrera, L. Y. (2020). *En comunidad: Lessons for centering the voices and experiences of bilingual Latinx students.* Heinemann.

Estrada, P., Wang, H., & Farkas, T. (2019). Elementary English learner classroom composition and academic achievement. *American Educational Research Journal, 57*(4), 1791–1836. https://doi.org/10.3102/0002831219887137

Fan, S. P., Liberman, Z., Keysar, B., & Kinzler, K. D. (2015). The exposure advantage: Early exposure to a multilingual environment promotes effective communication. *Psychological Science, 26*, 1090–1097. https://doi.org/10.1177%2F0956797615574699

Finn, J. D. (1998). Taking foreign languages in high school. *Foreign Language Annals, 31*(3), 287–306. https://doi.org/10.1111/j.1944-9720.1998.tb00577.x

Fishman, J. A. (1991). Reversing language shift. Multilingual Matters.

Fishman, J. A. (2001). 300-plus years of heritage language education in the United States. In J. K. Peyton, D. A. Ranard, & S. McGinnis (Eds.), *Heritage languages in America: Preserving a national resource* (pp. 81–97). Center for Applied Linguistics and Delta Systems.

Fisk, J. (2020). School-level implementation of the Seal of Biliteracy: One linguistically diverse suburban Illinois high school's journey. In A. J. Heineke & K. J. Davin (Eds.), *The Seal of Biliteracy: Case studies and considerations for policy implementation* (pp. 141–160). Information Age.

Flores, N. (2020). From academic language to language architecture: Challenging raciolinguistic ideologies in research and practice. *Theory into Practice, 59*(1), 22–31. https://doi.org/10.1080/00405841.2019.1665411

Flores, N., & Chaparro, S. (2018). What counts as language education policy? Developing a materialist Anti-racist approach to language activism. *Language Policy 17*, 365–384 (2018). https://doi.org/10.1007/s10993-017-9433-7

Flores, N., & García, O. (2017). A critical review of bilingual education in the United States: From basements and pride to boutiques and profit. *Annual Review of Applied Linguistics, 37*, 14–29. https://doi.org/10.1017/S0267190517000162

Flores, N., Tseng, A., & Subtirelu, N. (Eds.). (2021). *Bilingualism for all? Raciolinguistic perspectives on dual language education in the United States.* Multilingual Matters.

Fortune, T. W., & Tedick, D. J. (2015). Oral proficiency assessment of English-proficient K-8 Spanish immersion students. *Modern Language Journal, 99*(4), 637–655. https://doi.org/10.1111/modl.12275

Fortune, T. W., Tedick, D. J., & Walker, C. L. (2008). Integrated language and content teaching: Insights from the language immersion classroom. In T. Fortune & D. J. Tedick (Eds.), *Pathways to multilingualism: Evolving perspectives on immersion education* (pp. 71–96). Multilingual Matters.

Freed, B. F., Segalowitz, N., & Dewey, D. P. (2004). Context of learning and second language fluency in French: Comparing regular classroom, study abroad, and intensive domestic immersion programs. *Studies in Second Language Acquisition, 26*(2), 275–301. https://doi.org/10.1017/S0272263104262064

Fullan, M. (2007). *The new meaning of educational change.* (4th edition). Teachers College Press.

Gadoeworldlanguages. [@gadoeworldlanguages]. (2021, December 2). *Congratulations to Daisy for qualifying to receive the first Spanish Seal of Biliteracy in the history of Seminole County! The Seal is available to Ga students in over 100 languages. Yearly, 2,000+ graduating seniors in Ga earn the seal of Biliteracy in over 20 languages.* [Tweet]. Twitter. https://twitter.com/gadoeworldlang/status/1466390125215113219

García, O. (2009). *Bilingual education in the 21st century: A global perspective.* Wiley-Blackwell.

García, O. (2012) Theorizing translanguaging for educators. In C. Celic & K. Seltzer (Eds.), *Translanguaging: A CUNY-NYSIEB guide for educators.* https://www.cuny-nysieb.org/wp-content/uploads/2016/04/Translanguaging-Guide-March-2013.pdf

García, O. (2019). Decolonizing foreign, second, heritage and first languages: Implications for education. In D. Macedo (Ed.), *Decolonizing foreign language education* (pp. 152–168). Routledge.

García, O., Flores, N., & Woodley, H. H. (2015). Constructing in-between spaces to "do" bilingualism: A tale of two high schools in one city. In J. Cenoz & D. Gorter (Eds.), *Multilingual education: Between language learning and translanguaging* (pp.199–224). Cambridge University Press.

García, O., Ibarra Johnson, S., & Selzer, K. (2017). *The translanguaging classroom: Leveraging student bilingualism for learning.* Caslon.

García, O., & Otheguy, R. (2017). Interrogating the language gap of young bilingual and bidialectal students. *Multilingual Research Journal, 11*(1), 52–65. https://doi.org/10.1080/19313152.2016.1258190

García, O., & Wei, L. (2014). *Translanguaging: Language, bilingualism and education.* Palgrave Macmillan.

Gebhard, M., Accurso, K., & Chen, I. (2019) Paradigm shifts in the teaching of grammar in K-12 ESL/EFL contexts: A case for a social-semiotic perspective. In L. C. de Oliveira (Ed.), *Handbook of TESOL in K-12* (pp. 249–263). Wiley. https://doi.org/10.1002/9781119421702.ch16

Genesee, F. (1987). *Learning through two languages: Studies of immersion and bilingual education.* Newbury House.

Glastonbury Public Schools. (2021). *Glastonbury Public Schools world language department.* https://www.glastonburyforeignlanguage.org/curriculum/grades-1-5-curriculum

Glisan, E., & Donato, R. (2017). *Enacting the work of language instruction: High-leverage teaching practices.* ACTFL.

Glisan, E. & Donato, R. (2021). *Enacting the work of language instruction: High-leverage teaching practices* (Vol. 2). ACTFL.

Goldenberg, C., & Rutherford-Quach, S. (2012). The Arizona home language survey: The under-identification of students for English language services. *Language Policy, 11,* 21–30. http://doi.org/10.1007/s10993-011-9224-5

Goulette, E. (2020). Heritage language learners in a mixed class: Educational affordances and constraints. *Dimension, 55,* 64–81.

Grosjean, F. (1989). Neurolinguists, beware! The bilingual is not two monolinguals in one person. *Brain and Language, 36*(1), 3–15. https://doi.org/10.1016/0093-934X(89)90048-5

Grosjean, F. (2008). *Studying bilinguals.* Oxford University Press. https://doi.org/10.1017/S0022226709990089

Gross, N. (2016). *Dual-language programs on the rise across the U.S.* Education Writers Association. http://www.ewa.org/blog-latino-ed-beat/dual-language-programs-rise-across-us

Hakuta, K., Butler, Y. G., & Witt, D. (2000). *How long does it take English learners to attain proficiency?* Linguistic Minority Research Institute.

Hammond, Z. (2014). *Culturally responsive teaching and the brain.* Corwin.

Hancock, C., & Davin, K. J. (2020). A comparative case study: Administrators' and students' perceptions of the Seal of Biliteracy. *Foreign Language Annals, 53*(3), 458–477. https://doi.org/10.1111/flan.12479

Harklau, L. (1994). Tracking and linguistic minority students: Consequences of ability grouping for second language learners. *Linguistics and Education, 6*(3), 217–244.

Harklau, L. (2013). Why Izzie didn't go to college: Choosing work over college as Latina feminism. *Teachers College Record, 115*(1), 1–32.

Hawaii Revised Statutes, chapter 302H, sections 1–7. (2009). http://www.capitol.hawaii.gov/hrscurrent/Vol05_Ch0261-0319/HRS0302H/HRS_0302H-0001.htm.

Heineke, A. J. (2020). Language policy in practice: Implementing the Seal in state and local contexts. In A. J. Heineke & K. J. Davin (Eds.), *The Seal of Biliteracy: Case studies and considerations for policy implementation* (pp. 35–48). Information Age.

Heineke, A. J., & Davin, K. J. (2020a). Prioritizing multilingualism in U.S. schools: States' policy journeys to enact the Seal of Biliteracy. *Educational Policy, 34*(4), 619–643. https://doi.org/10.1177/0895904818802099

Heineke, A. J., & Davin, K. J. (Eds.) (2020b). *The Seal of Biliteracy: Case studies and considerations for policy implementation.* Information Age.

Heineke, A. J., & Davin, K. J. (2021). Implementing the Seal of Biliteracy: A multiple case study of six high-awarding districts. *Modern Language Journal, 105*(2), 395–411. https://doi.org/10.1111/modl.12708

Heineke, A. J., Davin, K. J., & Bedford, A. (2018). The Seal of Biliteracy: Considering equity and access for English learners. *Education Policy Analysis Archives, 26*(99). https://doi.org/10.14507/epaa.26.3825

Heineke, A. J., Davin, K. J., & Dávila, A. (2019). Promoting multilingual communities, schools, and students: A closer look at the Seal of Biliteracy in Washington state. *TESOL Journal, 10*, 1–5. https://doi.org/10.1002/tesj.451

Heineke, A. J., & McTighe, J. (2018). *Using Understanding by Design in the culturally and linguistically diverse classroom.* ASCD.

Heritage, M., Walqui, A., & Linquanti, R. (2015). *English language learners and the new standards: Developing language, content knowledge, and analytical practices in the classroom.* Harvard Education Press.

Herrera, S. G. (2016). *Biography-driven culturally responsive teaching* (2nd ed.). Teachers College Press.

Honig, M. I. (2006). Complexity and policy implementation: Challenges and opportunities for the field. In M. I. Honig (Ed.), *New directions in education policy implementation: Confronting complexity* (pp. 1–24). State of New York Press.

Honig, M. I., & Hatch, T. C. (2004). Crafting coherence: How schools strategically manage multiple external demands. *Educational Researcher, 33*, 16–30. https://doi.org/10.3102/0013189X033008016

Hornberger, N. H. (2003). *Continua of biliteracy. An ecological framework for educational policy, research, and practice in multilingual settings.* Multilingual Matters. https://doi.org/10.1017/S0047404505260116

Howard, E. R., Lindholm-Leary, K. J., Rogers, D., Olague, N., Medina, J., Kennedy, B., Sugarman, J., & Christian, D. (2018). *Guiding principles for dual language education* (3rd ed.). Center for Applied Linguistics.

Jefferson County Public Schools World Languages Rubrics. (2021a). *Guide to performance-toward-proficiency rubrics.* https://spinternal.jefferson.kyschools.us/gheenswebsite/_layouts/15/WopiFrame.aspx?sourcedoc=/gheenswebsite/Public%20Documents%20%20World%20Languages/Guide%20to%20Proficiency%20Rubric%2012-09-14.docx-&action=default

Jefferson County Public Schools World Languages Rubrics. (2021b). *Public documents: World languages.* https://spinternal.jefferson.kyschools.us/gheenswebsite/Public%20Documents%20%20World%20Languages/Forms/AllItems.aspx-#ServerFilter=FilterField1%3DLevel%255Fx-0020%255F1-FilterValue1%3DRubrics-

Jessner, U. (2008). Teaching third languages: Findings, trends and challenges. *Language Teaching, 41*(1), 15–56. https://doi.org/10.1017/S0261444807004739

Johnson, D. (2013). *Language policy.* Palgrave MacMillan.

Kahakalau, K. (2017). Developing an Indigenous proficiency scale. *Cogent Education, 4*(1). https://doi.org/10.1080/2331186X.2017.1377508

Kelleher, A. (2010). What is a heritage language? *Heritage Briefs.* Center for Applied Linguistics. http://www.cal.org/heritage/pdfs/briefs/What-is-a-Heritage-Language.pdf

Kersaint, G., Thompson, D., & Petkova, M. (2013). *Teaching mathematics to English language learners* (2nd ed.). Routledge.

Khiana, I. [@khiana_ayeisha]. (2013, April 17). *My pampo would be proud!* [Tweet; link toInstagram post included]. Twitter. https://twitter.com/khiana_ayeisha/status/324726526170001408

Kissau, S., & Adams, M. J. (2016). Instructional decision making and IPAs: Assessing the modes of communication. *Foreign Language Annals, 49*(1), 105–123. https://doi.org/10.1111/flan.12184

Krashen, S. D. (1981). Bilingual education and second language acquisition theory. *In Schooling and language minority students: A theoretical framework* (pp. 51–79). California State Department of Education.

Krashen, S. D. (1982). *Principles and practice in second language acquisition.* Pergamon.

Kroll, J. F., & Dussias, P. E. (2017). Language and productivity for all Americans. *Foreign Language Annals, 50*(2), 248–259. https://doi.org/10.1111/flan.12271

Kruger, T., Davies, A., Eckersley, B., Newell, F., & Cherednichenko, B. (2009). *Effective and sustainable university-school partnerships: Beyond determined efforts by inspired individuals.* Victoria University.

Language Opportunity Coalition. (2021). *Biliteracy pathway award criteria.* https://sealofbiliteracyma.org/pathway-award-criteria/

Language Testing International. (2021). *Understanding proficiency.* https://www.languagetesting.com/lti-information/understanding-proficiency

Larsen-Freeman, D. (2010). Having and doing: Learning from a complexity theory perspective. In P. Seedhouse, S. Walsh, & C. Jenks (Eds.), *Conceptualizing "learning" in applied linguistics* (pp. 52–68). Palgrave. https://doi.org/10.1057/9780230289772_4

Larsen-Freeman, D., & Cameron, L. (2008). *Complex systems and applied linguistics.* Oxford University Press. https://doi.org/10.2989/SALALS.2009.27.2.9.872

Larsen-Freeman, D., & Tedick, D. J. (2016). Teaching world languages: Thinking differently. In D. H. Gitomer & C. A. Bell (Eds.), *Handbook of research on teaching* (pp. 1335–1388). American Educational Research Association. https://doi.org/10.3102/978-0-935302-48-6_22

Latta, M. M., & Chan, E. (2010). *Teaching the arts to engage English language learners.* Routledge.

Lead with Languages. (2021). *Expand a language program.* https://www.leadwithlanguages.org/language-advocacy/expand-a-language-program/

Levinson, B. A. U., & Sutton, M. (2001). Introduction: Policy as/in practice – A sociocultural approach to the study of educational policy. In M. Sutton (Ed.), *Policy as practice: Toward a comparative sociocultural analysis of educational policy* (pp. 1–22). Ablex.

Lindholm-Leary, K. J. (2001). *Dual language education.* Multilingual Matters.

Lindholm-Leary, K., & Block, N. (2010). Achievement in predominantly low SES/Hispanic dual language schools. *International Journal of Bilingual Education and Bilingualism, 13*(1), 43–60. https://doi.org/10.1080/13670050902777546

Linquanti, R., & Cook, H. G. (2013). *Toward a common definition of English learner: A brief defining policy and technical issues and opportunities for state assessment consortia.* Council of Chief State School Officers.

Liu, N. (2010). *The role of Confucius Institutes in Chinese heritage language–community language (HL-CL) schools: Stakeholders' views.* Unpublished doctoral dissertation. Arizona State University, Tempe.

Liu, N., Musica, A., Koscak, S., Vinogradova, P., & López, J. (2011). *Challenges and needs of community-based heritage language programs and how they are addressed.* https://www.cal.org/heritage/pdfs/briefs/challenges-and%20needs-of-community-based-heritage-language-programs.pdf

Long, M. H. (1983). Linguistic and conversational adjustments to non-native speakers. *Studies in Second Language Acquisition, 5*(2), 177–193. https://doi.org/10.1017/S0272263100004848

López-Robertson, J. (2012). "Está página me recordó": Young Latinas using personal life stories as tools for meaning-making. *Bilingual Research Journal, 35*(2), 217–233. https://doi.org/10.1080/15235882.2012.703634

Lucas, T., Villegas, A. M., & Freedson-González, M. (2008). Linguistically responsive teacher education preparing classroom teachers to teach English language learners. *Journal of Teacher Education, 59*(4), 361–373. https://doi.org/10.1177%2F0022487108322110

Lyster, R. (2004). Research on form-focused instruction in immersion classrooms: Implications for theory and practice. *Journal of French Language Studies, 14*(3), 321–341. https://doi.org/10.1017/S0959269504001826

Lyster, R. (2007). *Learning and teaching languages through content: A counterbalanced approach.* Benjamins. https://doi.org/10.1075/lllt.18

Makoni, S., & Pennycook, A. (2015). Disinventing and reconstituting languages. In S. Makoni & A. Pennycook (Eds.), *Disinventing and reconstituting languages* (Vol. 46, pp. 1–41). Multilingual Matters. https://doi.org/10.1207/s15427633scc0304

Marichal, N., Roldán, A. R., & Coady, M. (2021). "My language learners seemed like ghosts": A rural teacher's transformational journey implementing the Seal of Biliteracy. *The Rural Educator, 42*(1), 52-56. https://doi.org/10.35608/ruraled.v42i1.1180

Martínez-Álvarez, P., & Ghiso, M. P. (2017). On languaging and communities: Latino/a emergent bilinguals' expansive learning and critical inquiries into global childhoods. *International Journal of Bilingual Education and Bilingualism, 20*(6), 667–687. https://doi.org/10.1080/13670050.2015.1068270

McCardle, T. (2020). A critical historical examination of tracking as a method for maintaining racial segregation. *Educational Considerations, 45*(2). https://doi.org/10.4148/0146-9282.2186

McCarty, T. (2011). *Ethnography and language policy.* Routledge. https://doi.org/10.1007/s10993-012-9237-8

McLeay, H. (2003). The relationship between bilingualism and the performance of spatial tasks. *International Journal of Bilingual Education and Bilingualism, 6*(6), 423–438. https://doi.org/10.1080/13670050308667795

McMillan, B. A., & Rivers, D. J. (2011). The practice of policy: Teacher attitudes toward "English only." *System, 39*(2), 251–263. https://doi.org/10.1016/j.system.2011.04.011

McTighe, J., Doubet, K. J., & Carbaugh, E. M. (2020). *Designing authentic performance tasks and projects: Tools for meaningful learning and assessment.* ASCD.

McTighe, J., & Willis, J. (2019). *Upgrade your teaching: Understanding by Design meets neuroscience.* ASCD.

Medina, C. L., & Martínez-Roldán, C. (2011). Culturally relevant literature pedagogies: Latinostudents reading in the borderlands. In J. C. Naidoo (Ed.), *Celebrating cuentos: Promoting Latino children's literature and literacy in classrooms and libraries* (pp. 259–272). ABC-CLIO.

Menken, K., & García, O. (2010). Introduction. In K. Menken & O. García (Eds.), *Negotiating language policies in schools: Educators as policymakers* (pp. 1–10). Routledge.

Menken, K., Hudson, T., & Leung, C. (2014). Symposium: Language assessment in standards-based education reform. *TESOL Quarterly, 48*(3), 586–614. https://doi.org/10.1002/tesq.180

Minnesota Department of Education. (2021). *Minnesota bilingual seals program.* https://education.mn.gov/MDE/dse/stds/world/seals/

Moll, L. C., Amanti, C., Neff, D., & González, N. (1992). Funds of knowledge for teaching: Using a qualitative approach to connect homes and classrooms. *Theory into Practice, 31*(2), 132–141. https://doi.org/10.1080/00405849209543534

Montrul, S. (2016). *The acquisition of heritage languages.* Cambridge University Press. https://doi.org/10.1017/CBO9781139030502

Moore, Z. (2005). African American students' opinions about foreign language study: An exploratory study of low enrollments at the college level. *Foreign Language Annals, 38*(2), 191–200.

Morales, J., Calvo, A., & Bialystok, E. (2013). Working memory development in monolingual and bilingual children. *Journal of Experimental Child Psychology, 114*(2), 187–202. https://doi.org/10.1016/j.jecp.2012.09.002

National Center for Educational Statistics. (2019). *English language learners enrolled in public elementary and secondary schools.* https://nces.ed.gov/programs/digest/d19/tables/dt19_204.20.asp

National Standards Collaborative Board. (2015) *World-readiness standards for learning languages* (4th ed.). Author.

NCSSFL & ACTFL. (2017a). 2017 *NCSSFL-ACTFL can-do statements.* Author. https://www.actfl.org/publications/guidelines-and-manuals/ncssfl-actfl-can-do-statements

NCSSFL & ACTFL. (2017b). *Reflection: Intercultural communication.* https://www.actfl.org/sites/default/files/can-dos/Intercultural%20Can-Dos_Reflections%20Scenarios.pdf

Negueruela-Azarola, E. (2013). The being and becoming of metalinguistic knowledge: Rules and categories of grammatical description as functional tools of the mind. In K. Roehr & G. A. Gánem-Gutiérrez (Eds.), *The metalinguistic dimension in instructed second language learning* (pp. 221–242). Bloomsbury.

New Hampshire Department of Education. (2021). *NH Seal of Biliteracy portfolio guide.* https://www.education.nh.gov/sites/g/files/ehbemt326/files/inline-documents/sonh/biliteracy-portfolio-option.pdf

New Mexico Statutes §22-23A-1 (2009). https://law.justia.com/codes/new-mexico/2009/chapter-22/article-23a/

Norton, B., & Toohey, K. (2011). Identity, language learning, and social change. *Language Teaching, 44*(4), 412–446. https://doi.org/10.1017/S0261444811000309

Nutta, J., Bautista, N. U., & Butler, M. B. (2010). *Teaching science to English language learners.* Routledge.

O'Rourke, P., Zhou, Q., & Rottman, I. (2016). Prioritization of K-12 world language education in the United States: State requirements for high school graduation. *Foreign Language Annals, 49*(4), 789–800. https://doi.org/10.1111/flan.12232

Ohio Department of Education. (2017, October 27). *ODE: Introducing Ohio's Seal of Biliteracy program* [Video file]. YouTube. https://www.youtube.com/watch?v=43aSTe2UBW8

Ohio Department of Education. (2021). *Rubrics for world languages.* http://education.ohio.gov/Topics/Learning-in-Ohio/Foreign-Language/World-Languages-Model-Curriculum/Model-Curriculum-for-World-Languages-and-Cultures/Instructional-Strategies/Scoring-Guidelines-for-World-Languages

Okraski, C., Hancock, C., & Davin, K. J. (2020). Promoting equitable access to the Seal of Biliteracy: The case of Minnesota. In A. J. Heineke & K. J. Davin (Eds.), *The Seal of Biliteracy: Case studies and considerations for policy implementation* (pp. 67–84). Information Age.

Olsen, L. (2020). The history of the movement: Enacting the State Seal of Biliteracy in the state of California. In A. J. Heineke & K. J. Davin (Eds.), *The Seal of Biliteracy: Case studies and considerations for policy implementation* (pp. 17–34). Information Age.

Ortega, L. (2011). SLA after the social turn. In D. Atkinson (Ed.), *Alternative approaches to second language acquisition* (pp. 167–180). Routledge.

Paris, D., & Alim, H. S. (Eds.). (2018). *Culturally sustaining pedagogies: Teaching and learning for justice in a changing world.* Teachers College Press.

Pratt, C. (2012). Are African American high-school students less motivated to learn Spanish than other ethnic groups? *Hispania, 95,* 116–134.

Public Law 101-477. (1990). *Native American Language Act.* Retrieved from https://www.govinfo.gov/content/pkg/STATUTE-104/pdf/STATUTE-104-Pg1152.pdf

Pufahl, I., & Rhodes, N. C. (2011). Foreign language instruction in U.S. schools: Results of a national survey of elementary and secondary schools. *Foreign Language Annals, 44*(2), 258–288. https://doi.org/10.1111/j.1944-9720.2011.01130.x

Randolph Jr, L. J. (2017). Heritage language learners in mixed Spanish classes: Subtractive practices and perceptions of high school Spanish teachers. *Hispania, 100*(2), 274–288.

Ricento, T. K. (2000). *Ideology, politics, and language policies: Focus on English.* John Benjamins. https://doi.org/10.1075/impact.6

Ritz, C., & Sherf, N. (2021). World language programming and leadership in K–12 Massachusetts public schools. *Foreign Language Annals, 54*(2), 476-504. https://doi.org/10.1111/flan.12519

Rodríguez, R. J. (2019). *Teaching culturally sustaining and inclusive young adult literature: Critical perspectives and conversations.* Routledge.

Roehr-Brackin, K. (2018). *Metalinguistic awareness and second language acquisition.* Routledge.

Rothman, J., & Iverson, M. (2010). Independent normative assessments for bi/multilingualism, Where art thou? In M. Cruz-Ferreira (Ed.), *Multilingual norms* (pp. 33–51). Peter Lang. https://doi.org/10.3726/978-3-653-00478-6

Saint Paul Public Schools. (2021a). *Hmong language and culture products.* https://www.spps.org/Page/5831

Saint Paul Public Schools. (2021b). *Immersion programs in St. Paul Public Schools.* https://www.spps.org/domain/10455

Sandrock, P. (2010). *The keys to assessing language performance: A teacher's manual for measuring student progress.* ACTFL.

Santos, R. (2019). *Framingham Public Schools proudly prepares for the official launch of the State Seal of Biliteracy.* https://www.framingham.k12.ma.us/site/default.aspx?PageType=3&DomainID=1920&ModuleInstanceID=11380&ViewID=6446EE88-D30C-497E-9316-3F8874B3E108&RenderLoc=0&FlexDataID=8322&PageID=6803

SB41. (2008). *International education initiative - critical languages program.* https://le.utah.gov/~2008/bills/sbillint/SB0041S01.pdf

Schoener, H. & McKenzie, K. (2016). Equity traps redux: Inequitable access to foreign language courses for African American high-school students. *Equity and Excellence in Education, 49*(3), 284–299. https://doi.org/10.1080/10665684.2016.1194099

Schwedhelm, M. C., & King, K. A. (2020). The neoliberal logic of state seals of biliteracy. *Foreign Language Annals, 53*(1), 12–27. https://doi.org/10.1111/flan.12438

Seal of Biliteracy (2021). Determine the level of pathway awards to be granted. https://sealofbiliteracy.org/steps/2-determine-level-pathway-awards-be-granted/

Shelby County Schools (2021). *Performance feedback tools.* https://scsworldlanguages.weebly.com/performance.html

Sherf, N. L., Hardy, P. R., & Solórzano, H. (2020). A collaborative model for Seal of Biliteracy implementation in the Massachusetts pilot program. In A. J. Heineke & K. J. Davin (Eds.), *The Seal of Biliteracy: Case studies and considerations for policy implementation* (pp. 85–104). Information Age.

Shohamy, E. (2007). Language tests as language policy tools. *Assessment in Education: Principles, Policy & Practice, 14*(1), 117–130. https://doi.org/10.1080/09695940701272948

Shrum, J. L., & Glisan, E. W. (2016). *Teacher's handbook: Contextualized language instruction* (5th ed.). Cengage.

Sims Bishop, R. (1990). Mirrors, windows, and sliding glass doors. *Perspectives: Choosing and using books for the classroom, 6*(3).

Smith, T. W., Marsden, P. V., & Hout, M. (2011). *General social survey, 1972-2010 [cumulative file]* (ICPSR31521-v1). National Opinion Research Center.

Smith, A. K., Watkins, K. E., & Han, S. (2020). From silos to solutions: How one district is building a culture of collaboration and learning between school principals and central office leaders. *European Journal of Education, 55*(1), 58–75. https://doi.org/10.1111/ejed.12382

Snyder, S., & Staehr Fenner, D. (2021). *Culturally responsive teaching for multilingual learners: Tools for equity.* Corwin.

Souto-Manning, M. (2009). Negotiating culturally responsive pedagogy through multicultural children's literature: Towards critical democratic literacy practices in a first-grade classroom. *Journal of Early Childhood Literacy, 9*, 50-74. https://doi.org/10.1177/1468798408101105

Spillane, J. P., Reiser, B. J., & Gómez, L. M. (2006). Policy implementation and cognition: The role of human, social, and distributed cognition in framing policy implementation. In M. I. Honig (Ed.), *New directions in education policy implementation: Confronting complexity* (pp. 47–64). State of New York Press.

Staehr Fenner, D. (2014). *Advocating for English learners: A guide for educators.* Corwin.

Suárez-Orozco, C. (2004). *Formulating identity in a globalized world. In M. M. Suárez-Orozco & D. B. Qin-Hilliard, Globalization: Culture and education in the new millennium* (pp. 173–202). University of California Press.

Subtirelu, N. (2020). Raciolinguistic ideology, the Seal of Biliteracy, and the politics of language education. In A. J. Heineke & K. J. Davin (Eds.), *The Seal of Biliteracy: Case studies and considerations for policy implementation* (pp. 161–176). Information Age.

Subtirelu, N. C., Borowczyk, M., Hernández, R. T., & Venezia, F. (2019). Recognizing whose bilingualism? A critical policy analysis of the Seal of Biliteracy. *Modern Language Journal, 103*, 371–390. https://doi.org/10.1111/modl.12556

Sugarman, J. (2018). *A matter of design: English learner program models in K-12 education.* Migration Policy Institute. https://www.migrationpolicy.org/research/english-learner-program-models-k-12-education

Surrain, S. (2018). 'Spanish at home, English at school': How perceptions of bilingualism shape family language policies among Spanish-speaking parents of preschoolers. *International Journal of Bilingual Education and Bilingualism.* https://doi.org/10.1080/13670050.2018.1546666

Swain, M. (1985). Communicative competence: some roles of comprehensible input and comprehensible output in its development. In S. Gass & C. Madden (Eds.), *Input in second language acquisition* (pp. 235–253). Newbury House.

Swain, M. (1993). The output hypothesis: Just speaking and writing aren't enough. *The Canadian Modern Language Review, 50*(1), 158–164. https://doi.org/10.3138/cmlr.50.1.158

Swain, M., & Lapkin, A. (2013). A Vygotskian sociocultural perspective on immersion education. *Journal of Immersion and Content-Based Language Education, 2*(1), 165–180. https://doi.org/10.1075/jicb.1.1.05swa

Swartzloff, J. [@WeGo94HR]. (2019, May 15). *Illinois, it's time to take a stand and provide equity for English learners and their WL learner peers. Let's start by making the English requirement more attainable on the IL State Seal of Biliteracy. @ISBEnews* [Tweet]. Twitter. https://twitter.com/WeGo94HR/status/1128825019763699723

Swartzloff, J. (2020, August 4). *Why earn your Seal of Biliteracy* [Video file]. YouTube. https://www.youtube.com/watch?v=1OgEfk0GIj4

TESOL International. (2018). *Standards for initial TESOL preK-12 teacher preparation programs.* Author. https://www.tesol.org/docs/default-source/books/2018-tesol-teacher-prep-standards-final.pdf?sfvrsn=23f3fffdc_6

Thomas, W. P., & Collier, V. P. (2002). *A national study of school effectiveness for language minority students' long-term academic achievement.* Center for Research on Education, Diversity & Excellence. www.crede.ucsc.edu/research/llaa/1.1_final.html

Torres, L. (2005). *Liliana's grandmothers.* Farrar, Straus and Giroux.

Turnbull, B. (2002). Teachers' participation and buy-in: Implications for school reform initiatives. *Learning Environments Research, 5,* 235–252.

Turnbull, M., Lapkin, S., & Hart, D. (2001). Grade 3 immersion students' performance in literacy and mathematics: Province-wide results from Ontario (1998-99). *The Canadian Modern Language Review, 58*(1), 9–26.

Umansky, I. M., & Reardon, S. F. (2014). Reclassification patterns among Latino English learner students in bilingual, dual immersion, and English immersion classrooms. *American Educational Research Journal, 51,* 879–912. https://doi.org/10.3102%2F0002831214545110

Valdés, G. (1997). Dual-language immersion programs: A cautionary note concerning the education of language-minority students. *Harvard Educational Review, 67,* 391-429. https://doi.org/10.17763/haer.67.3.n5q175qp86120948

Valdés, G. (2000). *Introduction. Spanish for Native Speakers, Volume 1.* AATSP Professional Development Series Handbook for Teachers K-16. Harcourt College Publishers.

Valdés, G. (2005). Bilingualism, heritage language learners, and SLA research: Opportunities lost or seized? *Modern Language Journal, 89*(3), 410–426. https://doi.org/10.1111/j.1540-4781.2005.00314.x

Valdés, G. (2018). Analyzing the curricularization of language in two-way immersion education: Restating two cautionary notes. *Bilingual Research Journal, 41*(4), 388–412. https://doi.org/10.1080/15235882.2018.1539886

Valdés, G. (2020). The future of the Seal of Biliteracy: Issues of equity and inclusion. In A. J. Heineke & K. J. Davin (Eds.), *The Seal of Biliteracy: Case studies and considerations for policy implementation* (pp. 177–204). Information Age.

Valdés, G., & Figueroa, R. A. (1994). *Bilingualism and testing: A special case of bias.* Ablex.

Valdés, G., Fishman, J. A., Chavéz, R., & Pérez, W. (2006). *Developing minority language resources.* Multilingual Matters.

Valdez, V. E., Freire, J. A., & Delavan, M. G. (2016). The gentrification of dual language education. *The Urban Review, 48*(4), 601–627.

Vygotsky, L. S. (1978). Mind in society: The development of higher psychological processes. Harvard University Press. https://doi.org/10.2307/j.ctvjf9vz4

Vygotsky, L. S. (1986). *Thought and language.* The MIT Press.

Vyn, R., Wesely, P., & Neubauer, D. (2019). Exploring the effects of foreign language instructional practices on student proficiency development. *Foreign Language Annals, 52*(1), 45–65. http://dx.doi.org/10.1111/flan.12382

Wang, J., & Goldschmidt, P. (1999). Opportunity to learn, language proficiency, and immigrant status effects on mathematics achievement. *Journal of Educational Research, 93*(2), 101–111. https://doi.org/10.1080/00220679909597634

Watzinger-Tharp, J., Rubio, F., & Tharp, D. (2018). Linguistic performance of dual language immersion students. *Foreign Language Annals, 51*(3). https://doi.org/10.1111/flan.12354

WIDA. (2020). *English language development standards framework.* Author. Retrieved from https://wida.wisc.edu/sites/default/files/resource/WIDA-ELD-Standards-Framework-2020.pdf

Wiggins, G. P., & McTighe, J. (2005). *Understanding by design*. ASCD.

Wiggins, G. P., & McTighe, J. (2007). *Schooling by design: Mission, action, and achievement*. ASCD.

Wiggins, G. P., & McTighe, J. (2011). *The understanding by design guide to creating high quality units*. ASCD.

Zhai, L. (2019). Illuminating the enactment of high-leverage teaching practices in an exemplary world language teaching video library. *American Educational Research Journal, 56*(5), 1681–1717. https://doi.org/10.3102/0002831218824289

Zhang, X., Winke, P., & Clark, S. (2020). Background characteristics and oral proficiency development over time in lower-division college foreign language programs. *Language Learning, 70*(3), 807–847. http://doi.org/10.1111/lang.12396

Zsiga, E., Boyer, O., & Kramer, R. (Eds.). (2014). *Languages in Africa: Multilingualism, language policy, and education*. Georgetown University Press.

Zyzik, E. (2016). Towards a prototype model of the heritage language learner: Understanding strengths and needs. In M. Fairclough & S. Beaudrie (Eds.), *Innovative approaches to heritage language teaching* (pp. 19–38). Georgetown University Press.

Appendix 1. External Proficiency Assessments

TEST (VENDOR)	DOMAINS ASSESSED	LANGUAGES OR CONTENT ASSESSED
AP Language & Culture Exam (College Board)	Listening Speaking Reading Writing	Chinese, French, German, Italian, Japanese, Spanish
AAPPL (Language Testing International)	Interpersonal-Listening/ Speaking Presentational-Writing Interpretive-Reading Interpretive-Listening	Chinese, French, German, Italian, Japanese, Spanish
IB Standard Level (SL) or Higher Level (HL) Exam (International Baccalaureate Organisation)	Listening Speaking Reading Writing	Arabic, Chinese (Mandarin), English, French, German, Hindi, Italian, Japanese, Korean, Portuguese, Russian, Spanish, Thai
STAMP 4S (Avant Assessment)	Listening Speaking Reading Writing	Arabic, Mandarin (simplified and traditional), English, French, German, Hebrew, Hindi, Italian, Japanese, Korean, Polish, Portuguese (Brazilian), Russian, Spanish
Avant STAMP 4Se (Avant Assessment)[1]	Listening Speaking Reading Writing	Arabic, Cantonese, English, French, German, Hebrew, Japanese, Korean, Mandarin (simplified and traditional), Portuguese (Brazilian), Russian, Spanish, Yup'ik
ALTA Language Tests (ALTA Language Testing)	Oral Proficiency (Listening & Speaking) Writing	Over 100 languages; please see https://www.altalang.com/language-testing/seal-of-biliteracy/
AAPPL Elementary (Language Testing International)[2]	Interpersonal Listening and Speaking	Chinese (Mandarin), English, Spanish
Avant STAMP 3S (Avant Assessment)	Reading Speaking Writing	Swahili, Yoruba
Avant STAMP WS (formerly called WorldSpeak; Avant Assessment)	Speaking Writing	Amharic, Armenian, Chin (Hakha), Chuukese, Czech, Filipino (Tagalog), Haitian Creole, Hawaiian ('Olelo Hawai'i), Hmong, Ilocano, Kannada, Marathi, Marshallese, Samoan, Somali Maay Maay, Somali Maxaa, Tamil, Telugu, Turkish, Urdu, Vietnamese, Yup'ik, Zomi
ACTFL OPI & WPT for the Seal of Biliteracy (Language Testing International)	Oral Proficiency (Listening & Speaking) and Writing Proficiency	Albanian, Amharic, Bengali/Bangla, Bosnian/Croatian, Bulgarian, Cantonese, Dari, Gujarati, Haitian Creole, Hebrew, Malayalam, Pashto, Polish, Swahili, Tamil, Tagalog, Turkish, Ukrainian, Urdu, Vietnamese, Yoruba
ACTFL Listening Proficiency Test (LPT; Language Testing International)	Listening	Arabic, Chinese, English, French, German, Italian, Japanese, Korean, Portuguese, Russian, Spanish Note: Because the AAPPL is available in all of these languages, the LPT is rarely, if ever, used for the SoBL.

TEST (VENDOR)	DOMAINS ASSESSED	LANGUAGES OR CONTENT ASSESSED
ACTFL Oral Proficiency Interview (OPI; Language Testing International)	Speaking	More than 120 languages; please see https://www.actfl.org/assessment-research-and-development/actfl-assessments/actfl-postsecondary-assessments/oral-proficiency-interview-opi
ACTFL Oral Proficiency Interview – Computer (OPIc; Language Testing International)	Speaking	Arabic, Chinese (Mandarin), English, French, German, Italian, Japanese, Korean, Pashto, Persian Farsi, Portuguese, Russian, Spanish, Tagalog, Vietnamese
ACTFL Reading Proficiency Test (RPT; Language Testing International)	Reading	Indonesian Note: Available in approximately 12 languages, but Indonesian is the only language not available via AAPPL, and thus the only language for which schools use the RPT for SoBL testing.
ACTFL Writing Proficiency Test (WPT; Language Testing International)	Writing	Albanian, Arabic, Chinese, Danish, Dutch, English, French, German, Greek, Haitian Creole, Hebrew, Hindi, Italian, Japanese, Korean, Persian Farsi, Polish, Portuguese, Russian, Serbo/Croatian, Spanish, Swedish, Turkish, Vietnamese
ACCESS for ELLs 2.0 (WIDA)	Listening Speaking Reading Writing	English language proficiency
ACT	Varies by state; some states require scores on English portion only, some accept minimum composite scores (math, science, reading)	Achievement test to determine college readiness
Advanced Placement English Language & Composition Assessment (College Board)	Reading Writing	English content knowledge
AAPPL (ACTFL Assessment of Performance Toward Proficiency in Languages; Language Testing International)	Interpersonal-Listening/Speaking Presentational Writing Interpretive Reading Interpretive Listening	English language proficiency
SAT Evidence-based Reading & Writing	Reading Writing	Achievement test to determine college readiness
SAT Reading Subtest	Reading	Achievement test to determine college readiness
STAMP (STAndards-based Measurement of Proficiency) 4S; Avant Assessment	Listening Speaking Reading Writing	English language proficiency

TEST (VENDOR)	DOMAINS ASSESSED	LANGUAGES OR CONTENT ASSESSED
TOEFL iBT	Listening Speaking Reading Writing	English language proficiency
ALIRA (Language Testing International)	Interpretive Reading	Latin
ASLPI (Gallaudet University)	Interactive, Receptive, Expressive	American Sign Language

Note: [1]Designed for 2nd to 6th grade students. [2]Designed for 3rd and 4th grade students.

Appendix 2. Self-Assessment to Determine Test Readiness Based on NCSSFL-ACTFL Intermediate Mid Can-Do Statements

Each of the statements below describes what an individual needs to be able to do to score Intermediate Mid on each section of a SoBL assessment. Please read each statement carefully and think about your world language abilities. If you respond with "yes" to each, you are ready to take the test. If you answer "no" to any of these statements, then you should continue practicing those skills.

Reading Abilities

I can understand the main idea and key information in short straightforward texts.

Listening/Viewing Abilities

I can identify the main idea and key information in short straightforward conversations.

Abilities in Conversations

I can exchange information in conversations on familiar topics and some researched topics, creating sentences and series of sentences and asking a variety of follow-up questions.

I can interact with others to meet my needs in a variety of familiar situations, creating sentences and series of sentences and asking a variety of follow-up questions.

I can exchange preferences, feelings, or opinions and provide basic advice on a variety of familiar topics, creating sentences and series of sentences and asking a variety of follow-up questions.

Abilities in Spoken, Signed, or Written Texts

I can tell a story about my life, activities, events and other social experiences, using sentences and series of connected sentences.

I can state/sign my viewpoint about familiar topics and give some reasons to support it, using sentences and series of connected sentences.

I can give straightforward presentations on a variety of familiar topics and some concrete topics I have researched, using sentences and series of connected sentences.

Appendix 3. Sample Interpersonal Speaking/Listening Prompts for Intermediate Mid

The following sample prompts were created using the steps in Tool 3.2. These prompts were designed to elicit interpersonal speaking/listening samples at the Intermediate Mid level. To elicit an interpersonal speaking sample, remember that this must be a conversation between two individuals. For example, with Sample Prompt 1, Student A would play the role of the president and Student B would play the role of the vice president. If there are not two students who speak the target language, a teacher or community member can serve as the conversation partner.

Remember that the conversation must be spontaneous and unscripted. While you might have a list of bullet points of requirements or pose some follow-up questions to elicit more speech, students should not have time to plan what they will say in advance. Be sure to record the conversation so that you can play it back to determine an appropriate rating.

Finally, we recommend that you provide students with the prompts in both English and the language in which they are pursuing the SoBL. In this way, you can minimize validity issues related to students' understanding of the prompt.

Intermediate Proficiency Benchmark: I can participate in spontaneous spoken, written, or signed conversations on familiar topics, creating sentences and series of sentences to ask and answer a variety of questions.

Sample Prompt 1

Strand	How can I exchange information and ideas in conversations?
Intermediate Mid Performance Indicator	I can exchange information in conversations on familiar topics and some researched topics, creating sentences and series of sentences and asking a variety of follow-up questions.
Prompt (in GRASPS format)	Because of a recent donation, your [language] teacher has announced that everyone in the [language] club will be going on a fieldtrip (Situation). As the president of the club (Role), he has asked you and the vice president to discuss options in the community (Audience). You must each share at least one potential location and why this place would be good for a field trip (Goal). Ask each other questions about the details of their idea (Product, Performance, and Purpose). Then, come to an agreement on the location, plan the details of the trip, including the date, time you will leave school, time you will return, lunch plans, and what you will do while at the location (Standards and Criteria for Success).

Sample Prompt 2

Strand	How can I meet my needs or address situations in conversations?
Intermediate Mid Performance Indicator	I can interact with others to meet my needs in a variety of familiar situations, creating sentences and series of sentences and asking a variety of follow-up questions.
Prompt (in GRASPS format)	You have a big project due at the end of the week, but your grandparents are in town for the first time in five years. You want to be able to spend some time with them after school each day instead of working on your project. Explain the situation to your teacher, describe the plans that your family has each evening, and ask about potential alternative due dates or point deductions if you turn the assignment in late.

Sample Prompt 3

Strand	How can I express, react to, and support preferences and opinions in conversations?
Intermediate Mid Performance Indicator	I can exchange preferences, feelings, or opinions and provide basic advice on a variety of familiar topics, creating sentences and series of sentences and asking a variety of follow-up questions.
Prompt (in GRASPS format)	You are president of the student body at a school that is trying to decide whether to offer some subjects in a virtual format rather than a face-to-face format. The principal of the school has requested a meeting with you to hear your opinion on the matter. Your goal is to share your opinions about the ideal format with the principal and convince her to adopt your suggestions. Be sure to ask the principal questions about which subjects she is considering putting online, when the change would occur, what other changes would occur, and other key details.

Appendix 4. Sample Interpersonal Speaking/Listening Prompts for Intermediate High

The following sample prompts were created using the steps in Tool 3.2. These prompts were designed to elicit interpersonal speaking/listening samples at the Intermediate High level. To elicit an interpersonal speaking sample, remember that this must be a conversation between two individuals. For example, with Sample Prompt 1, Student A would play the role of the student and Student B would play the role of the counselor. If there are not two students who speak the target language, a teacher or community member can serve as the conversation partner.

Remember that the conversation must be spontaneous and unscripted. While you might have a list of bullet points of requirements or pose follow-up questions to elicit more speech, students should not have time to plan what they will say in advance. Be sure to record the conversation so that you can play it back to determine an appropriate score.

Finally, we recommend that you provide students with the prompts in both English and the language in which they are pursuing the SoBL. In this way, you can minimize validity issues related to students' understanding of the prompt.

Intermediate Proficiency Benchmark: I can participate in spontaneous spoken, written, or signed conversations on familiar topics, creating sentences and series of sentences to ask and answer a variety of questions.

Sample Prompt 1

Strand	How can I exchange information and ideas in conversations?
Intermediate High Performance Indicator	I can exchange information in conversations and some discussions on a variety of familiar and some concrete topics that I have researched, using connected sentences that may combine to form paragraphs and asking a variety of questions, often across various time frames.
Prompt (in GRASPS format)	You are meeting with the school counselor to discuss what to do after graduating from high school at the end of the year. You are trying to decide between several options, including enrolling in a few different schools or taking some time off from school to work. Discuss the options with the counselor, explaining the pros and cons of each. Be sure to also ask the counselor for advice on the pros and cons of each.

Sample Prompt 2

Strand	How can I meet my needs or address situations in conversations?
Intermediate High Performance Indicator	I can interact with others to meet my needs in a variety of situations, sometimes involving a complication, using connected sentences that may combine to form paragraphs and asking a variety of questions, often across various time frames.
Prompt (in GRASPS format)	You love your job as a server at the Hamburger Shack, but your boss keeps scheduling you for lunch shifts instead of dinner shifts, which means that you earn less in tips. You decide to be brave and schedule a meeting with your boss to address the issue. In your conversation, describe the issue and provide examples of the low tips you have earned on your previous shifts. Compare those to what your friend makes on the dinner shift and explain why you would be an asset. Ask your boss about why you keep receiving lunch shifts and about possibilities for working dinner shifts in the future.

Sample Prompt 3

Strand	How can I express, react to, and support preferences and opinions in conversations?
Intermediate High Performance Indicator	I can explain preferences, opinions, and emotions and provide advice on a variety of familiar and some concrete topics that I have researched, using connected sentences that may combine to form paragraphs and asking a variety of questions, often across various time frames.
Prompt (in GRASPS format)	Your counselor is urging you to delete your social media accounts as you begin applying for a summer job. However, you do not believe this is necessary. Exchange opinions with your counselor about why social media may actually strengthen your prospects at finding a summer job. Explain how you have used the platforms in the past and how that might help you in the future. Ask your counselor why they feel so strongly about the issue and what evidence they have that social media can be harmful to finding a job.

Appendix 5. Sample Presentational Writing Prompts for Intermediate Mid

The following sample prompts were created using the steps in Tool 3.2. These prompts were designed to elicit presentational writing samples at the Intermediate Mid level. Remind students that they should write in paragraphs and complete sentences.

Intermediate Proficiency Benchmark: I can communicate information, make presentations, and express my thoughts about familiar topics, using sentences and series of connected sentences through spoken, written, or signed language.

Sample Prompt 1

Strand	How can I present information to narrate about my life, experiences and events?
Intermediate Mid Performance Indicator	I can tell a story about my life, activities, events and other social experiences, using sentences and series of connected sentences.
Prompt (in GRASPS format)	Your pen pal from [country] just found out that he/she/they is moving to the United States. He/she/they wants to play on the same high school sports team as you. Write your pen pal a letter that describes the process of trying out for a team. Provide details such as how many days tryouts typically last, what occurs during tryouts, how many people typically try out, and how the system of cuts works. Be sure to explain details regarding the next opportunity to try out.

Sample Prompt 2

Strand	How can I present information to give a preference, opinion or persuasive argument?
Intermediate Mid Performance Indicator	I can state my viewpoint about familiar topics and give some reasons to support it, using sentences and series of connected sentences.
Prompt (in GRASPS format)	You have been invited to write an editorial for a local newspaper published in [target language] on the best restaurant in town. Write an editorial that convinces readers that they should eat at this restaurant. Be sure to describe the type of cuisine, your favorite dishes, the atmosphere of the restaurant, the service, and the cost.

Sample Prompt 3

Strand	How can I present information to inform, describe, or explain?
Intermediate Mid Performance Indicator	I can give straightforward presentations on a variety of familiar topics and some concrete topics I have researched, using sentences and series of connected sentences.
Prompt (in GRASPS format)	You have been asked to write a blogpost on how your life in the United States changed as a result of the COVID pandemic. Describe the major changes to your daily routine, including school, sports, and ways that you spend time with friends and family. Be sure to explain how your pandemic life differs from your pre-pandemic life.

Appendix 6. Sample Presentational Writing Prompts for Intermediate High

The following sample prompts were created using the steps in Tool 3.2. These prompts were designed to elicit presentational writing samples at the Intermediate High level. Remind students that they should write in paragraphs and complete sentences.

Intermediate Proficiency Benchmark: I can communicate information, make presentations, and express my thoughts about familiar topics, using sentences and series of connected sentences through spoken, written, or signed language.

Sample Prompt 1

Strand	How can I present information to narrate about my life, experiences and events?
Intermediate High Performance Indicator	I can tell stories about school and community events and personal experiences, using a few short paragraphs, often across various time frames.
Prompt (in GRASPS format)	You have been asked to write an article for the school newspaper about what you did for your 10th grade service-learning project. The purpose of the article is to describe your own project so that incoming students have ideas on what they might do. Write an article that has at least three paragraphs, including details such as where you completed your project, who the project was designed to help, how long the project took, and what you learned.

Sample Prompt 2

Strand	How can I present information to give a preference, opinion or persuasive argument?
Intermediate High Performance Indicator	I can state my viewpoint on familiar or researched topics and provide reasons to support it, using a few short paragraphs, often across various time frames.
Prompt (in GRASPS format)	Your school's administration has decided to add one new sport or club to the current extracurricular offerings. To propose a sport or club, students must write a letter to the deciding committee that includes a persuasive argument for the sport or club of their choice. You are passionate that the new addition should be [choose something!]. Write a letter that includes at least 3 paragraphs describing the sport/club, explaining why it would be popular or valuable to the school, and detailing the resources that the school would need to make it happen.

Sample Prompt 3

Strand	How can I present information to inform, describe, or explain?
Intermediate High Performance Indicator	I can give detailed presentations on a variety of familiar topics and some concrete topics I have researched, using a few short paragraphs, often across various time frames.
Prompt (in GRASPS format)	Your [language] teacher has announced a contest with a prize of $200 for whoever can create the most informative flyer about the Seal of Biliteracy. The purpose of the flyer is to inform students, teachers, and parents about the program. The flyer must include one paragraph on what the Seal of Biliteracy is, one paragraph about the benefits of the Seal of Biliteracy, and one paragraph that explains how to earn the recognition. Your goal is to win that prize money and create the best flyer!

Appendix 7. Scoring Speaking Samples at the Intermediate Level

It is much easier to distinguish among the major proficiency levels (Novice, Intermediate, Advanced) than it is to distinguish the Low, Mid, and High sublevels on the ACTFL Proficiency Scale (ACTFL, 2012b). To ensure that a sample is accurately rated, we recommend that you attend ACTFL Oral Proficiency Interview Tester Certification. However, if that is not a possibility, the descriptions below can help you to distinguish among the sublevels. In this tool, we share the major differences between Intermediate Low, Intermediate Mid, and Intermediate High speakers so that you can assign a rating for a portfolio sample. For further details on how Intermediate-level language users differ from those at the Novice or Advanced level, we recommend you consult the ACTFL Proficiency Guidelines (ACTFL, 2012b), which are freely available online.

Intermediate-Level language users can

- Create with language when talking about familiar topics related to daily life
- Recombine learned material to express personal meaning
- Ask simple questions
- Satisfy personal needs and social demands to survive in the target culture
- Produce sentence-level language, ranging from discrete sentences to strings of sentences

INTERMEDIATE LOW	INTERMEDIATE MID	INTERMEDIATE HIGH
Can successfully handle a limited number of uncomplicated communicative tasks in social situations	Can successfully handle a variety of uncomplicated communicative tasks in social situations	Can converse with ease and confidence when dealing with routine tasks and social situations
Struggles to respond to direct questions or requests for information	Can respond to direct questions or requests for information	Can handle successfully uncomplicated tasks and social situations requiring an exchange of basic information
Can pose a few appropriate questions	Can ask a variety of questions about simple themes to satisfy basic needs	Can ask a variety of questions to satisfy basic needs
When asked to handle topics at the Advanced level, is restricted to the present tense and is unable to link ideas or provide paragraph-length discourse	When asked to handle topics at the Advanced level, can provide some information but struggles to link ideas, communicate accurately in various tenses, and use communicative strategies	Can narrate and describe in all major time frames, but when attempting Advanced-level tasks (e.g., narrating in past, dealing with a social situation with an unexpected complication), speech exhibits one or more features of breakdown, such as the failure to carry out fully the narration or description in the appropriate major time frame, an inability to maintain paragraph-length discourse, or a reduction in breadth and appropriateness of vocabulary
Communicates via short statements and discrete sentences	Communicates via sentences and strings of sentences	Communicates via connected discourse of paragraph length, but not all the time

INTERMEDIATE LOW	INTERMEDIATE MID	INTERMEDIATE HIGH
Oral communication is characterized by frequent pauses, ineffective reformulations, and self-corrections	Oral communication is characterized by pauses, reformulations, and self-corrections	Communication at Intermediate level is smooth, but pauses, reformulations, and self-corrections occur when attempting advanced-level tasks
Pronunciation, vocabulary, and syntax are strongly influenced by first language, but in spite of frequent misunderstandings that may require repetition or rephrasing, can generally be understood by sympathetic language users accustomed to the communication of non-native speakers	Can generally be understood by sympathetic language users accustomed to the communication of non-native speakers	Can generally be understood by native speakers unaccustomed to dealing with non-natives, although interference from another language may be evident (e.g., use of code-switching, false cognates, literal translations), and a pattern of gaps in communication may occur

Note: These descriptions are based on the ACTFL Proficiency Guidelines for Speaking (ACTFL, 2012b).

Appendix 8. Scoring Writing Samples at the Intermediate Level

It is much easier to distinguish among the major proficiency levels (Novice, Intermediate, Advanced) than it is to distinguish the Low, Mid, and High sublevels on the ACTFL Proficiency Scale (ACTFL, 2012b). To ensure that a sample is accurately rated, we recommend that you attend an ACTFL Writing Proficiency Tester Certification workshop. However, if that is not a possibility, the descriptions below can help you to distinguish among the sublevels. In this tool, we share the major differences between Intermediate Low, Intermediate Mid, and Intermediate High writers so that you can assign a rating for a portfolio sample. For further details on how Intermediate-level language users differ from those at the Novice or Advanced level, we recommend you consult the ACTFL Proficiency Guidelines (ACTFL, 2012b), which are freely available online.

Intermediate Level language users can

- Create with language when talking about familiar topics related to daily life
- Recombine learned material to express personal meaning
- Ask simple questions
- Satisfy personal needs and social demands to survive in target culture
- Produce sentence-level language, ranging from discrete sentences to strings of sentences

INTERMEDIATE LOW	INTERMEDIATE MID	INTERMEDIATE HIGH
Can meet some limited practical writing needs	Can meet a number of practical writing needs	Can meet all practical writing needs of Intermediate level (see description above)
Can create statements and formulate questions based on familiar material	Can write short, simple communications, compositions, and requests for information in loosely connected texts	Can write compositions and simple summaries related to work/school experiences
Sentences are largely recombinations of learned vocabulary and structures. Vocabulary is adequate to express elementary needs	Writing style resembles oral discourse	Vocabulary, grammar, and style of Intermediate High writers essentially correspond to those of the spoken language
Writing is framed almost exclusively in present time	Writing is framed in present time but may contain references to other time frames	Can narrate and describe in different time frames when writing about everyday events and situations
Sentences are short and simple using basic word order, often with repetitive structure	Writing consists of a collection of discrete sentences and/or questions that are loosely strung together with little evidence of deliberate organization	Narrations and descriptions are often but not always of paragraph length
Writing may contain basic errors in grammar, word choice, punctuation, spelling, and in the formation and use of non-alphabetic symbols	Writing shows evidence of control of basic sentence structure and verb forms	Writing provides some evidence of control of sentence structure, but contains errors when attempting advanced level tasks such as past or future narration or dealing with a social situation with an unexpected complication

INTERMEDIATE LOW	INTERMEDIATE MID	INTERMEDIATE HIGH
Writing is understood by natives used to the writing of non-natives, although additional effort may be required	Writing is readily understood by natives used to the writing of non-natives	Writing is generally comprehensible to natives not used to the writing of non-natives, but there are likely to be gaps in comprehension
When performing tasks at the Advanced level, writing deteriorates significantly and message may be incomplete	When performing tasks at the Advanced level, the quality and/ or quantity of writing declines and message may be unclear	When performing tasks at the Advanced level, writers may be inconsistent in use of appropriate major time markers, resulting in a loss of clarity

Note: These descriptions are based on the ACTFL Proficiency Guidelines for Writing (ACTFL, 2012b).

Appendix 9: Action Plan Example for Initiating SoBL Implementation

PLANNING STEPS	ACTION PLAN
Biliteracy Goals What do we seek to achieve with the SoBL?	**Long-term goals:** *(after five years of implementation)* Support 30 percent of graduating seniors in achieving the SoBL in at least ten different languages Support 80 percent of students enrolled in dual-language programming in receiving SoBL pathway recognitions Shift the mindset of educators from monolingual to multilingual **Short-term goals:** *(by the end of this school year)* Secure assessments in the top ten languages used in students' homes Assess how current programs and teachers support students' biliteracy Design systems for students to apply and track progress toward SoBL attainment Develop SoBL materials to share with students, families, and educators
Evaluation Plan How will we know we have achieved these goals?	**Formal data:** SoBL assessment data: Number and percentage of students achieving SoBL and SoBL pathway recognitions, number of languages recognized Annual survey of educators: Perceptions of languages/multilingualism, how they support biliteracy development in classroom practice **Anecdotal data:** SoBL assessment list, application process, and recruitment materials Annual student and teacher feedback on SoBL processes and efforts

PLANNING STEPS	ACTION PLAN
Implementation Plan What will enhance progress toward our goals?	**Programs:** Integrate the SoBL into the dual-language program, where students can achieve pathway recognitions in preschool, fifth, and eighth grades *(Dan will partner with elementary bilingual leads to work on this throughout the year.)* Put together survey to assess bilingual and world language teachers' approaches to curriculum and instruction *(José will take the lead and modify previously used survey that went to all bilingual teachers.)* Based on the above survey, support programs in refining program model, curriculum, and instruction to support biliteracy *(José will take the lead for bilingual, Ana for world language, Terri for ESL/ELA.)* **Partnerships:** Invite elementary and middle school bilingual leads onto SoBL team to develop and enhance pathway recognition *(ASAP; Dan will reach out.)* Reach out to neighboring districts already implementing the SoBL to gain insight and partnership *(Ana has contacts and will request meeting.)* Pitch goals, plan, and budget to superintendent and school board for approval *(José will draft presentation for next meeting.)* Conduct professional development with all teachers on value of biliteracy and how to incorporate into regular practice *(Next school year; will need PLC texts for each grade level and school administrator buy-in.)* **Promotion:** Use home language survey data to find and secure SoBL assessments in as many languages as possible *(Dan will request HLS data and take the lead on this for our next meeting.)* Develop application and self-reflection for students to indicate their interest in taking SoBL assessment *(Terri & Ana will draft.)*

Appendix 10: Action Plan Example for Refining SoBL Implementation

PLANNING STEPS	ACTION PLAN
Biliteracy Goals What do we seek to achieve with the SoBL?	Long-term goals: Support at least 80 percent of students in becoming biliterate by the class of 2030 Develop and maintain the heritage languages of all students with at least 80 percent of English learners (ELs) achieving the Seal of Biliteracy by the year 2030 Extend pathways to becoming bilingual and biliterate, including world language and bilingual programs from elementary through high school Short-term goals: Shift transitional to maintenance bilingual programs by 2023 Extend world language study into elementary schools by 2023 Build community partnerships to develop other heritage languages by 2023
Evaluation Plan How will we know we have achieved these goals?	Formal data (annual collection and analysis): SoBL recognitions: Number of students recognized as percentage of graduating class, number of current/former ELs as percentage of graduating current/former ELs, number of languages tested and recognized Language program enrollment: Annual number of students enrolled in each type, language, and grade level Anecdotal data (annual collection and analysis): Surveys/interviews: Provide students, families, and teachers opportunities to respond with perspectives and experiences related to program changes Partner profiles: Brief documents that outline the partner, focal language, programming, assessment, and other efforts to support students' biliteracy

PLANNING STEPS	ACTION PLAN
Implementation Plan What will enhance progress toward our goals?	**Moving from transitional to maintenance Spanish bilingual programs** (*Lead: Paty*): Meet with elementary bilingual teachers to discuss needed resources and supports to change language allocations in support of maintenance (ASAP) Meet with middle and high-school world language teachers about the potential for offering Spanish-for-native-speaker sections (ASAP) Amass team of educators from across schools to redraft goals for bilingual programs to focus on maintenance over transition (next year) Meet with administrators and the school board to approve change and seek out funds with any resources needed for programs (next year) **Extending world language study into elementary schools** (*Lead: Sara*): Meet with elementary school administrators to share vision and discuss logistics of using special-area time for world language study (ASAP) Develop plan to present to administrators and school board (ASAP) Reach out to universities to develop pipelines to recruit elementary world language teachers into the district (pending approval) Backward design K-12 world language curriculum using ACTFL standards, proficiency guidelines, and Can-do statements (next year) **Developing opportunities in heritage languages** (*Lead: Anushka*): Use home language survey data to explore other SoBL assessment options to offer in the district (e.g., STAMP 4S, AAPPL; ASAP) Reach out to state/university partners regarding languages not offered on existing assessments for support with alternative assessments (ASAP) Reach out to community language schools to share information about the SoBL and invite their participation in district efforts (ASAP) Work with each partner individually to determine best way to support biliteracy given time and resources (next year) As needed, seek out board approval for funds to develop on-site programs, such as afterschool language clubs or heritage language electives (pending) **Supporting and promoting the recognition with ELs** (Lead: Alex): Invite ESL teachers to serve on the SoBL planning committee (ASAP) Partner with bilingual counselors to develop informational materials (ASAP) Attend student groups to share information about the SoBL and related community partnerships (e.g., Polish Club, Indian Student Alliance; ASAP) Offer professional development for all teachers (target ESL and sheltered content teachers) on the value of students' home languages (next year) Ask recent recipients who are current/former ELs to make brief videos about their experience in becoming biliterate and earning the SoBL (next year)